3039300000647563

D0938951

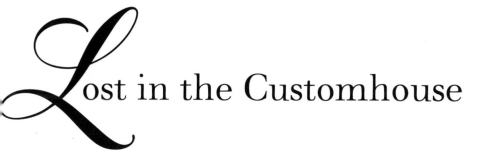

Lost in the Customhouse

Authorship in the American Renaissance

Lost in the Customhouse

Jerome Loving

University of Iowa Press Ψ Iowa City

University of Iowa Press,
Iowa City 52242
Copyright © 1993 by the
University of Iowa Press
All rights reserved
Printed in the
United States of America

Design by Richard Hendel

Printed on acid-free paper

FRONTISPIECE:
*Fur Traders Descending
the Missouri*, George Caleb
Bingham, 1845. Courtesy of the
Metropolitan Museum of Art,
Morris K. Jesup Fund, 1933
(33.61).

Library of Congress Cataloging-in-Publication Data
Loving, Jerome, 1941–
    Lost in the customhouse: authorship in the
American renaissance/by Jerome Loving.
        p.   cm.
    Includes index.
    ISBN 0-87745-404-3 (alk. paper)
    1. American literature—19th century—
History and criticism—Theory, etc.
    2. Authorship—Social aspects—United
States—History—19th century.
    3. Literature and society—United States—
History—19th century.   4. Self in literature.
    5. Canon (Literature).   I. Title.
PS201.L64   1993
810.9'003—dc20   92-33051
                                            CIP

97 96 95 94 93 C 5 4 3 2 1

DEDICATED TO ROGER ASSELINEAU

Contents

Prologue

he American Renaissance is defined here as com-
mencing with the magnum opus of Washington Irving
and extending to the first (and best) novel of Theodore
Dreiser in 1900. I have given special attention to the
word "Renaissance" as it denotes rebirth and con-
notes re-awakening. When F. O. Matthiessen (following the suggestion of Harry Levin) applied it to five
canonized male authors of our antebellum Romantic
Period, he meant the rebirth on American soil of a
number of European values and artistic concerns that
had been obliterated by puritanism. Yet in using the
term Matthiessen may have sensed in his vision of a
"native" American literature the same idea that I have
tried to develop in these pages: that the central experience in American literature in the nineteenth century (if not also in the twentieth) is essentially the
puritanical desire for the prelapsarian—that second
chance of coming into experience anew. Beginning
with Irving, the American canon is filled with narrators and characters who keep waking up to the central
scene of their adventures and not the end of the story.
Analeptic instead of proleptic, this pattern gives rise to
a literature of recurrent beginnings, stories about narrators who make it home to tell their stories because
they never really leave home in the first place. Rather,
they travel through a customhouse of the imagination
in which the Old World experience of the present is
taxed by the New World of the utopian past, where life
is always cyclical instead of linear.

For this study of American desire in literature, I

have selected what I consider the twelve most important American writers of the nineteenth century. The list could have been longer, but not without repetition in terms of charting the psychological (as well as social) landscape as I view it. These twelve are, not coincidentally, the most "canonized" writers of the American nineteenth century. I have followed the canon not only because I believe its best works give the most aesthetic pleasure and philosophical insight but *because* these texts were the ones to be canonized in our own century—the rapidly fading twentieth. Which is to say that they were chosen, primarily at least, for psychologically—not politically—urgent reasons; chosen for their passages backward in personal history rather than for the voyage forward in public ideology.

If my study has another "argument" (in the "political" sense that every analysis of any aspect of our culture must in the post-Vietnam era), it is that the writer is neither an autonomous romantic nor a cultural automaton. Rather, the most original product of his or her imagination comes from the interaction of the individual and society at a crucial juncture in the writer's emotional and intellectual life. In other words, every writer has finally only one great work—toward which every other product moves and which everything written afterwards probably reflects upon. It is a work such as *The Scarlet Letter* or *The Portrait of a Lady*, for example, that is most invested with the writer's identity and identity-theme. My book, therefore, is not a sociological study of literature. I am not interested here in "interpretative communities," "reader responses," or primarily the social forces that "wrote" the books or the "texts" that shaped the political and social landscape in America. In recent years, we have seen a preponderance of such studies in symbiotics, a few of them brilliant, premised generally on Michel Foucault's notion that literature is ideology rather than primarily the work of a creatively charged imagination. To insist in the late twentieth century that every literary act is "political" (or "ideological") is no more persuasive or capable of proof than to say—as the implication went in the age of Emerson and most of the nineteenth century—that every meaningful literary act is "religious." What was meant then, as it may also mean today, is that the act of creative writing, while inseparable from its social context, is an allegory of the personal and psychological, which is finally representative of the human condition and conflict.

The emphasis on "material culture" in criticism, of course, licenses the examination of *any* writing, certainly all the uncanonized literary works. Study in this vein has filled many gaps in our cultural history; one of the best recent examples is Cathy N. Davidson's *Revolution and the Word* (1986), which argues that this "minor" literature was working "revolutions" in the American social fabric long before the emergence of Washington Irving. My concern, however, is with the literary works in the nineteenth century that emerged as "major" productions in the twentieth and with why they continue to remain the principal objects of our critical discourse. My goal is not to argue directly against the claims for literature made by the New Historicists, but to allow my thesis to emerge indirectly through discussions of the literature as "literature" instead of "ideology" (i.e., "culturally shaped" literature). Indeed, the very act of such direct argument reduces criticism and literary history to a political debate and thus at best demonstrates unintentionally that everything is ultimately "political." Even the recent work of Sacvan Bercovitch, our "leading" New Historicist because he attempts to maintain a middle ground between aesthetics and ideology in his discussions of canon formation, is finally committed—as *The Office of the Scarlet Letter* (1991) so admirably demonstrates—to the demystification of the literary act.

Specifically, then, I argue that the major works from *The Sketch Book* to *Sister Carrie* reveal something about the basis and animus of American desire—about utopian consciousness in the face of psychological and social change. The writers discussed in Part One wake up primarily to psychological facts that blossom into the fiction of the self begotten out of the nothingness of existence. For Irving, it is the "blank page in existence" found on the voyage back to England; for Hawthorne, it is the sterile customhouse whose stories require an "authenticity of the outline," or the restructuring of history into personal myth. For Melville, it is biblical history that animates his best work—the story of Jonah in the womb of the leviathan that issues forth the dazed Ishmael, who is damned to relive his story every time we read it. Their stories are cyclical in the sense that the protagonists repeatedly wake up to a beginning without conclusion, or a life whose episodes are anything but episodic. Poe's *Narrative of Arthur Gordon Pym* follows this pattern, as its protagonist wakes up from one drunk after another to begin an adventure only loosely connected to the last but characterized by the same quest—in this case, the return to "Edgartown" and Edgar Poe instead of Edgar Allan Poe. Emerson's most analeptic work is "Experience" instead of *Nature* because it was the death of his first son in 1842 that jolted him out of a Transcendental confidence once strong enough to absorb another personal loss of supreme trauma, the death of his first love and wife Ellen Tucker. In "Experience" Emerson asks, "Where do we find ourselves?" and the answer is that we are back at the same inscrutable beginning with yet another stair to ascend. Thoreau writes his best work at (and about) the scene of his first memory, Walden Pond. In all cases, these literary journeys are mainly psychological and solipsistic rather than socially oriented and politically tinged. Their works are filtered through the customhouse of the imagination as it struggles with the paradoxes of experience.

It occurs to me, only after writing this book, that Melville first developed my metaphor in his famous apostrophe to Hawthorne. It comes from his letter of 16 April 1851 in which Melville expounds upon "the grand truth about Nathaniel Hawthorne": "He says NO! in thunder; but the Devil himself cannot make him say yes. For all men who say *yes*, lie and all men who say *no*,—why, they are in the happy condition of judicious, unincumbered travellers in Europe; they cross the frontiers into Eternity with nothing but a carpet-bag,—that is to say, the Ego. Whereas those yes-gentry, they travel with heaps of baggage, and damn them! they will never get through the Custom House." Though Melville, as critics have remarked both of this letter and the essay about his Lenox neighbor in *The Literary World* of August 1850, may be engaged in self-description, he is also reaching out to describe the antinomian spirit in American literature—the New World tendency of the spirit to rebel against itself. Not only do we find in these remarks the Puritan (and post-Puritan) insistence on separating the damned from the elect but also the relentless desire to separate the self along the same battle lines in search of a psychological victory. My original idea for the use of the customhouse in the imagery of my title stemmed from Hawthorne's "preface" to *The Scarlet Letter*. Yet juxtaposed with Melville's vision of the writer passing through the customhouse without "heaps of baggage," we have a clearer view of the burden of the American writer who desires to "cross the frontiers into Eternity with nothing but a carpet-bag,—that is to say, the Ego."

The result is to become "lost" on this frontier of the imagination, to find oneself—without the bag and baggage of a linear life—adrift in a representative role that reveals its solitary state.

Part One, therefore, is about Emerson's theory of literary representation and its paradoxes. Which is also to say that it is about the Homeric desire of coming home to the universal experience. Rip Van Winkle's twenty-year nap and return from the Catskills are, of course, prefigured by the twenty-year absence and impeded journey home in the first great work of western literature, *The Odyssey*—as well as those epic journeys in Dante, Cervantes, and others. Hawthorne's time in the customhouse recalls Dante in the Dark Wood. All the writers discussed in the first half of my study embark on the journey back to Ithaca and the beginning. Yet this desire extends throughout the American nineteenth century and—beyond the scope of this volume—into the twentieth, to be found, for example, in Sherwood Anderson's *Winesburg, Ohio* (1919), William Saroyan's *The Human Comedy* (1943), J. D. Salinger's *The Catcher in the Rye* (1951), and John Updike's middle-class saga, where the fourth volume (I dare not say the last), *Rabbit at Rest* (1990), is no less analeptic than the first, *Rabbit, Run* (1960). Indeed, all four accounts, or stages, of Harry Angstrom's existence are predicated on that time when life was a "perfect swish." Certainly it is true of John Barth's *Lost in the Funhouse* (1968). Barth, almost thirty years ago a teacher of mine, also contributed to my metaphor and title, not only with *his* title but with the mock-epic meditation on Homer in "Night-Sea Journey." There he invents the latest way of telling the American story in medias res, a literary method employed by Hawthorne in *The Scarlet Letter* and more indirectly by the other writers studied here. The pattern of analepsis is neither confined to the nineteenth century nor particularly American. Yet the American Renaissance, as traditionally defined, is more obviously intent on making the return because these writers were essentially the "first" generation of American "scribblers"—a mob damned by the English and Continental literary traditions.

The writers of the second half of the American century, those discussed in Part Two, had at least the advantage of a "native" literary tradition. Consequently, they did not have to evoke the Homeric myth so directly in order to overcome British and Continental influences. Indeed, Whitman, whose work starts part two of the Renaissance as I have redesignated it, made a point of not referring to traditional literary subjects. After Emerson, he could announce, as he does in his 1855 preface, that "the expression of the American poet is to be transcendant and new. It is to be indirect and not direct or descriptive or epic. . . . Let the age and wars of other nations be chanted and their eras and characters be illustrated and that finish the verse. Not so with the great psalm of the republic." In openly celebrating the American theme of rebirth and new beginnings, however, Whitman modified Irving's paradigm by taking the problem of identity outward as well as inward, by shifting the weight of the imagination away from the solitary pilgrim and toward the solitary singer who found his identity in the long catalogs of Americans and their occupations. His theme, while also logocentric, begins in the immediate wake of "Experience." Although it was the lecture on "The Poet" that Whitman heard Emerson deliver in 1842, both "Experience" and "The Poet"—as I have argued in *Emerson, Whitman, and the American Muse* (1982)—fracture the Cartesian creed while also attempting to justify it. Whitman also came along at a time of rapid advancement in print technology, which put books more cheaply into the hands of more Americans whose working-class experiences called for the gradual leveling of literary themes into social questions. The American self now found its prelapsarian pull much more clearly in the social cycle. It was to be found not so much any longer in the isolation of romance and its escape from everyday circumstances, but *within* those circumstances—where "the doings of the men correspond with the broadcast doings of the day and night." In the successive editions of *Leaves of Grass*, the social scopes and themes are broad and all-embracing. The editions paced out the century as America's best writers were energized by society as well as the writer's solitude.

Generally, what emerges from the antislavery movement, the women's movement, the Civil War, and the inequities of Reconstruction is the problem of democracy in a nation whose destiny was no longer so clearly manifest. Whitman's struggle with the problem centers on sex in a democractic society—the "doings of men" *and* women, and even more specifically the presence of women in that society as mothers, daughters, sisters, wives, and lovers. His newspaper editorials, descriptions in *Leaves of Grass*, recorded comments, and letters suggest the poet's lifelong preoccupation with the mother/lover division of the

American Eve, who became the focus of the fiction in the latter half of the century. This is not to say that Whitman was in any significant fashion a part of the "feminist" movement (his 1858 editorial against abortion in the *Brooklyn Daily Times* would by itself seriously disqualify him, at least today); rather, he celebrated the woman as an alter ego and a means of return to the same elusive self that had been the object of literary quests from Irving to Thoreau. Yet in freely announcing her as also representative of the generic American, Whitman set the stage for Dickinson's often androgynous narrator, Henry James's questing females, Kate Chopin's Aphrodite, and the purely utilitarian sex of Dreiser's un*lady*-like Carrie.

If there is an odd card in this newly stacked deck, it is Mark Twain. Yet he differs from the other postbellum writers only in subject matter, and not from any of the other writers in the American formula for locating and acting on a defining moment in the past. Scholarship of the last decade has demonstrated the diversity and depth of women's writing in America, which increased dramatically in the 1850s with the success of Harriet Beecher Stowe, then leveled off to steady production for the rest of the century. Twain, of course, contributed to the focus on women with his portraits of such mother-women as Aunt Sally and the Widow Douglas in *The Adventures of Huckleberry Finn* and, more remarkably, with his presentation of Roxy in *Pudd'nhead Wilson*. The latter, however, is also a slave—indeed a "white" slave to the curse of constitutionally approved bondage that was changed only by the will of war. For Samuel Clemens, a Southerner who resided in New England, the social and psychological emancipation most lacking and most motivating in his best works was the freedom of black—and white—America from the legacy of slavery. What makes Twain's focus on race so compelling and *Huckleberry Finn* so important in this regard is that he wrote on *our* side of the Emancipation Proclamation (1863). And it matters little whether his depictions (especially that of the runaway slave Jim, which will be debated as long as the novel is taught) are accurate because the nature of his concern—like those of the writers whose personae or central characters were female—is not exactly about the socially oppressed but about the *idea* of that oppression and its consequences upon the supposedly detached writer.

The "joke" in *Huckleberry Finn* as well as *Pudd'nhead Wilson* is that nobody was freed from slavery in 1863, certainly not America's white population. While black Americans continue to suffer from the legacy of inferiority enshrined in the pseudoscience of the nineteenth century (when the idea of returning blacks to Africa, even entertained by the president who freed the slaves, had lost all credibility), white Americans continue to carry the burden of guilt for slavery. Twain's effort in *The Adventures of Tom Sawyer, The Adventures of Huckleberry Finn, A Connecticut Yankee in King Arthur's Court, The Tragedy of Pudd'nhead Wilson*, and elsewhere is to get back in time before the "fall" into human corruption. In his magnum opus, the return is to a mythical period in youth and a fourteen-year-old who signs up for heaven when he agrees to "go to hell." *Huckleberry Finn* is our prototypical novel of adolescence, and it remains our quintessential bildungsroman because it presents the evolution of "Yankee" ingenuity without the guile of the capitalistic "pedlar." Huck's story ceases in innocence—on the frontier of freedom—rather than in an asylum, where J. D. Salinger's exhausted hero starts over, or in racism, where John Seelye's twentieth-century version of Huck resides. Even though the original Huck subscribes naively to the racist tenets of his society, he miraculously remains *innocent*. He bows out of his story with the "happy ending" that characterizes desire in American literature. It also saves Ishmael from the consequences of Ahab's madness (American idealism gone crazy). It brings Irving's Rip Van Winkle back from certain death, and it saves Dreiser's Carrie from Hurstwood's more realistic (and Zolaesque) fate. It provides Dickinson the "Wild Nights!" that could produce only a "virgin birth," and it allows James's Isabel and Chopin's Edna the luxury of an adventure with the self that had been traditionally reserved for males.

Whereas the writers in the second half of my study, and in the second half of the century, are more visibly affected by the social problems of their day, those in antebellum America were, of course, not unaffected by the society in which they wrote "literature." For Irving and Hawthorne, it was mainly the challenge of authorship in a practical nation that then considered writers "idle scribblers." For Melville and Poe, it was the more economically threatening problem of "making a living" out of writing—thus, their similar endeavors to put "facts" to work in their fiction. For Emerson and Thoreau, it was the American "notion that the scholar should be a recluse, a valetudi-

narian,—as unfit for any handiwork or public labor as a pen-knife for
an axe." They were, of course, also shaped indirectly by the ideology
and political questions of their times, but perhaps not to the extent of
the later writers in the century. And neither group—it is the firm
premise of this study—was primarily shaped and tutored by ideology.
The very fact of the Puritan-inspired return to a New World (or
Eden) argues against this theory of social automatism because "salvation"—although it was approached on a group basis—was also
thought to be determined individually. Furthermore, the Puritan jeremiad may have threatened the future, but it did so—psychologically
and biblically—only by suggesting that such a "destiny" had been
"seen before."

It is not so much that the writers of the latter half of the American
century were more directly affected by social developments—even
Thoreau's single-person utopia in *Walden* responded in part to the
interest in Fourierism, popularized in the 1840s on the front pages of
Horace Greeley's *New York Tribune*. They did write, however, during
a period whose postwar economy and redistribution of political power
emphasized class inequities, while also ushering in the rise of profes-
sionalism and an ever-growing dependence upon technology (cf.
Twain's use of fingerprinting in *Pudd'nhead Wilson*). Also, beginning
with Whitman, Americans in literature *work* for a living; except for
Henry James's major creations, they have "occupations." On the
other hand, Irving's most memorable character survives not only a
twenty-year, unattended coma but is somehow beyond the depriva-
tions of poverty under both the British and American flags. Whitman's
narrator loafs at his "ease," though this American *flâneur* is also hard
at work (as Whitman himself had been in the 1840s as a newspaper
editor looking for column material) inventing the "divine average"
out of the Puritan divine. The same American aspiration for life without death abounds in the nineteenth century as it did in the seventeenth; the same desire that animated the writers from Irving to Thoreau energized those from Whitman to Dreiser (and beyond, of
course). The difference between the early and latter parts of the century, therefore, is merely one of degree.

Yet this book, as I have said, is not an argument in the New Historicist sense (or directly against its premise for an ideologically influenced text). The reader, for instance, will not encounter here the long,

argumentative notes we have come to expect from the New Historicists: citation piled, often redundantly, upon citation and references to
"magisterial" studies published yesterday. (It is remarkable that so
much documentation is marshaled to *prove* that the "truth" of art is a
sociological fiction.) Rather, I present a narrative in which I encounter
and *experience* these twelve writers, after twenty-five years of reading
and teaching American literature. I have set out to celebrate their
works in the enjoyment of *writing* about them as they deserve to be
perceived—as literary geniuses instead of ingenious ideologues. Although the field of canonized writers has expanded in the last decade
(as the "expansion" in the late nineteenth and twentieth centuries
admitted the likes of Whitman, Dickinson, and Chopin), these twelve
remain central to America's claim for an original literature. Without
them, American literature of the last century, with few exceptions, is
largely sociological and "political." With them, we at least have a
standard of literary expression to explore—and even to condemn!

Acknowledgments

I t is always a pleasure to thank friends and colleagues (both on one's campus and elsewhere) for their thoughtful help and encouragement. Naturally, with a book of this scope, I called upon a great many for their reactions to particular chapters and upon a few to give me their impressions of the work as a whole. It has taken me so long to write this book that many of them, I suspect, have already forgotten the debt I owe them. I have not, and now want to record their names— while, as the obligatory statement goes, claiming all the errors for myself.

I would like to thank (in the order of the chapters they read and critiqued, from Irving to Dreiser) Philip McFarland, Terence Martin, Larry J. Reynolds, Daniel Hoffman, Benjamin Franklin Fisher IV, John J. McDermott, Lawrence Buell, David S. Reynolds, Justin Kaplan, Alan Gribben, James M. Cox, John Seelye, Charles Gordone, Vivian R. Pollak, Joan Templeton, Barton Levi St. Armand, Susan Goodman, Elaine Jude Leyda, and Richard D. Lehan. For help with useful information, materials, and ideas, I thank Paul Christensen, James H. Justus, Clinton MacHann, D. G. Myers, Kenneth M. Price, William J. Scheick, Bruce Thornton, Dorothy Van Riper, and Warwick Wadlington. Norman S. Grabo graciously and promptly read the entire manuscript of the penultimate draft and advised me as he has in previous books. Roger Asselineau (to whom this book is dedicated) sent me glad tidings about the manuscript from Paris. Ed Folsom took time out from his busy schedule as editor of *The Walt Whitman Quarterly Review* to give me his encouraging as well as cautionary advice. Finally, my colleague of fifteen years, at Texas A&M University, William Bedford Clark, read almost every chapter as the book developed and offered his encouragement and advice.

I was also assisted by a faculty development leave from Texas A&M University during the spring semester of 1987 as well as the opportunity to "try out" many of my chapters before the recently formed American Literature Association, the Modern Language Association, the South Central Modern Language Association, the Thoreau Society, the Whitman conference at Rutgers University at Camden, and the Universities of Graz, Vienna, and Paris. An earlier version of "Whitman's Idea of Women" (chapter 7) appeared in *The Mickle Street Review* 11 (1989), pp. 17–33. An earlier version of the Epilogue appeared as "The One Book for Whitman Studies" in *Études Anglaises* 45 (1992), pp. 333–39.

Most of all, I want to thank my wife, Cathleen C. Loving, who over the many years of our marriage has allowed me, with her unstinting support, to safely lose myself in these scholarly endeavors. Along with her, I thank my son, David C. Loving (who long ago reminded me that I was merely a "doctor of words"), and my daughter, Alison Cameron Loving (who will probably become "a doctor of words"), for enduring the lives of "academic children."

The American Renaissance
PART ONE

1 : Irving's Paradigm

Probably the most significant and yet paradoxical fact about American literature is that it begins in the middle of its official history and in the work of a dreamer, Washington Irving. Nothing before him in the brooding spirit of the Colonial writers or in the rational wisdom of the eighteenth century quite anticipates *The Sketch Book* (1819–20) as America's first acknowledged contribution to world literature as well as the first true, or candid, account of the American Self.[1] In a nation then committed to relentless industry, American literature begins—wakes up—not in the works of such men of action as Benjamin Franklin or Thomas Paine, but in the idle and apolitical character of a belated and beleaguered aristocrat from "Tarry Town" who chose for many years as his residence and as his theme the nostalgic antiquity of Europe. It originates with a gentleman of leisure (really in a story about another dreamer and lounger) who—as Irving's literary persona says in the "Author's Account of Himself"—"had longed to wander over the scenes of renowned achievement—to tread as it were in the footsteps of antiquity—to loiter about the ruined castle—to meditate on the falling tower—to escape in short, from the commonplace realities of the present and lose [himself] among the shadowy grandeurs of the past."[2] American literature begins not in a book written by Brother Jonathan or even "Jonathan Oldstyle," but in one by "Geoffrey Crayon, Gent." who finds the American experience to be essentially prelapsarian.[3] It finds its oneiric voice in a transplanted

[3]

folktale and in the character of Rip Van Winkle, whose first name serves as an acronym to bid our literary past in England and elsewhere to REST IN PEACE.

It is, to be sure, ironic that the book that liberated America's literary present from the past should dwell almost entirely on England. Of its thirty-two sketches, only four are set in the United States. And of those, two (about American Indians) were written much earlier, and the plots of the others were filched from German legend. In one sense, *The Sketch Book* marks the first time one of our writers went abroad to discover America. Many others had gone on grand tours of the Continent (as Irving himself had done between 1804 and 1806), but as Geoffrey Crayon, Irving went on a night flight into himself. Whereas in the Knickerbocker Papers he had relied on the example of Swift and other English literary precursors, Irving woke up in *The Sketch Book* as a literary foundling with nothing to write about but "a blank page in existence." In the opening sketch, entitled "The Voyage," the narrator speaks of "being cast loose from the secure anchorage of settled life, and sent adrift upon a doubtful world" (p. 11). And so it is in this *head*less flight, which renders the author's "account" of himself as baffling at times as that of Ichabod Crane in the shadows of Sleepy Hollow. With such a literary voyage, the book—and it *is* a book, America's first tall tale of "human frailty and sorrow"—gets under way in every way that is a departure from the "landlocked" themes of Colonial and eighteenth-century American literature. The first sighting on the seas that Crayon describes as all "vacancy" is appropriately the mast of a nameless ship whose full story can never be known. For nothing can ever be known for sure in *The Sketch Book* except through the prism of language and memory. Crayon— or Irving—wakes up to the stories he sketches much in the way of Rip Van Winkle, who scrambles off to the ancestral Catskills, described significantly as "a *dismembered* branch of the great Appalachian family" (p. 29; my italics). The tale parallels the author's self-imposed exile from America, which allowed him the freedom to conceive of the first American "gentleman," perhaps a laughable but not lamentable creature who sleeps through the best part of his life.

As an allegory for the state of American letters and life at the beginning of the nineteenth century, "Rip Van Winkle" also suggests that the Revolution had not yet separated us from our past in English literature. Like Rip, the American Scholar had slept through it—as soundly as the town drunks in the work of another pseudonymous writer, Mark Twain. Like his American hero (possibly Rip in adolescence), the American writer required a more western "territory" in order to discover the "neutral territory" of an emerging national identity and literary voice. With the advent of the American Renaissance, this became a self-begotten self, a persona without a past or a future that lingered in the "blank page" or nothingness of his existence. This individual, projected in Rip's case by an unemployed laborer, originates in *The Sketch Book*, America's first full-blown sketch of the melancholy figure—Adam, and by the end of the century, Eve— reincarnated in a world of psychological change as well as physical challenge. Writing abroad (from America and himself), Irving as Crayon sketched out not only the "gradual dilapidations of time" but the New World Self that had finally become a "gentleman" without either a social pedigree or a profession in literature. With the success of the Revolution, he had lost his innocence and was condemned like his European precursors to contemplate his secular existence in a world that the eighteenth-century notion of "progress" could never really change. Before—even with the burden of a termagant wife— life had been something of a dream: "Here [under the "rubicund portrait" of George the Third] they used to sit in the shade, through a long lazy summer's day, talking listlessly over village gossip, or telling endless sleepy stories about nothing" (pp. 31–32). In other words, fiction was safely an escape from reality rather than a matter of identity. After Rip's ascent and modern man's fall, however, the American dreamer is "completely confounded. He doubted his own identity, and whether he was himself or another man." Like Melville's Billy Budd when asked the origin of his identity, Rip exclaims, "God knows." At his "wit's end," he confesses: "I'm not myself—I'm somebody else—that's me yonder—no—that's somebody else got into my shoes—I was myself last night; but I fell asleep on the mountains—and they've changed my gun and every thing's changed—and I'm changed—and I can't tell what's my name, or who I am!" (pp. 38–39).

Later, in "Experience," Emerson would refine the question by asking, "Where do we find ourselves?"[4] Rip returns home in a daze, a "Chauncy Gardener" to his daughter Judith Gardenier, who had long given up her father as either having shot himself or been carried off by Indians. In fact, Rip was carried off by one of Irving's more enduring fits of melancholy that invests American literature with what would later be refined into the "damp, drizzly November" of the writer's soul. Later, as our first internationally successful author, Irving would retire to Sunnyside on the Hudson and write about George Washington instead of Washington Irving, but in 1819, at almost the same age that another New Yorker and "loafer" would begin to write about himself in the first *Leaves of Grass*, Irving was anticipating in "Rip Van Winkle" and throughout *The Sketch Book* the major theme of the literature he inaugurates. It is therefore an injustice to dismiss this work as merely a precursor to the works of the American Renaissance as outlined by F. O. Matthiessen or to call his themes temporal instead of timely—if not "timeless" in the prehistoricist sense.

Indeed, Rip's dilemma is as timeless as that of Whitman's dreamer, who, at the rising height of American industrial progress in the nineteenth century, leans and loafs at his ease, "observing a spear of summer grass." Like the narrator of "Song of Myself" (the ex-journalist who has written about everybody else), Rip, who has minded everybody's business but his own, now has nothing but himself to celebrate. A "descendant of the Van Winkles who figured so gallantly in the chivalrous days of Peter Stuyvesant," he has inherited "little of the martial character of his ancestors" (p. 29). Disenfranchised of his ancestral power (which has its source in the Old World), he is reduced to the level of "an obedient, henpecked husband" who "loafs" precisely because he thinks he has nothing of interest or importance to do. In one allegorical sense, this is a psychological portrait of stymied America on the eve of the Revolution; but in another way the character also represents the American writer facing the postwar bleakness of a land wrested from his ancestors but largely fashioned into another (British) empire. Before it had been all work and no play; now he has come of age and discovered the New World settled but not civilized in the way European culture has examined itself through the medium of art. The story expresses America's writing block, its linguistic paralysis in the absence of visible adversity, to articulate itself, its new self. Rip simply has nothing to say (for himself), and so his "sole domestic adherent was his dog Wolf" (p. 31). In fact, several of the sketches in Irving's book suggest that the author was experiencing his own writing block. Although "The Christmas Dinner" is one of the all-time favorites, its success is due largely to its subject, a holiday now widely celebrated and one that induces nostalgia. As an exercise in fiction, it may go on too long about nothing. At the close of the sketch, Irving feels the excess and offers the following apologia: "Methinks I hear the question asked by my graver readers, 'To what purpose is all this—how is the world to be made wiser by this talk?' Alas! is there not wisdom enough extant for the instruction of the world? And if not, are there not thousands of abler pens labouring for its improvement?—It is so much pleasanter to please than to instruct—to play the companion rather than the preceptor" (p. 191). In other words, the nothingness of the past is the most significant "companion" after all else has failed to instruct us about ourselves in the waking present. He continues by asking what "mite of wisdom" he could possibly throw "into the mass of knowledge" and concludes that he ought to write only to amuse, and if he fails the only evil is his own disappointment.

But Irving is also our preceptor as the companion of his own psyche in the book. The regretful tone is set in "Rip Van Winkle," the *real* "Author's Account of Himself."[5] Re-embodied into a present without a future (except for the inevitable and "undeconstructible" grave), Rip longs for the lazy and innocent past. With the best part of his life over, he now knows that life's dream is also something of a nightmare. What had seemed particularly odd about the dream he has awakened from, Irving tells us, was that although the party of revelers Crayon encountered in the Catskills "were evidently amusing themselves, yet they maintained the gravest faces, the most mysterious silence, and were, withal, the most melancholy party of pleasure he had ever witnessed" (p. 34). The scene presents such a dreamlike contradiction that we can hardly imagine it. The characters are real enough but inactive in the sense of actually living their lives. Like the scenes in Whitman's "The Sleepers," there is in the pastoral that Rip observes a certain coldness. The theme pervades the book. As Kenneth S. Lynn notes, "*The Sketch Book* suggests that England in the wake of Waterloo was nothing more than a picturesquely mouldering ruin."[6] Nothing really happens in the England Irving surveys.

Nothing *was*, it seems clear, Irving's subject and his obsession in *The Sketch Book*. Disheartened by the bankruptcy of his family's business in 1818, he returned to writing in order to escape from "the common-place realities of the present" (p. 9). Like Melville's Ishmael, who can no longer endure the landlocked reality of his existence and signs aboard the next available whaling vessel, Irving's Crayon went to sea and to sleep again—to dream about a past that is better precisely because it is muted in memory. Dusty with age, it has a grave-like quality, he says in "Rural Funerals," that "buries every error— covers every defect—extinguishes every resentment" (p. 116). Irving is speaking literally about the grave here, which holds "the only sorrow from which we refuse to be divorced" (pp. 115–16). But the irony for the mourner is the same for the American writer because he denies present facts in order to hold on to what has been reduced to nothingness. Possibly, Irving still had in mind the memory of Matilda Hoffman's death in 1809. As the bride-to-be that no longer was, she symbolized the blankness that—beginning with Irving—becomes the dominant theme in nineteenth-century American literature.

With the possible exception of Charles Brockden Brown, the American writer before Irving always had something "real" to write about. From William Bradford to Jonathan Edwards, from Benjamin Franklin to Hugh Henry Brackenridge, these writers had as their subject the frontier experience, whether it was spiritual, mercantile, or political. The earlier, Puritan writers at least had Scripture, and the later, more quotidian ones had the balance sheet. Angry or benevolent, their god clearly existed. With Irving, all that changes. Of course he is often conventionally sentimental in his references to the deity, but his focus is not on afterlife so much as on the absence of *this* life. The grave is "a place for meditation" (p. 116). It is the place for forty winks, and so it is appropriate that *The Sketch Book* gets under way with Rip's (and Irving's) mid-life nap. Having reached middle age if not forty himself, Irving retreated to a more desirable past and discovered it laden with dust. This was his crisis—to wake up like Rip and discover himself in "somebody else." This wakeful self cannot any longer find himself or know so exactly just who he is. He is a "sojourner" who can never go home again to the self of summer days and Christmas dinners. Now he is Ichabod ("the inglorious") fleeing from the headless horseman of his greed for life.

Essentially framed by Rip's innocence and Ichabod's knowledge, *The Sketch Book* establishes the pattern in American literature in which the Isolato runs away from home in order to envision his (and later *her*) place in it. Looking back at America from abroad, Irving was the first of our writers "to choose his own country for the scene of his story." The words are not Irving's but James Fenimore Cooper's in his preface to *The Spy* (1821). Cooper thought that, after Brown, he was the first to make effective use of the native landscape. He did, of course, investigate the duality of the American political experience by setting his historical tale in the "neutral ground" of political sentiment, yet the Revolution, or its fictionalizing in Cooper, merely precedes—and never anticipates—the Evolution that followed it—that of the American consciousness waking up to a world already made. In one way, *The Spy* is another national allegory in the fashion of *The Sketch Book*, yet Cooper's novel lacks the psychological penetration of Irving's book because it is about the American Politico and not the American Scholar or *thinker* for whom—in the definition of Emerson—action is "subordinate" if also essential.[7] Cooper wrote about the active Americans, the Harvey Birches and Natty Bumppos who eventually grew up in American literature to become characters in the fiction of Horatio Alger and Jack London. Although this level of fiction, especially the western, has received much critical attention lately, it must perforce be based on sociological grounds rather than literary ones. This is because the Rip Van Winkles of our literature—Emerson's Central Man, Thoreau's Utopian Hermit, Whitman's Solitary Singer, Poe's Man of the Crowd, Hawthorne's Pilgrim in the Dark Wood, Melville's Lone Survivor, Dickinson's Supposed Person, and others to be examined in this book—all grow old instead of up. They might go west like their more adventurous compatriots in American fiction, but like Natty Bumppo of *The Prairie* (1827) they do not conquer it.

Like Rip Van Winkle, they wake up as somebody else and are transported to another time that they do not quite recognize. Rip's life had stood a "Loaded Gun" before the Revolution, and now it was "an old firelock . . . the barrel incrusted with rust, the lock falling off, and the stock worm eaten." Irving's persona, the prototypical quester of the American Renaissance, determines to return to his other life, "to revisit the scene of last evening's gambol," but like the psychic drunk who on the morning after tries to climb out of bed, "he found himself stiff in the joints and wanting in his usual activity" (p. 35). Rip is not the town drunk per se, but he might as well be. His situation is as confusing as that of Bartleby the Scrivener—or Washington Irving the Scrivener. He returns to the village, like Goodman Brown or Arthur Dimmesdale, completely bewildered by the change he finds, never knowing for sure whether it is internal or external. He "comes to" like Ishmael to tell a story that is (like all of Melville's finest work) full of "ragged edges." In rags himself, Rip experiences the confusion that makes Washington Irving our first important writer of the true or internalized American scene: "His mind now misgave him; he began to doubt whether both he and the world around him were not bewitched" (p. 36). Rip is bewitched but also begotten into an identity he now suspects is a fiction. Everything has changed, even "the ruby face of King George." Cooper's characters fight in a war that brings about national identity, but Irving's most memorable creation sleeps through the war and wakes up to the fiction that is *The Sketch Book*. In the episodes—or canvases—that follow "Rip Van Winkle," the past is sketched more abstractly than the historical past of Cooper. For Irving writes about a past that never existed *except* in the present.

In "Rip Van Winkle," what was once poetry in its capacity to dream becomes propaganda in its capacity to restrict and to regiment the imagination. In place of Nicholas Vedder's idle sagacity and Derrick Van Bummel's useless information, Rip returns from his dream to find "a lean bilious looking fellow, with his pockets full of handbills . . . haranguing vehemently about rights of citizens—elections—members of Congress—liberty—Bunker's Hill—heroes of seventy-six—and other words which were perfect babylonish jargon to the bewildered Van Winkle" (p. 37). Like the American writer who finds himself in another country, Washington Irving realizes that he does not readily fit into a society that has lost its ability to dream and to wonder about the nature of experience. He much prefers the past or "Rural Life in England," the title of the sketch that follows closely "Rip Van Winkle." There the knowledge that literature conveys is more pristine and suggestive, seemingly original instead of imitative and corrupted by modern or industrial concerns. In "The Art of Book Making," Geoffrey Crayon—really Rip on the "lam" now—suffers from the "habit of napping at improper times and places." The scene is the British Museum, where scholars are in "the very act of manufacturing books." They exploit literary classics, we are told, in order "to swell their own scanty rills of thought," and thus they are "manu-facturing" books instead of writing them. In the dream that follows, our dreamer imagines that whenever these bookmakers "seized upon a book, *by one of those incongruities common to dreams* [my italics], methought it turned into a garment of foreign or antique fashion, with which they proceeded to [dress] themselves." He also notices that "no one pretended to clothe himself from any particular suit" (p. 64). Like the "bilious looking fellow, with his pockets full of handbills," the objects of the narrator's description are somewhat chaotic in appear-ance. In both cases, their concerns and productions are mishmashes of modern confusion. They are "harangues" about everything instead of nothing.

To harangue about nothing, or nothingness, of course, is to be ni-hilistic, and this is not finally the result in Irving. It may be partially the case in the "sketch books" of Hawthorne and Melville, even Poe and Emerson, who take the implications of Irving's paradigm beyond the limits of New World idealism, but in *The Sketch Book* the effect is often sentimental, if not "domestic"—as in, for example, "The Bro-ken Heart." There Irving confesses his belief "in broken hearts and the possibility of dying of disappointed love." The ideas in this sketch stand in strange contrast to those in "Rip Van Winkle," where the husband is not only subordinate to his wife but also subordinate to his previous notion of himself. For the author of "The Broken Heart" states—in yet another "account" of himself—that the malady is not often fatal to his own sex but that "it withers down many a lovely woman into an early grave" (p. 56). This from the mourner of Matilda Hoffman! Rip himself "dies" from a termagant wife, and Irving "dies"—into writing *The Sketch Book*—from a terminal wife-to-be. The distinction between men and women in "The Broken Heart" comes from Irving the male ideologue and American patriot, that in-dividual who is not supposed to cry at funerals. It is his attempt to surface from the dream-vision of Geoffrey Crayon, to turn from that magical and mystical past to the present and its concern about "some-thing." And it is Irving at his worst, whether read today or yesterday, because its privileging of the male over the female is merely self- (or gender-) serving sentimentality. But Irving waxes sentimental in an-other, more legitimate, literary way—through nostalgia. It is this sense of the apolitical past that gets him back to the nothingness of the present. For the past was never any better than the present, and to insist that it was simply highlights the "blank page" of existence in the here and now.

The point is underscored in the plot of "Rip Van Winkle." When Rip wakes up from his twenty-year sleep and returns to the village, the political situation is improved to the extent that an independent nation now exists, and its people are (temporarily) free from foreign threats of oppression. Despite these changes, Rip remembers the past as a better time. He is alienated from the present and thus from himself. For Rip personally, of course, the present is rather bleak. But that is merely because he has missed the best part of his life (the middle), and consciousness of the present usually induces a sense of nostalgia or belatedness. Irving sensed that humans were destined to live "after the fall" and never before it in the *literary* past. Thus, *The Sketch Book*, as an exercise in metastasis, is full of precious memories instead of present moments—of old country inns and London antiques. Even the sketch of "John Bull" reads like an obituary. If not dead, this caricature of England is at best old and worn down by "pecuniary embarrassments and domestic feuds" (p. 255). In another sense, the sketch is yet another version of Rip, who later appears as "The Angler" and goes fishing in order to get out from beneath the burden of the present. At the end of this sketch Irving says, "I have done, for I fear that my reader is growing weary" (p. 271). But we think it is Irving who is growing weary of the world he has simultaneously avoided and confronted for thirty-one sketches. The end is near, and in the final "sketch" the author will be chased out of his dream-vision of the present as fast as Ichabod Crane is scared out of the town that held his fantasy of the future.

William L. Hedges notes that "next to nothing 'happens'" in "The Angler,"[8] but the fact is that next to nothing happens in the sketch itself—or at least the sketch in Irving's hands. This is true not only because the narrator (as Hedges also observes) is removed from the scene but because the scene itself is removed from the world of change. The only change in the sketches comes from the feeling of loneliness we sense in an aging bachelor who would half like to get married. In other words, he would like to "complete" himself, but with the past instead of the present. Hence, the self-begotten self, or hopeful persona, Irving projects is finally a misbegotten self—

misbegotten in the prescient present rather than begotten in the nostalgic past where life is a comfort instead of an absence and a threat. Nothing happens in the nostalgic past because everything has already happened; closure has been effected, and yet the protagonist of this dream is still alive to talk about it. To dwell in dreams, of course, is to keep moving, as Irving does from sketch to sketch; for if he ever settles down (and gets married), he is doomed to relive the past in the present and thus to suffer the "gradual dilapidations of time" (p. 134). Better to be a "sojourner" in what Emerson called "a fool's paradise" than to become a permanent resident of Sleepy Hollow. Indeed, when the itinerant Ichabod Crane thinks of settling there—if only long enough to win the hand (and land) of Katrina Van Tassel—he is run out of town by his superstitious nature.

The writer, according to Irving in "Westminster Abbey," is never an "active" participant in his own present. Admittedly, today such a defining characteristic of the writer might appear decadently "traditional," but then the tradition of American literature (which Irving defines and dispatches) thrives on the sense of belatedness. For Irving, therefore, the writer shuts "himself up from the delights of social life, that he might the more intimately commune with distant minds and distant ages." At Poet's Corner he notes the paucity of statues because "the lives of literary men afford no striking themes for the sculptor" (p. 136). Statues denote the state of having *lived* in a present. Writers, on the other hand, live in the past of their own imaginations in order to write for the future. In Irving's case, the (American) writer invents a past and a persona—an Adam, or an Eve, in the Garden again (to echo Emerson, roughly)—whose scenario provides the paradigm for the literature of the American Renaissance. Like Rip, its hero wakes up to the "New World" of George Washington and Washington Irving. It is a world, of course, of Poe's "sweets and sours" and of Dickinson's "certain slant of light," but these are the necessary imperfections that bring out the irony of the American writer who was promised a new world instead of the same old story that life is a fiction. In "Rip Van Winkle," we will recall, the protagonist finally wakes up, or comes to life again, as a storyteller: "He used to tell his story to every stranger that arrived at Mr. Doolittle's Hotel. He was observed at first to vary on some . . . points, every time he told it, *which was doubtless owing to his having so recently awaked* [my italics]. It at last settled down precisely to the tale I have related and not a man woman or child in the neighbourhood but knew it by heart" (p. 41). Confronted by the contradictions of his new identity, Rip finds something to do that is better than doing nothing at all. He immerses himself in language instead of history and becomes a teller of Washington Irving's tall tales instead of Fenimore Cooper's more factual sense of the past. And the tallest tale of all is the dream. "Some always pretended to doubt the reality of it," Irving concludes in his own tall tale, "and insisted that Rip had been out of his head, and that this was one point on which he always remained flighty" (p. 41). Like Hawthorne's Dantesque creations, Rip is never sure whether his tale is based on a dream or reality. And neither is the writer of the American Renaissance, who always finds *something* on the "blank page in existence."

In both cases, however, their stories cancel out the more sobering perception of reality in favor of the oneiric adventure. The resulting fantasies are what Terence Martin has called "negative structures," and they define what I am calling the self-begotten self. In an essay on "beginnings" in American literature, Martin observes a pattern in which European complexity is canceled out "in favor of an American emptiness." His first example is from Sylvester Judd's *Margaret: A Tale of the Real and the Ideal* (1845), where one of the characters asserts that "our ancestors were very considerably cleansed by the dashing waters of the Atlantic."[9] As a result, Americans are defined by the lack of what they left behind: monarchs, Catholicism, legends—in other words, an established and generally verifiable past. They have gone to sea in the fashion of Irving when he sets sail in *The Sketch Book* for an England that is New England—or, more precisely, New York at the foot of the Catskills. He wakes up a storyteller, and his story of an unverifiable past becomes the foundation for the "negative structures" that make our literature original. In Rip's case, it is worth noting again that the story "at last settled down precisely to the tale I have related, and not a man woman or child in the neighbourhood but knew it by heart" (p. 41).

Rip's tale becomes the American Dream of beginning again in the New World. Rip is free of his termagant wife, as Americans were of Old England after the Revolution. Yet at the same time he is bewildered by his newfound liberty and thus misremembers himself in a nostalgic story. Such a storyteller launches the American Renaissance by waking up America to its originality in sheer absence. Beginning with Irving and his sketches about nothing (in any present), the displaced Englishman or misbegotten American becomes self-begotten. Reborn in such a New World, Rip now knows no limits to his imagination. Once awakened to the power of the dream, that recycled imagination came to compensate for—and indeed celebrate—the absence of a literary tradition in America.

More will be said about the literary heritage established by what we ought to call Irving's "Dream Book" instead of *The Sketch Book*. Even *The Spy* was influenced by its meditation on the missed opportunity in the sense that although the novel celebrates the victory of American ingenuity over British hegemony, none of its victors can ever escape the political and ethical doubts of the "neutral ground." Yet Cooper's "neutral ground" is—as inviting as it might appear in this era of "New Historicism"—merely the surface of the "neutral territory" surveyed by Hawthorne and others for whom the specters of Irving's fiction were a source of their American originality. In *The Scarlet Letter* Dimmesdale may wake up as a minister again, but he can never tell whether he now dwells in the New World or the Old World. In *Moby-Dick* Ishmael is a neutral narrator in the civil war between humanity and God. In *The Narrative of Arthur Gordon Pym* Poe—or Pym—cannot finish the story. These and other protagonists in America's wakefulness of words tell the story of Rip Van Winkle. Just as they are about to settle for the New World of New Testament answers, they are harkened back to the old world of the self whose existence is inexplicable and elusive: "As he was about to descend [from the ancestral mountain] he heard a voice from a distance, hallooing, 'Rip Van Winkle! Rip Van Winkle!' He looked around, but could see nothing but a crow winging its solitary flight across the mountain. He thought his fancy must have deceived him and turned again to descend, when he heard the same cry ring through the still evening air" (p. 33). The encounter with Hendrick Hudson and his crew reminds him of his ineluctable past in the old country—"of the figures in an old Flemish painting, in the parlour of Dominie Van Schaick, the village parson, and which had been brought over from Holland at the time of the settlement" (p. 34). In the Catskills Rip discovers his past and his beginning in the New World as a storyteller. He goes to sleep as "somebody" who ought to work for a living and wakes up as the first "nobody" in our literature—that individual whose story is the lie that returns the American Adam—and Eve—to nakedness and nothingness. This was Irving's achievement in *The Sketch Book*: to wake up as Geoffrey Crayon and to arouse literary America to a past that never quite existed before except as a sketch or outline—or, as he said, the "frame" on which he stretched the materials of his "reborn" imagination.

It is not enough, of course, to say that Irving liberated the literary imagination of his country without observing the particular nerve in the American psyche that *The Sketch Book* exposes. Part of the answer is to be found in the enduring popularity of the book, especially the two "American" stories that emerge from sketches of European life. "Rip Van Winkle" and "The Legend of Sleepy Hollow" are clearly "sketched" in the American consciousness to the extent that almost every American child has been told—in various forms, including a Walt Disney production of "Rip"—the story of the man who fell asleep for twenty years or the Headless Horseman who chases somebody (the figure of Ichabod Crane has largely faded from our national memory of the tale) out of Sleepy Hollow. One reason for the lasting effect of these figures is that they convey at the subversive level a sermon about the consequences of failing to take advantage of opportunities or of acting too late. Rip, of course, sleeps through the Revolution, and the Headless Horseman dies during it. While the latter, a British mercenary, is the nameless victim "in some nameless battle during the revolutionary war" (p. 273), the haunting legend of Sleepy Hollow is fleshed out historically with an allusion to Major John André, who was summarily executed in the area in 1780 for conspiring with Benedict Arnold. Today, the name of Arnold is still as "household" in the American vernacular as Rip's, yet in the period in which Irving wrote, the name of André carried its own legendary aura, becoming the subject of plays named for him by William Dunlap and Philip Freneau. His case is also discussed in *The Spy*, but it is his memory that plays in *The Sketch Book*. With the dream of Rip and the memory of André, Irving was toying with the power of the past to inflict pain on the present—to fill it with a Calvinistic sense, or trace, of guilt. André has disappeared today to all but antiquarians (and perhaps New Historicists), probably because he lost his life and not merely his head, but Rip has to face the fact that while he slept in the mountains, others—including André, who haunts and hunts Ichabod—died in the valley of Sleepy Hollow.

As the final "story" in *The Sketch Book*, "The Legend of Sleepy Hollow" concludes like a bad dream, evoked by darkened shapes and ended in nervous laughter and relief. It dissuades Ichabod from his dream of becoming rich in the West, as he becomes instead a lawyer and local politico in the East. Though this information is made available to the residents of Sleepy Hollow, Ichabod never becomes a legend in the fashion of André:

> The old country wives . . . maintain to this day that Ichabod was spirited away by supernatural means; and it is a favourite story often told about the neighbourhood round the winter evening fire. The bridge [where André was apprehended] became more than ever an object of superstitious awe, and that may be the reason why the road has been altered of late years, so as to approach the church by the border of the millpond. The schoolhouse, being deserted, soon fell to decay, and was reported to be haunted by the ghost of the unfortunate pedagogue; and the plough boy, loitering homeward of a still summer evening, has often fancied his voice at a distance, chanting a melancholy psalm tune among the tranquil solitudes of Sleepy Hollow. (p. 296)

This is the voice that summons Rip up the mountain.

As experience fades into myth, the story comes into being for the next generation. Rip's story becomes—in the fiction of *The Sketch Book*—the first myth of the new nation, and Washington Irving's myth (of himself) is the first story of that nation. *The Sketch Book* establishes the oneiric pattern that characterizes American literature in general and its nineteenth century in particular, going well past Whitman to Chopin and Dreiser in *The Awakening* and *Sister Carrie*. In these two books, it concludes where it began in "Rip Van Winkle," with a "termagant" wife and a runaway husband. Actually, Chopin's protagonist is "terminal" and so is Dreiser's Hurstwood, for neither dreamer ever makes it back to tell the story. The conclusion to Edna Pontellier's experience is achieved only by a fatal revision of Whitman's "Out of the Cradle Endlessly Rocking," and Hurstwood's tale is concluded by Carrie, who unlike Hester Prynne has no intention of abandoning her womanhood and worldly ways. The American story changes radically with these two novels, coming as they do in the very last years of the nineteenth century. Their stark domestic realism at first appears to contrast sharply with the *story* of "Rip Van Winkle." Yet a closer reading of *The Awakening* and *Sister Carrie* suggests that the specter of Irving's dreamer is, to use Whitman's words, "tireless and cannot be shaken away."

2 : Hawthorne's Awakening in the Customhouse

It is appropriate that the author of America's next "Sketch Book" is "A DECAPITATED SURVEYOR"—another dreamer who loses his head in the abyss of the imagination. In recounting the story of his removal from the Salem Custom House, Nathaniel Hawthorne compared his "decapitated state" to that of "Irving's Headless Horseman, ghastly and grim, and longing to be buried, as a politically dead man ought."[1] The parallel is perhaps more significant than even Hawthorne realized, for the author of *The Scarlet Letter* (1850) had been, like Irving, a scribbler of many sketches and, like Rip, the "idle" conclusion to generations of busy ancestors. Although his seclusion was initially exaggerated by modern critics, Hawthorne abandoned the world of the novel—and thus the realm of "something"—after writing the abortive *Fanshawe* (1828) and became—like Irving in *The Sketch Book*—a "sojourner" in sketches. In fact, *The Scarlet Letter* was conceived as a sketch, and it was Hawthorne's original expectation that it would be only the central one of several tales in yet another collection. The "romance" that resulted is a watershed in Hawthorne's career as an American writer because it records the point at which he saw something of the "blankness" of his own pages. As with Irving, the lifting of this writer's block was indirectly the consequence of the death of a loved one—in this case, Hawthorne's mother. He began writing *The Scarlet Letter* shortly after her death, for his grief had enabled him to cut through to the nothingness or "neutral territory" of a self-begotten self. This was personified by Hester Prynne in America's second great "tale of human frailty and sorrow."

In reaching back in *The Scarlet Letter*, Hawthorne doubtless became aware that he had lost a lover as well as a mother in the summer of 1849. Hester's singular blend of maternal and carnal qualities suggests it. Having grown up in Salem without a father to "castrate" him, this now "decapitated surveyor" began to realize in the wake of his three and a half years' literary sleep in the customhouse and in the imminent loss of his mother that he had finally found the proper, and hence personal, context for the guilt he had explored at a more comfortable remove in the numerous sketches he had written. After visiting his mother's bedside the day before her death, he acknowledged a son's natural love for his mother but added that "there has been, ever since my boyhood, a sort of coldness of intercourse between us, such as is apt to come between persons of strong feelings, if they are not managed rightly."[2] Without adopting wholly the Freudian paradigm, we can nevertheless appreciate how the trauma of Elizabeth Hawthorne's death led her son to the second story of the customhouse and the dream of Hester and her Pearl.

Hawthorne remembered kneeling that day at his mother's bedside and shaking "with sobs." He recorded the moment as the "darkest hour" he had ever lived. Yet that moment was contrasted brilliantly in the very next with the "spirit and life" of his daughter Una playing in the grass below his mother's bedroom window. He saw at once in this drama of life and death, he said, "the whole of human existence."[3] What he also saw, however, was "the authenticity of the outline" he would claim for *The Scarlet Letter* (p. 33). As with Irving at *his* literary apex, the only thing and the very thing Hawthorne required for his genius to pass through the "customhouse" of his imagination was the proper "frame" of experience. For the first and really last time in his writing career he would pass through it, as Melville later suggested, without the bag and baggage of a "nay-sayer" disguised as a yea-sayer, or at best one who pretends to survey "something" instead of "nothing" in life. In spite of the moralistic close of Hawthorne's tallest tale, what emerged from the summer of 1849 was the figure of self-begotten beauty—"Divine Maternity" with a consecration of her own.

Although the customhouse sketch was written after all but the final three chapters of the romance it introduces,[4] as Hawthorne attempted to distance himself emotionally from the tale he had thus far told, its autobiographical nature reveals the author's proximity to Hester's powerful sense of self and his initial need to explore to its full conclusion the dream he had been merely sketching for the past two decades. Rebuked by the past because he had not (until the writing of *The Scarlet Letter*) embraced its full meaning, he stands before his grimly active ancestors as one who has become little more than "a writer of tolerably poor tales" and "a tolerably good Surveyor" (p. 38) in a relatively idle customhouse. Like Rip in *The Sketch Book*, Hawthorne in the customhouse appears to have nothing of interest or importance to do and thus wanders aimlessly until he finds the significance of his "blankness"—or in Hawthorne's case, his "blackness." *His* ancestral mountain, however, is the second story of the customhouse, where he finds the "authenticity" of his outline. Today, that outline or "story" is as finished as *The Scarlet Letter* with its final three chapters, but it was unfinished in Hawthorne's mind and time because it held the tale he was compelled to tell upon the death of his mother. Its "brick-work and naked rafters," Hawthorne writes, still awaited "the labor of the carpenter and mason" (p. 28). It seems clear that while he concocted his "introductory" sketch, he was also getting ready to plaster and paper over the "second story" he had already revealed. Enough of that dusty attic remains, however, to reveal the true writer of the customhouse. Like the surveyor the sketch introduces, Hawthorne had finally found a subject that was nothing to customhouse clerks and everything to the human heart in competition with its primordial sense of itself. Surveyor Pue's story of Hester serves as Hawthorne's outline because his documents, unlike the first ones Hawthorne finds in the attic, were "not official, but of a private nature, . . . written in his private capacity, and apparently with his own hand" (p. 30). They speak of a love that had flourished long ago, indeed even prior to the plot of *The Scarlet Letter*, which appropriately begins in medias res. In the customhouse of his imagination, in the Salem of his birth, Hawthorne returned, like his fictional and fecund Hester, to the scene of the crime. "Here [Hester] said to herself"—as Hawthorne perhaps said to himself as he took up directly now the burden of his unconscious past in *The Scarlet Letter*—"had been the scene of her guilt, and here should be the scene of her earthly punishment; and so perchance, the torture of her daily shame would at length purge her soul, and work out another purity than that which she had lost" (p. 80).

When Hawthorne turned from the figure of his dying mother to the sprightly image of his daughter, the theme of his "romance" flashed subliminally before him. For the God that gives Hester a lovely child "as a direct consequence of the sin which man thus punished" (p. 89) is the same great satirist who gave Hawthorne his own Pearl "of great price." Named from Spenser's Una in Book I of *The Faerie Queene*, the daughter who lived as Hawthorne's mother died became the model for the child worthy to have been left in Eden "after the world's first parents were driven out" (p. 90). Like the wild rosebush "rooted almost at the threshold" (p. 48) of the prison door from which Hester emerges, Pearl represents the "wildlife" that survives the death of every ecstatic moment. As an extension of Hester's character and crime, she is unamenable to rules because "in giving her existence, a great law had been broken" (p. 91). She is the "wildlife" of the Dark Wood that was supposedly leveled to make way for the settlement of the New World. But as Hawthorne tells us in his truest "romance" of the self, its symbol had "been kept alive in history . . . after the fall of the gigantic pines and oaks that originally overshadowed it" (p. 48).

Ultimately the fable of humankind emerging from the vast forest of its origin in inexplicable sin, *The Scarlet Letter* sets out to consecrate that crime in the tragic triumph of Hester over the human (if not social) condition. In one sense, her character resembles that of Melville's Ahab in the capacity to sustain her sense of wholeness in the face of despair and public contumely. But Hawthorne realized all too well before the end where his "sketch" was taking him and left off writing the conclusion (or what became the final three chapers) until he had revived his former or social sense of himself by immersing himself in the customhouse sketch. By backing out of his story and giving instead this "Author's Account of Himself" (one at the same time as deceptive and revealing as Irving's had been in *The Sketch Book*), Hawthorne probably saved himself from writing the "Wicked book" Melville thought he had written in *Moby-Dick*.[5] As one critic put it, perhaps more astutely than he may have realized, once the sketch had been written, "Hawthorne felt free to write the last three chapters in a triumphant dash."[6] The author's last-minute retreat from the primordial sense of himself in *The Scarlet Letter* may have preserved his sanity to some extent—as well as his chance to publish a novel deemed worthy of family reading under the standard "of the evening lamp." But it also cost him (and us) the true ending of the novel, for what Hawthorne really left posterity was the middle of his story, one that not only begins in medias res but ends there as well. Like Melville, who would tell Hawthorne that he had baptized his magnum opus in the name of the devil,[7] Hawthorne admitted to Horatio Bridge on the day he completed *The Scarlet Letter* that his book was "positively a h—ll-fired story, into which I found it almost impossible to throw any cheering light."[8] But in fact the sunshine floods this "tale of human frailty" in the last three chapters in which Dimmesdale repents, Hester becomes a "nun," and Pearl lives happily ever after.

In sending James T. Fields everything but the last three chapters, Hawthorne urged his publisher to read the customhouse sketch first, for it served as a frame and as a foil to the confessional story of Hester—and Hawthorne. "'The Scarlet Letter' is rather a delicate subject to write upon," he added, "but in the way in which I have treated it, it appears to me there can be no objections on that score."[9] He was referring, of course, to the tale's commencement in medias res—long after that delicate moment between Hester and her lover. And yet he must have realized that his skillful handling of one delicacy had led him to a greater one. It had taken him back to the scene of the universal "crime," that of Job in the bewilderment of his sinful existence. In avoiding Hester's actual crime, Hawthorne stumbled onto his own and now found himself—by the end of "The Minister in a Maze"— falling into the same nihilism that Hester considers seven years after her fall and public punishment. *The Scarlet Letter* had indeed "not done its office" (p. 166). In "Endicott and the Red Cross," England's symbol is cut from "New England's banner." The deeds of the past are punished instead of preserved: the young woman in the sketch "whose doom it was to wear the letter A on the breast of her gown"[10] was thus far in *The Scarlet Letter* acting out the script from the part of the novel that Hawthorne—like Endicott—had already cut out.

As Hawthorne emerged from his "romance" to write the customhouse sketch, he may have indeed felt like Dimmesdale upon his

emergence from the Dark Wood of Hester. He desperately needed a
beginning and an ending that would save him from the self he had
revealed in the true text, or middle, something that would also save
the book from the sensationalist and erotic fiction described recently
by David S. Reynolds.[11] For the true "customhouse" was to be found
in the novel where Hawthorne had already passed from the illusion
about a world of good and evil to the discovery of one of good *in*
"evil." In *The Scarlet Letter* Hester experiences "a new birth, with
stronger assimilations than the first" (p. 80). Her so-called sin—the
lovemaking for which she is punished—becomes a means by which
she establishes an identity that can never be decapitated by the "custom" of a John Endicott. She develops, at least up to the composition
of the customhouse sketch, complete faith in the solitary self and de-
served, in Hawthorne's inversion of contemporary morality, to be pardoned and not punished because she has betrayed no one but the
sense of her fragmented self in the present. Consecrated instead of
castigated by the letter, Hester had, however, gone about as far as
Hawthorne—and his genteel readership—would allow. Indeed, it is
she as well as Dimmesdale who lacks penitence in their forest meeting. Both have done their penance, but Dimmesdale is also very sorry
for what he did in the Dark Wood and, like Aylmer in "The Birth-
mark," strives to erase the blemish without killing off the patient (in
this case, himself). Hester, on the other hand, relishes the new identity
the "sin" has given her and is ready to do it again (and perhaps does)
in the wilderness. "Doth the universe lie within the compass of yonder
town?" she asks her former lover, teasing him with a language whose
sexual connotations are hard to miss: "Wither leads yonder forest-
track? Backward to the settlement, thou sayest! Yes, but onward, too!
Deeper it goes, and deeper, into the wilderness, less plainly to be seen
at every step; until, some few miles hence, the yellow leaves will show
no vestige of the white man's tread. There thou are free!" (p. 197).
Before Hawthorne can stop his Hester, she practically undresses before him, for undoing the letter also undoes the sense of Puritan guilt
about what John Winthrop called "natural liberty." In what has been
recently described as "the loveliest erotic moment in nineteenth-century American literature,"[12] Hester's "sex, her youth, and the whole
richness of her beauty, came back from what men call the irrevocable
past" (p. 202). What "men" call the irrevocable past is in fact a version

of the verboten present in which one is endlessly free of the consequences of freedom. Hence, "the whole richness" of Hawthorne's irrevocable but also unforgettable past came back with this scene. For the sin committed had been—as Hawthorne says of Hester and Arthur's—one "of passion, not of principle, nor even purpose" (p. 200). It had been the sin of the self—a fictive self, to be sure—but one whose fiction is the only fact it chooses to acknowledge.

Prior to writing *The Scarlet Letter* Hawthorne had usually managed to squeeze a moral out of his near-heretical visions of the past in the present. In "Young Goodman Brown" and "Rappaccini's Daughter," two stories mirroring *The Scarlet Letter*'s theme of the self-consecrated self, the lesson is that the head ought always to be tempered by the heart, suspicion offset by trust. Such tales with their moralistic frames ultimately tell no tales on their author, and finally neither does Hester's. Before she can take Dimmesdale deeper into her wilderness, Hawthorne takes them both into the customhouse. From there they return, like Dimmesdale after his (second) night in the forest, as other people. No longer Adam and Eve enjoying the "sympathy of nature" (or "natural liberty"), they hear the voice in Hawthorne's puritanical garden and reappear in the story as priest and nun. Fifty years later another "sister" would slip through the American customhouse, but Hester went to bed with a druid instead of a drummer. This difference draws the line between the literary treatment of women in the nineteenth century and at its close with Dreiser in *Sister Carrie*, a point I develop in my final chapter. For now and for Hawthorne's time, it is necessary only to realize the necessary subversions Hawthorne had to entertain in order to write about "human frailty and sorrow." The fact is that Hawthorne had lost his head in what he described to Horatio Bridge as a "delicate subject" and found it again only in the customhouse (sketch). Like Shakespeare at the end of *Hamlet*, he needed a stage device to remove the characters slain by their desire for life.

Part of the problem, as he must have seen it, was the inadequacy of his Unpardonable Sinner, whose role in the tales had usually saved them from heresy. In *The Scarlet Letter* Chillingworth is but a minor player; he in fact does nothing truly illicit or unethical (other than administer a doctor's care and a few herbal drugs to the individual who has cuckolded him), and thus his defeat could not redeem the tale or dissipate its nihilistic thunder. Having the old man shrivel up did little to hide the fact that Hawthorne had thus far written a dangerous allegory in which man is reborn again through the power of sex. Whitman would explore the same idea much more boldly in the "Children of Adam" poems and find himself reviled by the literary class's demand for conventional morality in its literature. Yet Hawthorne's reticence goes much deeper than simply a concern about middle-class censure (though it was always a concern to him). That is to say, he was Emersonian (and neopuritanical) enough to look for nature's compensation in the scenes he surveyed. Although the contrast between life and death had led him to his dialectic in *The Scarlet Letter*, he went on in the same notebook entry (as he would in the novel) to modify the mockery he found in the loss of a mother and the "gain" of a daughter: "God would not have made the close so dark and wretched [he wrote], if there were nothing beyond; for then it would have been a fiend that created us, and measured out our existence, and not God. It would be something beyond wrong—it would be insult—to be thrust out of life into annihilation in this miserable way. So, out of the very bitterness of death, I gather the sweet assurance of a better state of being."[13] The speaker here is Dimmesdale and not Hester—or Hawthorne on the "first story" of himself. It is the same individual who at the close of the novel feebly asks Hester if confession and death are not better "than what we dreamed of in the forest" (p. 254). Hawthorne's true confession would be at least partially concealed by the ending he found in the customhouse. Safely out of the Dark Wood of his imagination, indeed out of the Inferno and up the Purgatorial Mount, Hawthorne would make his way to the public paradises of children's books and Transcendentalist utopias. Resurrected as Coverdale in *The Blithedale Romance*, the former surveyor would claim "a license with regard to every-day Probability" (as he wrote in the preface to that novel) that would keep his probable characters "entirely fictitious." Unlike the use of autobiography in *The Scarlet Letter*, here it would be autobiography in the third person. "In short," he wrote, "his present concern . . . is merely to establish a theatre, a little removed from the highway of ordinary travel, where the creatures of his brain may play their phantasmagorical antics, without exposing them to too close a comparison with the actual events of *real lives*" (my italics).[14] "Be true! Be true!" he had said at the end of *The Scarlet Letter.* "Show freely to the world, if not your worst, yet some trait whereby the worst may be inferred!" (p. 260). Yet all we can infer from the revealed Dimmesdale or the concealed Coverdale is a self misbegotten instead of self-begotten.

It is important that we do not hear the actual words of Dimmesdale's election sermon, only its cadences. Although Hawthorne reports its message as the "complaint of a human heart" (p. 243), he does not allow his priest to confess it directly. What comes through, therefore, is a censured instead of self-begotten self, whose sermon does "its office" and turns Hester into a pillar of salt—as she stands "statue-like, at the foot of the scaffold." The only remaining wildness belongs to Pearl, who flits about during the sermon like "a humming-bird": "She ran and looked [a] wild Indian in the face, and he grew conscious of a nature wilder than his own" (p. 244). In other words, all that remains of their consecration is its soundless symbol, plucked from a rosebush by the prison door. The child was, Hawthorne tells us, "the scarlet letter in another form; the scarlet letter endowed with life!" (p. 102). But this life cannot escape the sobered vision of Hawthorne. Time and again in the tale Pearl—the symbol of her parents' consecration—is about to fly away from it all, but in the end she becomes the heir of Chillingworth instead of Dimmesdale.

In other words, Hawthorne takes the whole affair back through the customhouse and this time stamps it public instead of private. What happened in the forest must be declared in the marketplace, as Pearl herself suggests by asking her mother why the minister fails to acknowledge them on the day of the procession. Driven out of the forest by its own sense of guilt, this secret self now stands on the scaffold thinking not of its own consecration but of the law it broke by coming into existence. The exposure kills off more than Dimmesdale, for with the public confession Hester finally becomes penitent, and Pearl becomes a person. All the characters lie dead on this moral stage, awaiting the arrival of the customhouse officer who will claim for the story only the authenticity of an outline. Hawthorne's "White Whale" concludes as a white lie that calls life a tale of sin and redemption instead of one of "human frailty and sorrow" (p. 48).[15]

Hawthorne's ultimate denial of Hester's (and his own) subversive nature is anticipated, of course, in "Young Goodman Brown," where that pilgrim also loses faith in the possibility of returning to the libidinous Garden of Eden. Hester, Hawthorne tells us in the customhouse sketch, had "flourished" and so had Faith. Standard readings of that sketch find Goodman Brown losing faith in the goodness of human-kind, but our pilgrim really loses faith in himself. He wakes up to find himself isolated from the world and unable to re-experience the passion he had once enjoyed in the Dark Wood. Instead of finding a lover there, he finds a perfidious wife who has given herself to the devil. Dimmesdale imagines the same fate as he comes out of the forest.[16] To become self-begotten, to go back to one's beginning, is itself as adulterous as the passion of Hawthorne's two lovers. To go back before the Fall in order to experience perfection is to cheat the present, or the Emersonian principle of loss and gain. Dimmesdale had been there once, but the sense of wholeness was as "irrevocable" as Hester's original beauty, its garden now a Dark and Dead Wood. And thus his song of himself is nothing more than the "unfinished sermon" to which he returns.

This is also the fate of Hawthorne's dream of himself in *The Scarlet Letter*. His song becomes a sermon that condemns with one voice both "unpardonable" and pardonable sinners—not only the Chillingworths who never live (or love) but the Dimmesdales who dare to make their lives "a twice-told tale," a second story of election instead of a sentimental sermon about sin and repentence. We are told that when Pearl kissed the minister's lips, "a spell was broken" (p. 256). Yet the spell had already been broken back in "The Minister in a Maze." Hawthorne, too, emerged from the Dark Wood of the imagination—from what he called "The Interior of a Heart"—to a headiness that left him reeling. Like Dimmesdale, he found himself back in New England and not in the New World of the imagination. Now Dimmesdale has "something" to do again, and so does Hawthorne. In the next chapter (and the last before he broke off to write the customhouse sketch), he reclothes his Hester "in a garment of coarse gray cloth." It had the effect, he says, "of making her fade personally out of sight and outline; while, again, the scarlet letter brought her back from this twilight indistinctness, and revealed her under the moral aspect of its own illumination." Her face returned to "the marble quietude" the townspeople knew: "It was like a mask; or rather, like the frozen calmness of a dead woman's features" (p. 226).

This is Hawthorne's pasteboard "mask" that can finally never be removed in public.

In a well-known passage in the customhouse sketch where Hawthorne defines the Romance, he also gives himself away. For what enters his "neutral territory" is "a form, beloved, but gone hence, now sitting quietly in a streak of this magic moonshine, with an aspect that would make us doubt whether it had returned from afar, or had never once stirred from our fireside" (p. 36). We might imagine that this is Elizabeth Hawthorne come back from her fresh grave to call her son back to himself in the present as the father of Una instead of Pearl. Because it is the lover of Hester *and* Elizabeth that launches this romance, but the penitent son who brings it to a close. Sorry for what *he* did in the Dark Wood—the moonlight of memory—Hawthorne returned to the novel to change the meaning of the Scarlet Letter. It now stood for "adulteress," not "able" or "angel," after all. No longer able himself, this adulterer makes his public confession, one that is as obscure as Dimmesdale's, but also as bathetic. Somehow, we are supposed to believe that his two pilgrims had wronged themselves by becoming themselves—consecrated by passion and not by principle or purpose. But *The Scarlet Letter* in its original and unfinished version is not about faking it through life but about that other word that invokes the shame of our own illicit beginning. Hester and Arthur break through the "paste-board mask," but only Hester lives to tell about it. As Hawthorne's "Lone Survivor," she outlasts both her Arthur and her Author. Penitent perhaps, but in a noble and stoical way that surely reveals Hawthorne's ambivalence about the tale he has told (on himself), Hester Prynne is the Anne Hutchinson of our literature—always self-begotten and never misbegotten, even in defeat.

We will remember from John Winthrop's journal the description of the "monstrous birth" that followed Anne Hutchinson's self-consecration and sanctification here on earth. In "open assembly at Boston," Winthrop recorded that John Cotton held up the birth as a living sermon against the mother's theological errors.[17] Hester's "sin-born infant" reintroduces that text with an ironic twist. For the birdlike Pearl springs from a "virgin birth" whose conception precedes and thus eludes the action of the novel. As the offspring of the same kind of egotism for which Hutchinson was banished, she is the elixir that makes *The Scarlet Letter* a romance instead of a novel in which Hester, like Anne Hutchinson, would have been driven out of New England and into the hands of savages. For Pearl exists only as evidence of her parents' ecstasy, and when that ecstasy is finally denied she disappears as a viable part of the drama. Before we know it, she is whisked off to the Old World of novels involving letters "with armorial seals" or early maiden graves. Hawthorne's uncertainty as to Pearl's exact fate belies the fact that she was always a chimera and never a character in the novelistic sense. In *The Blithedale Romance* Hawthorne would write a novel, more or less, but in *The Scarlet Letter* he had truly written as Coverdale. His text playfully and secretly rejected the moral code that finally defeats his two lovers. The floor of his "familiar room" had indeed become a neutral territory in which the ghosts of our unknown past might enter, "without affrighting us" (pp. 35–36).

Hawthorne was quite frankly embarrassed about his tour de force and spent the next year or so comparing it unfavorably to his other work. In a letter to Evert Duyckinck, he called *The House of the Seven Gables* "a more natural and healthy product" of his mind.[18] He told his sister Elizabeth that it had "more merit" than *The Scarlet Letter.*[19] It appears that despite the book's commercial success, he was trying to bury it the way he had tried to bury *Fanshawe*. Both novels had been the work of his "youth." Each had been gothic, *The Scarlet Letter* in the sense that it had taken Hawthorne back to his ancestral self. After reading the manuscript to his wife, he boasted to Horatio Bridge of having sent her to bed "with a grievous headache—which I look upon as a triumphant success." But privately, in his notebook, he confessed to having broken down himself during the reading.[20] *The Scarlet Letter*, it should now become clear, was secretly dedicated to the memory of Elizabeth Hawthorne almost as surely as *Moby-Dick* was dedicated to her son. It was dedicated to the memory of a love so primordially deep that it made Hawthorne swim for his authorial life. The book was conceived in the sorrow that brings every man full circle with himself. With the death of his mother, he is in effect reconceived as a father instead of a son, a brother at best, and never again a lover. Hester had "flourished" long ago, and so had Hawthorne. He had been conceived, and for many years had lingered about the scene of the crime—always allied with his mother, but also somewhat alienated.

In the romance that sprang from Hawthorne's belated sense of Oedipal displacement, Dimmesdale comes to Hester the second time as a little boy, helplessly beseeching her to get him out of trouble. "Be thou strong for me!" he begs. "Advise me what to do." It is at this point that he is beckoned back into her forest, beckoned to "begin all anew! . . . give up this name of Arthur Dimmesdale, and make thyself another" (pp. 196, 198). But the way inward is also the way outward in this case, for his lover is also Hawthorne's mother. Dimmesdale, as he confesses, lacks the courage "to venture into the wide, strange difficult world, alone!" (p. 198). Under the spell of Oedipus, he had been strong and virile. But this "open ignominy" is simply too much—so much in fact that he never really gives a clear confession. What makes this novel compelling, therefore, is not that it is a love story of two but an allegory of one who *is* two. It is a tale of twisted feelings, of a "polluted priest" who commits the sin he officially forgives. The priest and his parishioners pray together, but no one stays together for very long in this moonlit drama of the psyche. One might say, though certainly over Poe's objections, that *The Scarlet Letter* concerns the death of a beautiful woman. And with her death the son died, too, and was reborn as a husband instead of a lover. Surely, this was the narrator who finished the tale and gave his wife a headache, not the desperate Dimmesdale who broke down in the middle of the story.

Actually, Hawthorne records that he broke down while reading the "last scene" of the book, but he adds that his "very nervous state" was the result of "having gone through a great diversity and severity of emotion, for many months past."[21] As Arlin Turner observes, in the wake of Elizabeth Hawthorne's death, "there followed six months of creativity that he did not equal in intensity or achievement at any other time in his life."[22] So great had been the strain of genius that Hawthorne remarked that he had "never overcome [his] own adamant in any other instance" than during the reading aloud of *The Scarlet Letter*. If Hawthorne's "adamant" or shell had been cracked, however, his wife refused to acknowledge (to others, at least) this Dimmesdalian confession. In writing to her sister, Sophia Hawthorne wondered what she would think of the story. "It is most powerful, & contains a

moral as terrific & stunning as a thunderbolt." And she added significantly: "It shows that the Law cannot be broken."[23] The same woman
would challenge (in a private letter to her mother) Melville's discovery
of "blackness" in Hawthorne's *Mosses from an Old Manse.* "But it is
funny," she wrote, "to see how he does not know how this heart and
this intellect are enshrined." Insisting upon the balance of head and
heart instead of a heart beheaded as her husband's theme, Sophia
could not share her husband's confession in *The Scarlet Letter.*
Rather, his heartache gave her a headache.[24]

Hawthorne's "tale of human frailty" opened in the memory of his
mother and closed in the presence of his wife. In the middle his
daughter hovered over the drama as a symbol of the fleeting self he
had dared to celebrate in the novel. Yet its symbolic center is of course
Hester, who is a composite of all three in their various relationships to
the author: as a "daughter" she confides in her father-confessor; as a
"wife" or sexual partner she comes to Dimmesdale in the Dark Wood;
and as a "mother" she hears his confession in the forest. "So pictur-
esque in her attire and mien," Hawthorne establishes at the outset,
Hester is "the image of Divine Maternity, which so many illustrious
painters have vied with one another to represent." Yet she is *unpaint-
able* because her beauty contains "the taint of deepest sin in the most
sacred quality of human life, working such effect, that the world was
only the darker for this woman's beauty, and the more lost for the
infant she had borne" (p. 56). Just as Poe's apostrophe to the sensual
Helen was inspired by the *mother* of one of his schoolmates, the sensuality of Hawthorne's Hester resides in her "Divine Maternity"—one that ultimately bears and nurtures a Christ that must be
crucified. If not crucified, at least "decapitated"—as are most of Hawthorne's protagonists, from Fanshawe to Dimmesdale (and beyond),
who lose their heads in an affair of the heart. When Ellen Langton in
Fanshawe offers herself to the reclusive hero of that romance, she
receives the same answer Dimmesdale ultimately gives to Hester.
Both Fanshawe and Dimmesdale subsequently die out of the drama
that castrates, crucifies, and decapitates them.

In *The Scarlet Letter* Hawthorne allowed himself the same freedom
he gives his two protagonists (however vicarious it is in Fanshawe's
case). Like Dimmesdale in "A Flood of Sunshine," he gazed into
Hester's face with a look of "hope and joy" but finally fled from the

"horror of her boldness" (p. 199). Decapitated by what he had surveyed, he chased himself out of the tale as surely as Ichabod Crane is chased out by the decapitated Irving at the end of *The Sketch Book.* Another dream book, *The Scarlet Letter* is the same kind of headless invasion of the heart, which takes the author into "a moral wilderness" that is indeed a Dark Wood. In "The Minister's Vigil," for example, we find Dimmesdale "walking in the shadow of a dream, as it were, and perhaps actually under the influence of a species of somnambulism," until he reaches "the spot, where, now so long since, Hester Prynne had lived through her first hour of public ignominy." His destination is the scaffold, of course, "black and weather-stained with the storm or sunshine of seven long years, and foot-worn, too, with the tread of many culprits who had since ascended it" (p. 147). The number seven has a long tradition in literature, but it is worthwhile to remember that Hawthorne had married Sophia almost exactly seven years before the death of his mother. The engagement had been a strained affair, kept secret by Hawthorne from his mother and two sisters until only a month or two before the wedding on 9 July 1842. No member of the groom's family attended the ceremony. All three family members resented the concealment of the engagement, but Hawthorne's mother—according to her daughter[25]—was especially pained to hear of the coming wedding from her prospective daughter-in-law instead of from her introspective son. The marriage must have been a kind of "public ignominy" to the woman who had raised the groom without a father. With his secret engagement, Hawthorne had, in a sense, abandoned his mother on the scaffold of public opinion, much in the way Dimmesdale allows Hester to stand there alone. Seven years later they both return to the scene of the crime.

In 1849, when Hawthorne got the "authenticity" of his outline, he had acknowledged, we will remember, "a sort of coldness" in the relationship with his mother that (he said) often comes between "persons of strong feelings." Whatever the source of that coldness, it was possibly renewed by Hawthorne's secret love and subsequent marriage. Hawthorne had commited adultery, as it were, in 1842, and so seven years later he was ready—like Dimmesdale—to make his confession in *The Scarlet Letter.* For the book, in one sense at least, is the story of an abandoned mother and lover, the story of betrayal. Indeed, Hawthorne had betrayed his deepest feelings, but like Dimmesdale's confession we never hear the actual words of penitence but only the cadences of the self in conflict with itself. In "The Minister's Vigil," it is important to note, Dimmesdale can acknowledge his intimacy with Hester (and Pearl) only at night. Ominously, this mother-lover has just returned from Governor Winthrop's deathbed after taking "his measure" for a funereal robe. Because he cannot yet acknowledge (either publicly or privately) the consequences of his frailty and ultimate fatality as a human being, Dimmesdale will not promise Pearl to remount the scaffold in the light of day. And when he finally does—in the chapter ironically called "The Revelation of the Scarlet Letter"—the confession is as obscure as Hawthorne's final three chapters are in terms of *his* confession. In both cases, Dimmesdale's auditors and Hawthorne's readers are not quite sure of the text, not quite sure whether it is a confession or a sermon, and never sure they can abide anything other than its hopeful ambiguity. Whatever Hawthorne reveals in *The Scarlet Letter*, he also cleverly conceals. In *Fanshawe* and the sketches leading up to Hawthorne's greatest sketch of himself, as well as beyond it in what might be termed "aborted" romances, Hawthorne had kept his perspective (and his sanity), but in *The Scarlet Letter* the case was different. He would have agreed with Melville in *Moby-Dick* that "when Leviathan is the text, the case is altered." [26]

3 : Melville's High on the Seas

If telling the primordial truth was the result of Hawthorne's dream in *The Scarlet Letter*, Herman Melville in *Moby-Dick* probably realized that such "truth" was too deep to tell completely. He found it, as he says in the chapter on "Cetology," "full of leviathanism, but signifying nothing."[1] He had already learned from Shakespeare *and* Hawthorne that it was "a tale told by an idiot" whose lunacy was the proper text and test for his imagination. No more "crazy" after his fall from "something" into "nothing" than Rip or Dimmesdale, the narrator of *Moby-Dick* wakes up to "that damp, drizzly November" of his soul with absolutely *nothing* to do. "Having little or no money in my purse, and nothing particular to interest me on shore," Ishmael confesses, "I thought I would sail about a little and see the watery part of the world" (p. 12). Once again we find the American writer on the "blank page in existence,"[2] headed for the myth of his identity in the fluid element Melville calls "an everlasting terra incognita" (p. 235). Columbus may have discovered the dry land of America, but en route he "sailed over numberless unknown worlds." From these we were, like Ishmael, perennial outcasts despite the alleged progress of our civilization. However much "baby man may brag of his science and skill, and however much, in a flattering future, that science and skill may augment; yet for ever and for ever, to the crack of doom, the sea will insult and murder him, and pulverize the stateliest, stiffest frigate he can make" (p. 235). Such is the fate of Ahab and the *Pequod*, of course, in this dialectic of the Leviathan.

Whereas *The Scarlet Letter* lacks a beginning and an ending in its myth of man in the Dark Wood and womb of his imagination, *Moby-Dick* lacks a discernible middle in its effort to recreate the myth of Jonah in the belly of the whale. It consists of episodes and stories that recommence the voyage of the self into the unknown, which hides its beginning and assures its ending. From "Loomings" to "Epilogue" this whale's tale keeps starting over with sketches about a crew that is in fact as fictional as Irving's crew of revelers in the Catskills. Like the abandoned Bulkington, their tales signify nothing more than the fate of every fiction about an identity outside the present. One tale that stands out for its fiction in this assemblage of "facts" about whaling is "The Town-Ho's Story." Like the raft passage in *Huckleberry Finn*, it exists outside the larger story to remind us that the first-person narrator is a storyteller and not an "eyewitness" to the events he recounts. In Mark Twain's "aside," the tall tales or boastings of the raftsmen are cut down to reality by another tall tale—that of the shortest combatant whipping the two bigger men. In "The Town Ho's Story," the hissed threat of Steelkilt defeats the fiction of the captain's supremacy at sea. Yet another fiction, the lakeman's warning serves as fact for the captain and, indirectly, as fate for his first mate, Radney. Interestingly, both the raft passage and "The Town-Ho's Story" appeared prior to the publication of the fiction to which they originally belonged.[3] Because he had dedicated his passage to another story (to which it did not belong), Twain never returned the part to the whole of *Huckleberry Finn*, but Melville had already exhausted his stories of shipboard "youth" and so was compelled to put his tale back into the larger lie of his literary maturity. This was the myth he created in *Moby-Dick*, for the other is merely a "story" in the sense that it ends happily instead of not at all. *Moby-Dick* begins every time it ends with the awakening of the orphan in a coffin. As in the epilogue, the writer in Melville's fiction is always waking up as an orphan, yearning in the present for the living past.

In his biography of Melville, Edwin Haviland Miller has already argued perceptively for this identity-theme, that of the orphan whose genius is shaped largely by his sense of alienation from his parents and parental love.[4] "Call me Ishmael," Melville announces at the beginning of his book, and we do because the story begins with an aura of loss and abandonment. As it begins (again), the narrator has lost his crew and captain in the pursuit of a greater loss, the whale and womb which the biblical Jonah inadvertently sought out in what has become one of the western myths of our being in the beginning. In earlier works, Melville had carefully (if not altogether consciously) avoided the whale as a symbol of the human enigma in his attention to the sea as a field of adventure. In *Moby-Dick*, however, the whale finally breaches to lure us into an "adventure" that happened long ago. This is the myth of man enwombed again, and as such it is a retracing of the Book of Jonah. In that story we remember most clearly the scene in which God comes to Jonah in the belly of the whale and not—because of the analeptic nature of desire—its conclusion east of the wicked city of Nineveh. It is as if Jonah were never "vomited" back upon "dry *land*" but forever entombed in his "true" beginning. In other words, in our memory of that story, we keep waking up to the central scene and never to the end of the story.

In his study of patients suffering from *encephalitis lethargica*, or "sleeping sickness," Oliver Sacks notes that their awakenings often forty or more years later (induced by the drug L-dopa) involved what he calls a "forced reminiscence." That is to say, such patients wake up with a profound sense of loss that allows them to recall with un- canny precision the events of the year in which they went to sleep. In the case of one patient, a "Miss R." who was first stricken by the disease in 1926, Sacks writes that she felt her past as present, that perhaps it never felt "past" for her. "Is it possible that Miss R. has never, in fact, moved on from the 'past'?" He adds that this patient knew "perfectly well" that it was forty-three years later and that she was sixty-four instead of twenty-one. Yet she *felt* as if it were 1926 because she had "never really experienced" the intervening years.[5] As a result, her "nostalgic state" seemed more real than the present one. Although Sacks's study may be more popular than professionally con- vincing, the case presents on its face a dramatic illustration of the power of memory to drive us out of the present and back to a time when we were timelessly happy. For Miss R., 1926 had been the hap- piest and most productive time she could remember, the last year be- fore her long "dream" of helplessness to help herself. In waking up, therefore, she experienced another beginning, and we do the same every time we invoke the myth of our existence in something larger than the flawed present. We exorcize our sense of belatedness with fictions about a past that never quite existed—not with stories that end happily but with myths that are full of beginnings. Appropriately, *Moby-Dick* invokes that sense of origin with the Old Testament and the Books of Genesis and Jonah. Ishmael, the illegitimate son of Abraham and Sarah, springs from it, and so does possibly the whale, who is named after Moab, the "illegitimate" son of Lot by his daughter. It is also a story of the sea, where all life supposedly began, and concerns a sperm whale, seamen, and a captain named after another Old Testament figure (1 Kings 16–22). Full of facts about whaling, *Moby-Dick* is yet another myth that recycles our fantasy as orphans of something instead of nothing.

What "looms" at the close of the *Pequod*'s voyage is what follows the conclusion of every human journey, or cycle of it: a burial at sea and a "sleep" that awaits another awakening and the desire for a new beginning. Ahab might as well join Jim and Huck in their search for the *other* wooden leg as pursue the whale that only Jonah found in his dream and in our dream-vision about a prenatal and primordial harmony that must precede what we call the "human condition." It is, in fact, a *condition* to our identity as orphans of a world that is older than time itself. Just as the lascivious daughters of Lot seduce their father in order to preserve his seed, so Ahab seduces his crew into undertaking a suicidal mission in order to rediscover his connection with a paternity that is as elusive as the sperm whale. Its whiteness represents the same "blank page in existence" that drove Irving to sea and Hawthorne to its edge in the customhouse. In 1850 Melville had already been to sea and was yet to spend twenty long years in a customhouse. He woke up in the middle of his literary life and started over as the biblical Ishmael—the "lone survivor" who is destined to tell our story in *Moby-Dick* every time we read it. In other words, he wakes up in our present and tells a story as old as Jonah's, as if the intervening years had never been experienced.

I have remarked in another book that the narrative voice in *Moby-Dick* becomes so heterodiegetic that it might as well be the voice of God that we hear.[6] The book opens in the autobiographical but soon deepens into a disembodied voice that clearly blends with Ahab's. One might say that in the course of the novel Ishmael "dies" into Ahab, and indeed the reviewers of the English edition complained—more literally—that it was a story told by a dead man. One incredulous critic wrote: "It is canon . . . that nothing should be introduced into a novel which is physically impossible for the writer to have known: thus, he must not describe the conversation of miners in a pit if they *all* perish. Mr. Melville hardly steers clear of this rule . . . by beginning in the autobiographical and changing *ad libitum* into the narrative."[7] Emily Dickinson might safely adopt the posthumous, or proleptic, point of view, but she chose not to publish. Melville, on the other hand, was "damned by dollars," as he told Hawthorne,[8] and thus compelled to publish his identity-dream. In *The Whale*, as the English edition was called, he did allow for the possibility of a surviving narrator—in the form of the third man in Ahab's whaleboat who is observed "helplessly dropping astern, but still afloat and swimming" (p. 466). In the epilogue added to the American edition, of course, we discover that this person is the narrator called Ishmael.

Clearly, the conclusion to *The Whale* is more realistic (and less dreamlike) than the close of *Moby-Dick; or The White Whale*. And had the British edition begun with the omniscient point of view, its critics would have been more satisfied with its fiction. The American conclusion, or "Epilogue," brings the autobiographer back on stage to reflect on his tale as a dreamer trying to make sense of his dream. As a literary frame, it is as fantastic as the one used by Hawthorne in "Young Goodman Brown." That dream-vision of connubial guilt is brought to a close by asking whether the hero had "fallen asleep in the forest, and only dreamed a wild dream of a witch meeting."[9] Brown's dazed condition is similar to Dimmesdale's confusion about what went on the evening before in the Dark Wood with Hester. This is the American Romance, the lie whose truth must ultimately be questioned and consigned to the impossible realm of myth.[10] When the narrator surfaces from the "closing vortex" of his story, he retells it pseudonymously because it signifies an identity lost long ago but remembered as if it were yesterday.

There are no notable women in *Moby-Dick* except for the absent girl-wife whom Ahab has effectively "widowed" by running off to sea after leaving but "one dent" in his marriage pillow. Like Goodman Brown, he is another womb-quester who flees the role of father for that of son. In Melville's largely single-gender world, that possibility is symbolized not with a mother-lover such as Hester but with a

Jonah-whale such as Moby-Dick. Moab, whose biblical meaning is "the seed of the father," courses the globe as so many protozoa and thus represents life *before* the fall of Adam into Eve. Figuratively at least, it is a whale's womb that entombs Jonah and Ahab in this fiction of a beginning in the autobiographical instead of the omniscient, or "narrative," point of view. The autobiographical is analeptic, whereas the omniscient is proleptic: the first looks back at life before birth, the second at life after death. Irving told his dream as Geoffrey Crayon, or as another person; and Hawthorne had told his in medias res, or "after the fact." Melville, on the other hand, told his tale as if it had not yet happened, or as it always happened in the cycle of beginnings—"cruises" that punctuate the sailor's life.

Ahab has been married for almost three such cruises, or almost nine years, allowing him virtually no time with his young wife and only son. Like Melville himself, whose personal relationship with his wife and children was sometimes turbulent, Ahab keeps voyaging out from the dry land of his present existence in search of the year or day in which he knew life without death. Like Dickinson, who was "widowed" by every life experience and looked anew for a lover or "master," the Berkshires poet was always returning from each cycle—or like Ahab, each circumnavigation of the globe—at the beginning of the next one and thus at the *beginning* of the story of life and death. The narrator of *Moby-Dick*, therefore, is both autobiographical and omniscient, both American and all that is—in terms of American idealism—dramatically *un*-American: he wakes up at the beginning of every life cycle in this fiction to be drawn into his drama and almost *drowned* by it. For Melville's reenactment of Jonah's tale is a burial at sea in a coffin whose wood—like that of the *Pequod*, as Ahab exclaims—"could only be American!" (p. 468). In the British version there are no really credible survivors, but the American dreamer is always waking up again to tell his story as if it really happened.

This is the *real* American Dream, a reverse ideology that posits our sanctity in the past instead of the future. In a land of renaissances, revivals, reborn Christians, and the psychology of endless second chances, the writer is also *reborn*—but only once. "Until I was twenty five," Melville confessed shortly before the publication of *Moby-Dick*, the signature of his awakening after so many literary "cruises," "I had no development at all. From my twenty-fifth year I date my life. Three weeks have scarcely passed, at any time between then and now, that I have not unfolded within myself. But I feel that I am now come to the inmost leaf of the bulb, and that shortly the flower must fall to the mould."[11] He was writing, of course, to Hawthorne, who had already revealed too much of himself in *The Scarlet Letter* and was in fast retreat with the recent publication of *The House of the Seven Gables*. The actual house on which the Pyncheon mansion was modeled in that novel had in fact only five gables at the time (two others were added in the twentieth century to take capitalistic advantage of art), but Hawthorne was hiding more than that after the publication of *The Scarlet Letter*. Melville no doubt suspected as much, and in his epistolary review of *The House of the Seven Gables* (in an earlier letter to Hawthorne), he described the book as "abundantly" but "judiciously furnished." "We think the book, for pleasantness of running interest, surpasses the other works of the author. The curtains are more drawn; the sun comes in more; genialities peep out more."[12] In other words, this well-wrought novel, with its firm story line and gothic embellishment, takes place in society and not in a Dark Wood—or on an open(-ended) sea. While hinting at his disappointment, Melville was also telling Hawthorne what he probably wanted to hear, what Hawthorne had said to his sister Elizabeth and to Evert Duyckinck about the novel's having "more merit" and being "a more natural and healthy product" of his mind. Earlier and—it is important to note—pseudonymously, Melville had boldly declared that it was Hawthorne's "blackness" and not his lightened room with its "genialities" that had so fixed and fascinated him. In writing "Hawthorne and His Mosses," he had, in fact, discovered the clear and candid voice of Ishmael, who as an orphan of God has nothing to lose. The essay appeared in successive issues of *The Literary World* of late August 1850, and over the next eight months, as he wrote (or rewrote) *Moby-Dick*, Melville obviously pressed his reluctant neighbor in the Berkshires for confirmation of what he called in the essay "the shock of recognition." Even though he would proclaim in the spring of 1851 that there was "a grand truth about Nathaniel Hawthorne," that he had said "NO! in thunder," Melville was more than likely celebrating the earlier work and not *The House of the Seven*

Gables, which brought Hawthorne back to the customhouse with its "heaps of baggage"—its marriage of Holgrave and Phoebe instead of the mirage of Arthur and Hester in the American Wood.

As Hawthorne resumed his duties in the customhouse of children's tales and Coverdales, Melville went farther and farther out to sea in *Moby-Dick*. "We incline to think," he told his reformed mentor, "that God cannot explain His own secrets, and that He would like a little information upon certain points Himself. . . . But it is this *Being* of the matter; there lies the knot with which we choke ourselves." He described himself as having reached "the last stages of metaphysics," having exhausted most of the "plain facts" that would keep *Moby-Dick*, as he wrote in chapter 45, from becoming some "monstrous fable, or still worse and more detestable, a hideous and intolerable allegory" (p. 177). In other words, life, or language, could not ultimately span—as Nietzsche and his heirs, the psycho-linguists, or Lacanians, of today, have theorized—the unbridgeable difference and distance between "vehicle" and "tenor" in every metaphorical equation. For "as soon as you say *Me*, a *God*, a *Nature*," Melville complained, "so soon you jump off from your stool and hang from the beam."[13] That is to say, what we *were* is forever elusive—lost in the space of time before time was. The longest distance between two places *was* time; this was the "*Being* of the matter." Life itself, as Melville suspected, *was* "a monstrous fable, or still worse and more detestable, a hideous and intolerable allegory" from which we could never quite wake up. For as soon as we did, it began all over again as if it were yesterday.

This is of course a problem of language and its mythmaking possibilities. In *Moby-Dick* it is dramatized by Melville's use of the Jonah myth. Father Mapple tells the biblical truth in chapter 9, but the problem with such a "truth" is taken up in chapter 83, provocatively called "Jonah Historically Regarded." The myth itself is a metaphor in the sense that it applies the life of man to a scene that is not literally applicable. Some Nantucketers, we learn, "rather distrust this historical story of Jonah and the whale"—

One old Sag-Harbor whaleman's chief reason for questioning the Hebrew story was this:—He had one of those quaint old-fashioned Bibles, embellished with curious, unscientific plates; one of which

represented Jonah's whale with two spouts in his head—a pecu-
liarity only true with respect to a species of the Leviathan (the Right
Whale, and the varieties of that order), concerning which the fish-
ermen have this saying, "A penny roll would choke him"; his swal-
low is so very small. But to this, Bishop Jebb's anticipative answer
is ready. It is not necessary, hints the Bishop, that we consider Jonah
as tombed in the whale's belly, but as temporarily lodged in some
part of his mouth. (p. 307)

Another reason for the Sag-Harbor lack of faith in biblical truth is
that Jonah would have been consumed by the whale's gastric juices.
"But this objection," Melville writes with obvious reference to the
High Critics' scrutiny of the Bible, "likewise falls to the ground, because a German exegetist supposes that Jonah must have taken refuge
in the floating body of a *dead* whale." Other explanations are that
soon after Jonah was thrown overboard from the Joppa ship, he was
rescued by a vessel "with a whale for a figure-head"; or that "the
whale mentioned in the book of Jonah merely meant a life-preserver"
(p. 307). There is also the problem of the great distance between the
Mediterranean, where Jonah is tossed overboard, and the city of Nineveh, where Jonah is restored to land after three days' journey. Not
only is the journey much more than three days, but the Tigris waters
approaching Nineveh are too shallow "for any whale to swim in."
Finally, Jonah in making the trip would have had to weather the Cape
of Good Hope—thus preceding its discoverer Bartholomeu Dias and
making "modern history a liar" (p. 308).

The myth, therefore, contradicts history. Jonah found the whale
and miraculously stood in the sight of God, but the quotidian fact for
Ahab is that, as the captain of the dejected *Delight* tells him, "the
harpoon is not yet forged" that will kill Moby-Dick (p. 441). Ahab is
faced with the fact that the whale—like Faulkner's bear—is unkill-
able: God always *was* and never *is* a possibility. And this "fact" is the
fiction which merges myth with history—merges it to the ultimate
exclusion of either because the blend is a "blind" that makes even
"plain facts" the linguistic materials for "a hideous and intolerable
allegory" called life. In using language, we are as blind as the whale,
whose eyes are planted in the sides of its head and who can thus look
only to port and starboard and never straight ahead. "The position of

the whale's eyes," Melville writes, "corresponds to that of a man's ears" (p. 279). Which is to say that we "see" with our ears, or through the use of metaphor, where the ultimate meaning of the "plain facts" is always just out of sight. Moby-Dick is always just out of reach until the collapse of metaphor and Ahab's necessary death. For the novel is a memory play, and as such it finally brings down the curtain on every attempt to unite "vehicle" and "tenor," or physical fact with spiritual fiction.

Like Hawthorne's pilgrim in the romance of "Young Goodman Brown," the protagonist of *Moby-Dick* must wake up before the end of the dream or die in his sleep. Which is to say that Truth exists only as a necessary myth, beyond which there is no "story" to tell. Ishmael, whose autobiography has during the course of the novel become absorbed by Ahab's narrative, wakes up as another Dantesque pilgrim to tell the story of the hell that lies beyond the "dark wood of life." "If I thought my answer were to one who could return to the world," Guido da Montefeltero tells the poet in the twenty-seventh canto of the *Inferno*, "this flame would shake no more." [14] But Dante and Ishmael—or Melville—travel with the impunity of language and thus *do* return to tell their stories. Or rather, they tell them only up to the point beyond which the terrain is postlinguistic. For this reason, Dante's *Commedia* can be said to end—in terms of the metaphorical quest—at the Wall of Flames, at the close of the *Purgatorio;* for here the language of Virgil, Dante's pagan philosopher and guide, fails, and he must proceed into Eden on faith alone. At the same point in *Moby-Dick*, where Ishmael witnesses the showdown between Ahab and the whale, the narrator almost drowns. The important difference is that he does not die, but rather than going, as Dante does, on faith alone, he wakes up to the failure of language to reveal more than "plain facts," or at best the *dream* that lies beyond them. "My Faith is gone!" Melville might as well have had Ishmael exclaim as he wakes up from the dream of Ahab and Moab, for the author has to resort to stage trickery in order to tell his story. Unlike Dante's allegory, *Moby-Dick* must conclude as an "intolerable" allegory that cannot venture beyond the limits of language. In order for its *American* fiction to remain symbolically factual, the narrator must wake up.

Dante's failure to do this, or his success at getting to heaven, points up Henry Adams's argument in "The Dynamo and the Virgin" that an "American Virgin would never dare command; an American Venus would never dare to exist."[15] Dante's Beatrice could take him straight up the Ladder of Love to paradise, but in the New Eden of America such sexual symbols had been replaced by sentimental "Faiths" in the future—instead of maidenhood, motherhood that rendered the cruise of the self a fait accompli. Like Goodman Brown, the frustrated Ahab leaves his wife for the *means* of his salvation, for the epic or heroic adventure that only the Old World seemed to enjoy. In America one woke up already "saved," feeling he had missed the middle or best part of his life. Irving, Hawthorne, Melville, and the other American writers Adams spoke for were "damned by dollars" and not by any deity that would later save them. Their mortgaged paradise always put them at the end of the story, where they were unmasked as the signifiers of nothing more than "the sound and the fury" of pilgrims without a meaningful past and thus an interesting future. They woke up not in Dante's European paradise but *from* the American entelechy whose disappearance revealed only the "plain facts" of a Hudson River village where nothing has really changed; in an idle customhouse and not in the Dark Wood of Hester; or in a coffin instead of the warm belly of a Jonah's whale.

Another English reviewer of *The Whale* called it "an ill-compounded mixture of romance and matter-of-fact." He noted that "the idea of a connected and collected story" had obviously occurred to Melville "again and again in the course of the narrative," but that the author's "purpose must have changed, or his power must have fallen short." Melville's American power to write a traditional romance had indeed fallen short, and that was the rub; for *Moby-Dick* was an attempt to re-enact the European myth in America—to find in his country's "matter-of-fact" not simply evidence of predetermined justification and salvation but of virgins and Virgils who would lead us *through* the confusion of the Dark Wood. In attempting the American epic he discovered its contradiction because—according to the psychology of the jeremiad and the national literature it had helped produce—Americans had already completed the journey back to Ithaca. They had already been saved by "history," or its ideological projection, which they embellished into the myth of the Chosen Few and a Promised Land in the here and now. Melville had told Hawthorne in the spring of 1851 that all his books were "botches." He meant that

Literature did not sell in America (a complaint Hawthorne himself would make a few years later), but he was anticipating a greater failure—one in which *Moby-Dick* would be (in the words of the same English reviewer) "neither so utterly extravagant as to be entirely comfortable, nor so instructively complete as to take place among the documents on the subject of the Great Fish." [16] Whereas the *Commedia*, Spenser's *Faerie Queene*, Cervantes' *Don Quixote*, and other Old World allegories had successfully invoked the mythical power of language, Melville's *Moby-Dick*, with its idiomatically American emphasis on "plain facts" as evidence of spiritual facts, undercut the myth in its act of revising history.

Myth, as Melville wrote, threatened to make "modern," or American, history a liar. It revealed the American experience as proleptic instead of analeptic in its ideological fusion of the present with the future instead of with the past, in its attempted fusion of signifier and signified in every literary quest. The truth was not to be found in such ideology but in the history of an idea whose origins were buried at sea. Although *Moby-Dick* is about a burial at sea on a grand scale, it has, surprisingly, only one such literal scene—the burial of the fifth sailor from the *Delight* in chapter 131. The other four "were buried before they died" (p. 441) in the ship's ideological pursuit of the White Whale. The scene is an eerie one because *a* coffin surfaces—or, rather, comes into view—immediately after the body has been committed to the sea, anticipating the survival of Queequeg's coffin in the epilogue. It is in fact the same coffin that the *Pequod* has been pulling astern when it meets the *Delight*. Ordinarily, no coffin is used in a sailor's burial, except in peacetime, and it is then not infrequent that the corpse plunges through the lightweight wooden container upon impact with the water, allowing the empty coffin to assume a life of its own on choppy seas. In *Moby-Dick* the same irreverent and ominous effect is accomplished when the life-buoy coffin comes into "conspicuous relief" following the "sound of the splash that the corpse made as it struck the sea." In other words, *Moby-Dick* as an American epic is a ship pulling its own coffin: "Ha! yonder! look yonder, men!" cries the captain of the *Delight*. "In vain, oh, ye strangers, ye fly our sad burial; yet but turn us your taffrail to show us your coffin." In trying to escape the sound of the burial at sea (or the past), the *Pequod* sees evidence of its own imminent sinking (or future). Ahab, as he is told, already sails upon the tomb of the four sailors "buried before they died" (pp. 441–42).

Contrary to at least one version of the American Dream, one cannot be buried alive and live; which is to say again that the gap between subject and object in every metaphorical quest is finally unbridgeable. Try as he might, Ahab cannot align the two. In chapter 99 he paces before the symbolical doubloon riveted to the mainmast. Like Hawthorne's rosebush in *The Scarlet Letter* that flourishes amidst the "grass-plot, much overgrown with burdock, pig-weed, apple-peru, and such unsightly vegetation,"[17] Melville's doubloon "of purest, virgin gold" shines "amidst all the rustiness of iron bolts and verdigris of copper spikes, yet, untouchable and immaculate to any foulness." Revered by the crew as "the white whale's talisman," it also represents the unresolvable duality of Ahab's not-so-monomaniacal quest. This is because the coin means—by its contrast with the "plain facts" surrounding it—something beyond itself. As Ahab tries to interpret what significance might "lurk" there, he is convinced that "some certain significance lurks in all things, else all things are [of] little worth, and the round world itself but an empty cipher" (pp. 358–59). The White Whale ought to mean something because Jonah's whale meant something; otherwise, all we had was history, and "the round world itself [is] but an empty cipher" and cycle. Dreams meant something because they consisted of burials in the sea of our beginning in the sight of God; whereas history always left us landlocked in Nineveh, where God is full of riddles instead of tall tales.

They were our myths, fabrications of the prescientific mind but modified by the discoverable designs of natural history. Melville, as Albert Camus once said, was "un créateur de mythes,"[18] but he would not have entirely agreed with Camus that we must become anthropocentric, for the myth derives not only from our fancy or imagination alone but from our imaginative perception of natural facts.[19] Camus was perhaps too much taken by the teachings of Nietzsche and the Russian Formalists, but Melville would have preferred "not to" write in a world in which words were merely signs of other words. Under such linguistic circumstances, at the prospect of unanchored tropes, his Bartleby simply runs out of psychic gas. He has no place to go except the Tombs, anything but a burial at sea. Jonah had gone below on the Joppa ship and fallen asleep—to dream what he could not witness awake. Ahab, on the other hand, finally refuses to go below deck. "I will have the first sight of the whale myself," he contends. "Aye! Ahab must have the doubloon!" (p. 439). The gold piece, of course, has been promised to the first sailor who sights Moby-Dick. Yet to claim the symbol, as Ahab ultimately does, is to finish the story, as Melville does with the whale's sinking of the *Pequod*. Rather than going below deck and dreaming Jonah's dream, Ahab wants to see directly. He wants a "Great Awakening"—something that cuts through the "paste-board mask" of language. He wants the story of Jonah explained *literally*. Like those Sag-Harbor skeptics, he wants its details to be as understandable as the rest of the "plain facts" about whaling so abundantly available in *Moby-Dick*. For a sailor is nothing if not "squared away" in his life at sea. Sailors, of course, have their sea stories such as "The Town-Ho's Story," but those are for the sailor's idle times. "When he can read God directly," Emerson had said of another kind of American voyager, "the hour is too precious to be wasted in other men's transcripts" of the so-called truth.[20]

The fictional Steelkilt might have his way with the facts, but in the "fish story" of *Moby-Dick* the "linked analogies" of Body and Soul are "far beyond all [such] utterance" (p. 264). As a symbol, the whale is something outside of Ahab that signifies something inside himself. Yet as Ishmael complains in chapter 42 in a voice now fully blended with Ahab's: "it was the whiteness of the whale that above all things appalled me" (p. 163). In other words, this nocturnal quester and dreamer encounters the same blankness that characterizes the "strong poetry" (to use Harold Bloom's term[21]) of Irving and Hawthorne. Melville hitched his wagon to the same star, or Milky Way of the world. The result was a quest that questioned language itself, for the thing it signified was not meaning but the visible absence of meaning. The whale's whiteness, Ishmael observes, "is not so much a color as the visible absence of color, and at the same time the concrete of all colors . . . a dumb blankness, full of meaning." By its meaninglessness, therefore, the whiteness of the whale *means* something: "it is at once the most meaning symbol of spiritual things" and the "colorless, all-color of atheism from which we shrink" (p. 169). Emerson had said in "Experience" that "dream delivers us to dream . . . [that] life is a train of moods like a string of beads, and as we pass through them they prove to be many-colored lenses which paint the world their own hue."[22] For Melville that "hue" was always white, but Emerson had seen God directly, had become "a transparent eye-ball" through which circulated "the currents of the Universal Being."[23] He had, he alleged in *Nature*, seen through the blankness—though later in his career, in "Experience," he would find himself—as I argue in chapter 5—dazed and back on the mortgaged land of Nineveh.

Melville found meaning in its very absence—in what must end as Ishmael's dream and not Ahab's (Emersonian or Platonic) vision. To put the matter another way, God's appearance before humanity was not in the future but in the past—as if the universe contracted instead of expanded and time ran backward toward the Promised Land. All we had was the dream, or our *sense* of the past. Such psychological time allowed us to remember the "future," as it were, and not forget the past in our rapture over a future we would never see. Better an absence of something than the presence of nothing at all. The fact that we dreamed, or that myth—that larger dream—existed, was evidence enough of a prelapsarian existence. If Jonah could return to that past, so could Ahab, but only in Ishmael's dream—or Melville's myth, in which everybody perishes except the orphan who, because of his estrangement from the life that was before *life* began, can tell the story without dying and going to heaven. The important point in the *Commedia* is not that Dante gets to heaven but that he returns to the Garden of Eden as the Adamic orphan of God—that is, the writer. The important point in *Moby-Dick* is not that Ahab perishes but that Ishmael lives to tell about it. He wakes up to the story as if it were yesterday and calls himself "Ishmael," signifying the existence of a story *worth telling*. For it is the orphan's dream that takes us back before the moment of present confusion to savor the remembered life.

Robert Frost defined poetry as a "momentary stay against confusion,"[24] and it is because poetry—or poesy—allows us to slip out of the matter of our existence and into its metaphorical if not metaphysical foreground. Dreams do the same for us because they are the essence of literature, or what Matthew Arnold called "the best that is known and thought in the world."[25] This is true and not simply a false consensus (reflecting the recent "consensus" about literature) because art takes us backward instead of forward. In *Moby-Dick* it is Ahab's ideology about language that fails, not Ishmael's dream and Melville's novel. Ahab cannot advance from natural facts, but Ishmael can take us back to the belly of the primordial whale. Call him Ishmael, and the story—humankind's original story—begins all over again every time. By calling our storyteller an orphan, we conjure up our own orphaned condition as dreamers awakened in the confusion of the present. We set sail on the Pacific, which embraces the troubled world, "the Indian Ocean and the Atlantic being but its arms." It connects with "the same waves" the most recent California towns with "the faded but still gorgeous skirts of Asiatic lands, older than Abraham." There is, Melville affirms, a "sweet mystery about this sea, whose gently awful stirrings seem to speak of some hidden soul beneath; like those fabled undulations of the Ephesian sod over the buried Evangelist St. John" (pp. 399–400).

Here Melville invokes the myth or universal dream that sleeps below our surface. Like the fabled sleep of St. John, who lies in his grave as a man sleeps in his bed, our fabled past stirs the surface. Beneath are "millions of mixed shades and shadows, drowned dreams, somnambulisms, reveries; all that we call lives and souls, lie dreaming, dreaming, still; tossing like slumberers in their beds; the ever-rolling waves but made so by their restlessness" (p. 399). As a "terra incognita," the sea was Melville's literary vehicle and version of Hawthorne's Dark Wood and Irving's "blank page." Each represents humanity's existence in nothing instead of something—in what we are instead of what we ought to be. It is enough to know it exists—that this inscrutable past is our catalyst to being. The White Whale was always in Ahab's past but never to be (conquered) in his future because that future was ideologically mistaken for the present. To *see* the actual future would be to bring one full circle and cycle to the past that can be apprehended only in "stories," or through metaphorical language. To actually kill Moby-Dick rather than to simply chase him would allow Ahab instead of Ishmael to finish the story. With such a paradigm, the memorable moment of Jonah's story would be on the dry land of Nineveh instead of in the belly of the whale. And instead of biblical myth, we would be left with ideology, or the theme of the Promised Land that Father Mapple emphasizes when he retells the story in the Whaleman's Chapel—that "if we obey God, we must disobey ourselves." The Book of Jonah has only four chapters—"four yarns," Mapple suggests, but nevertheless important "strands in the mighty cable of the Scriptures" (p. 45). Mapple's telling suggests that we mortgage our present for the future, that like the repentant Jonah, we go to the end of the story in Nineveh and listen to God's rhetorical questions about whether he should spare the wicked city. But just as *Moby-Dick* is a whale's tale, so is Jonah's. It is as memorable as the story of "Rip Van Winkle" or *The Scarlet Letter* not simply because the cast includes a whale, as of course *Moby-Dick* does, but because it is a story that dramatizes a past that probably never happened and has been happening ever since we woke up to the knowledge of our existence. As a result, we remember most clearly Jonah in the belly of the whale. It is one of our fables—as are the American productions of Irving, Hawthorne, and Melville. Like the Book of Jonah, each one is part of the literary mythology because it ends for us before its fatal conclusion. It "ends" in the middle with Rip waking up after a twenty-year sleep, with Hester and Arthur in the Dark Wood of passion, and with Ahab in hot pursuit of the whale.

The central question addressed in *Moby-Dick* is the one that animates all great works of art: "What is it," Ahab asks on the eve of the three-day chase, "what nameless, inscrutable, unearthly thing is it; what cozzening, hidden lord and master, and cruel, remorseless emperor commands me; that against all natural lovings and longings, I so keep pushing, and crowding, and jamming myself on all the time; recklessly making me ready to do what in my own proper, natural heart, I durst not so much as dare?" (pp. 444–45). Poe had already asked the question more idiosyncratically in "The Imp of the Perverse." Why is the life drive essentially suicidal? "We stand on the brink of a precipice," Poe wrote. "We peer into the abyss—we grow sick and dizzy. Our first impulse is to shrink from the danger. Unaccountably we remain."[26] To dramatize Ahab's question *un*historically, Melville employed two principal characters instead of one. The first acts, the second reflects; and in tandem they reproduce the cycle of being. Even in reflection Ahab is surely acting. Indeed, his question is a defiant gesture, one that lays the blame squarely on God and not on humanity: "Is Ahab, Ahab? Is it I, God, or who, that lifts this arm? . . . God does" (p. 445). Ishmael, while he admires Ahab's courage, also withdraws from the action—even while in the midst of it during the chase. As we know, he ultimately withdraws to tell Ahab's story. Ishmael, like Whitman's speaker in "Song of Myself," is "both in and out of the game." Or, should we say, "both in and out of the *dream*"?

As the proverbial and perennial orphan, he can play *at* life as if it were a game. This is the privilege of the storyteller: to talk about the actual as if it were the subjunctive. Ahab cannot ask his questions, without, as Melville told Hawthorne, jumping off from his stool and hanging himself from the beam. Neither could Melville, whose final work is at least open to the argument of *why* Billy must die. Only Ishmael can remain in the middle between the teller and the told, the signifier and the signified. In other words, life is most clearly perceived as a dream from which we occasionally wake to ask Ahab's question. It can be answered (or countered), however, only in myth: in that psychological fiction that we exist as more than divine automatons who, as Ahab complains, "are turned round and round in the world, like yonder windlass, and Fate is the handspike" (p. 445). Ishmael the Orphan has nothing to lose and everything to gain because he is human, or representative of that condition. Once he had everything, and now he has nothing but its memory.

4 : Poe's Voyage from Edgartown

In Edgar Allan Poe's *The Narrative of Arthur Gordon Pym* (1838) it is difficult to know whether the tale has a proper ending. Indeed, its title reflects palindromically back on its author, whose three-part name is euphonically similar to the name of his character. The "Note" at the close announces "the late sudden and distressing death of Mr. Pym" but adds that he survived long enough after his adventure to relate it to Mr. Poe—or almost all of it, "the few remaining chapters" being "irrecoverably lost through the accident by which he had perished himself."[1] In other words, we know from the "Note" that Pym finished *his* story, but can we be sure Poe finished his? Or is Poe's story like the drunken experience that launches it—one that has no ending but only a beginning in aching sobriety? Is this another of Poe's manuscripts in a bottle—or *from* one in the sense that the voyage from Edgartown is, like Rip Van Winkle's, a drunk and a dream to which there is no proper or satisfactory ending? It begins well, as the idyllic American dream of running off to sea always does,[2] then quickly becomes a nightmare from which there is no ending but only a waking up. The very act of regaining consciousness is, in the context of the fiction it concludes, unrealistic; and yet there is no other way to get out of a story that threatens to take the protagonist beyond mortal limits. Dead men tell no tales, and so our survival depends on the very negation of what began as our grandest dream. In *Moby-Dick* the hope is victorious confrontation with the White Whale, and in *Pym* it is a similar success with a menacing giant whose skin "was of the perfect whiteness of snow" (p. 1179). In both cases, the way out is waking up to a reality that is beyond belief. Ishmael survives waters infested with sharks because *"they glided by as if with padlocks on their mouths."*[3] Pym and his companion, Dirk Peters, endure the "embraces" of a vast cataract by nature of the Symmes Theory, a contemporary belief that the currents of the sea are emptied through a vortex at the South Pole, emerging at the North Pole and recirculating around the globe. "Once that idea is entertained," writes Daniel Hoffman, "it is evident that Pym and Peters need not perish when their canoe hurtles into the vortex. No, like the fisherman in ["A Descent into the Maelstrom"], they have gone down into the vortex and have been cast up alive."[4]

Pym concludes with a "vortext" that empties the tale of all credibility, and yet its protagonist—like Ishmael—insists that his story is true. Both entertain the fear of not being believed,[5] but Pym feels so orphaned from his past that he has Poe tell the first two chapters, or numbers, in *The Southern Literary Messenger*, *"under the garb of fiction"* (p. 1008). The "ruse" was so successful that Pym, having overcome his fear of "popular incredulity," decided to tell the rest of the story himself, saying that it would "be unnecessary to point out where his portion ends and my own commences." He insists that "the difference in point of style will be readily perceived," but of course there is no difference between the style of Arthur Gordon Pym and Edgar Allan Poe. It is *their* story as much as *Moby-Dick* is the joint enterprise of Ishmael and Ahab. Melville perhaps remained slightly more detached from his story through the pseudonymous authorial voice of Ishmael, whereas Poe was swept up by his drama as much as Hawthorne became for a time in his identity-dream. Pym, as James M. Cox suggests, is an anagram for "imp"[6] and thus the lure of the perverse. *Pym* is a voyage from the heart of *Edgar*town—from the heart of darkness in Edgar Allan Poe, who becomes much more than the editor and amanuensis for this tale of perversity.

Poe began his tale by asking the reader to call him "Arthur" instead of the author because such candor would have removed the pose of objectivity that as an editor and magazinist he had tried to maintain in his writings. Always endeavoring to write with an eye cocked toward the literary marketplace, he set out in *Pym* to write in the American genre of the "western"[7]—in this case, the sailor's voyage narrative—in order to profit from the contemporary interest in the remote and unexplored, and—like Melville in *Mardi* and *Moby-Dick*—he went too far into the remote and unexplored region of his psyche. Poe revealed so much that he was forced to kill off his Ishmael before he could finish the story—or publish all of it. Like Hawthorne in *The Scarlet Letter*, Poe probably wrote the "Preface" as well as the "Note" after finishing the work—giving it a literary frame that, in both cases, separated the identities of the "Arthur" and the "author." The "Note" gives the clear impression that Pym succumbed shortly after conveying the twenty-five chapters of his story, and the "Preface" states that the adventure happened only "a few months ago" (p. 1007). Yet in his desire to give his intimate role in the story a premature burial, Poe forgot Pym's mention in chapter 5 of the "many years" that have elapsed since the voyage from Edgartown (p. 1052). Surely, Pym would have had ample time to provide the concluding chapters during this long hiatus between deposition and disposition.

Fiction is the lie that supposedly tells the truth, but in this narrative it is the *garb* of fiction that lies. Poe is telling the truth about the lie that narrates his deepest fear, which is the destiny of his literary drunkenness. Like Pym's, Poe's narratives often begin in ecstasy and abandonment but conclude with the horror of not being able—or not wanting—to remember what happened the night before. Generally, Rufus Wilmot Griswold is blamed for the reputation that many high-school English teachers have preserved, but Poe himself is really to blame because his narrators are so violently drawn into the facts of their fiction. There is something "alcoholic" about their narratives. They take us on a drunk that often ends like a bad dream. In descriptions that often strain with double vision after detail, we lose hold of our identities as readers to become the visitor in "The Fall of the House of Usher," the traumatized widower in "Ligeia," or the all-too-sober avenger in "The Cask of Amontillado." Poe's narratives are successful at getting the reader to envision in their gothic scenes of heavily draped compartments and consuming catacombs the claustrophobia of death, its smothering but also mothering effect. In such a macabre world of drunkards and dreamers, life is indeed a *pre*mature burial, a return to rather than a "turn" of events.

In "The Imp of the Perverse" Poe's narrator complains that justifications of human conduct are a priori rather than a posteriori because we strive after the logic of our being: "The intellectual or logical man, rather than the understanding or observant man, set himself to imagine designs—to dictate purposes to God. Having thus fathomed to his satisfaction, the intentions of Jehovah, out of these intentions he built his innumerable systems of mind." Yet the narrator—enchained for a crime he not only committed but "convicted" himself of—insists that it is wiser to define man "upon the basis of what man usually or occasionally did, and was always occasionally doing, rather than upon the basis of what we took it for granted the Deity intended him to do" (pp. 826–27). What man "was always occasionally doing" in his most reflexive moments was running off to the primordial sea of himself. He was returning to a past that only a posthumous narrator can talk about; which is to say one who is either literally dead, such as the narrator of *Pym*, or "dead" in the sense of having no viable future, such as the condemned murderer in "The Imp of the Perverse" or the yet-to-be condemned one in "The Cask of Amontillado." In almost every case in the Poe canon, the "murderer" is compelled to tell his story and so to succumb by waking up to it belatedly. And what is clearly a fiction in the presence of this fact, Poe suggests, is the a priori definition of ourselves. "It might be supposed," Pym (or officially Poe here) confesses in chapter 2, "that a catastrophe such as [the *Ariel's* outing] would have effectually cooled my incipient passion for the sea. On the contrary, I have never experienced a more ardent longing for the wild adventures incident to the life of a navigator than within a week after our miraculous deliverance" (p. 1018).

Rather than being deductively delivered, Pym is lost in the induction that proves nothing more than the sum of its examples or episodes that follow one another with the regularity of tidal currents. And thus in *Pym* we follow the protagonist as he "dies" out of one crisis only to be "reborn" into another. After almost drowning in his initial experience on the *Ariel*, Pym is buried in a coffin-like box as a stowaway in the hold of the *Grampus*—saved from that premature burial only by the threat of another premature death at the hands of mutineers. As Dickinson would have described it, our hero is throughout the narrative, "just lost, when [he] was saved!"[8] He is drawn headlong every time to the very precipice Poe speaks of in "The Imp of the Perverse." He calls the compulsion our perversity—"a *mobile* without motive, a motive not *motiviert*." Hoaxer that he is, Poe takes great liberties with language, mixing Latin and German words stemming from the Latin infinitive *movere* (to move) to suggest that our genuine actions are perverse not only because they are not necessarily motivated by God but because they contradict the established social desire to move constructively and thus morally through life. The meaning of both phrases is essentially the same: "movement without motive," or in the context of Poe's story, "movement against movement"—clearly the definition of perversity. John Barth, a later Baltimore writer, would develop the same idea with his theme of stasis (where, for example, the protagonist in *The End of the Road* [1958] literally runs out of a motive for any action but inaction), but Poe is using *motive* not only in the sense of *incentive* or *inducement* but in the sense of the inner urge that prompts a person to action: "Through its promptings we act without comprehensive object; or, if this shall be understood as a contradiction in terms, we may so far modify the proposition as to say, that through its promptings we act, for the reason that we should *not*. In theory, no reason can be more unreasonable; but, in fact, there is none more strong" (p. 827). He calls this "tendency to do wrong for wrong's sake" a "radical, a primitive impulse."

Human motive, therefore, cuts both ways to slice up any meaning in our conduct other than the fact of the conduct itself. Language merely reflects this dilemma, which repeatedly draws the Poe protagonist into fictions that are either fatal or filled with the threat of fatality. In *Pym* each cycle or premature burial is accompanied or followed by a reverie or—as after the avalanche on the island of Tsalal—"*a longing to fall*; a desire, a yearning, a passion utterly uncontrollable" (p. 1170). Pym falls, of course, into the arms of Peters, the half-breed who represents the darkness of our nativity. Or, to quote Hoffman again, "It is *the longing of the living body to die*, of the organic to become inorganic, of the differentiated consciousness in the agony of its separateness to experience the frightening ecstasy of its reintegration into the unity from which it has been exiled—the unity of personal annihilation."[9] "The Imp of the Perverse" is the unconscious desire or death wish for a freedom that is prelapsarian in the sense that it has no endings but rather beginnings that are always original. Hoffman asserts that Pym's burial in the belly of the *Grampus* represents the desire "to be entombed to be enwombed, buried to rise again—as though to a new destiny."[10] Yet every *earthly* beginning must have—another—ending, and Pym's ending is finally lost, while Poe's story has no proper ending at all. The only one who can possibly conclude both stories (which are of course the same story) is the post-natally oriented Peters, and he *has* no story to tell, except the one that would send him to the gallows for mutiny and murder. *The Narrative of Arthur Gordon Pym* is thus utterly without *motive*, or movement toward a "new destiny" based on the deductive definition of God. It ends instead with Poe as Pym on the precipice of the original beginning that only (literary) drunkenness can simulate.

Peters disappears from the story with the expediency of Melville's Bulkington from *Moby-Dick* or Steelkilt from "The Town-Ho's Story." All three characters by their continued presence as stereotypes in the fiction of life as linear instead of circular threaten to tell stories with endings; thus, their tales must disappear from stories that are true—such as *Moby-Dick* and *Pym*. These are true in the sense that they conclude only as dreams conclude: with awakenings in the beginning of the adventure, which ends after "a good night's sleep," with a dream or dreams whose traces are remembered. Just as the dreamer conjures up his past and present together—events that happened long ago with the day's activities, conversations between the dead and the living—so the writer of the true story takes us on a dream whose "motive" is backward rather than forward. Such a tale can have no ending, only a recycling—as in the case of Rip Van Winkle under the rule again of "King George" or Dimmesdale returned to the Dark Wood. In the instances of Melville's and Poe's stories, the narrator is realistically posthumous *except* in the reverie of his beginning. In the end, Ishmael wakes up to yet another adoption, and Pym wakes up to yet another "premature" burial.

Leslie Fiedler has already commented on how the "dusty, fiendish" Peters replaces Augustus in the male bonding of drinking and dreaming up new adventures. The initial drinking partner's revelry on the *Ariel* and excitement on the *Grampus* can be found only in a bottle—or with one. Like Rip's story, it is a tale that strains credulity. Pym acknowledges the problem but also complicates it in Poe's "Preface" to what is perhaps more accurately called *The Narrative of A. Gordon Pym* (at the head of chapter 1 and as the running title in the original Harper & Brothers edition), because like J. Alfred Prufrock, another American drunk, or at least dreamer, who wakes up and dies, he is hiding something. He says that he had "several reasons" for initially declining to make his story public—"some of which were of a nature altogether private, and concern no person but myself" (p. 1007). Perhaps too sober by the time of the "Preface" to re-enact his fantasy in public, he wishes Augustus were still alive to lend credibility to their quest for exotic lands, or the state of the self before it was misbegotten in the horror of the human condition. For the story relates how the dream of Augustus devolves into the nightmare of Dirk Peters, that bestial figure who becomes Pym's new compatriot during the ordeal on the *Grampus* and beyond.

We do learn of horrible events—of putrefaction, execution, amputation, starvation, mutilation, cannibalism—but what else happens to Peters and Pym on the *Grampus*? The mutiny is resolved when Peters, hoping to be ultimately pardoned, joins with Arthur and Augustus in a plan to overthrow the other nine mutineers. It involves, literally, another "garb of fiction"—Pym's dressing up as one of the dead crewmembers. Playing on "the thousand superstitions which are so universally current among seamen," Peters and Augustus engage the others in a discussion of the dead man's decay (pp. 1070–71). Thus when Pym appears as the "revivication of [a] disgusting corpse," the hoax succeeds, and all but one of the opposition are slain. The hoaxers, however, find themselves the victims of a greater hoax or death threat because a storm renders their vessel "a complete hulk" drifting at will (p. 1075). The subsequent scenes both anticipate and exceed those of Stephen Crane's "The Open Boat" in the drama of man's helplessness in the face of "open" nature. Instead of cigars to sustain the illusion of life as a continuum, Poe's survivors—"rolling about at the mercy of every wave"—have only port wine, which makes them the dying drunks who eventually cry out to the dead of "a large hermaphrodite brig" whose marriage of lifelike movement and rotting flesh renders them as frenzied as those their hoax had so recently overcome (p. 1084).

The true hoaxer—not only for Poe's characters but also for his readers—is the fear of death, which tricks them time and again into the nightmare of a premature burial. In "The Premature Burial," a tale which treats more directly this phenomenon of waking up and thinking oneself dead, or buried alive, the cataleptic narrator discovers that despite his precautions (which include equipping the family tomb with a bell in the event he is buried during one of his seizures) he has—or thinks he has—been placed in "some common coffin" (ironically, the fate of Poe himself in 1849). This story, however, is something of a hoax itself, for after baiting his reader with "a vast number of such interments [that] have actually taken place" (p. 667), the narrator relates his own premature burial, which turns out to be simply a case of waking up in a strange environment. Poe, it appears, was trying to scare himself (and the reader) into the state of half-death where a glimpse of the beginning of life might be possible. That is to say, a premature return to the womb of mother earth is a way of living more intensely in life. The narrator of "The Premature Burial" says that the "tortures" of entombment were life-enhancing: "for their very excess wrought in my spirit an inevitable revulsion. My soul acquired tone—acquired temper. . . . In short, I became a new man, and lived a man's life" (p. 679).

Fear of the inevitable ending, therefore, produces the illusion of another beginning in which Pym becomes "a new man" who forgets his past in the course of events called destiny, or that movement from the womb to the tomb. Rather, he is entombed to be enwombed in the beginning again. Poe might have subtitled his novel "Out of the Coffin Endlessly Rocking." Repeatedly, he is cradled out of the clutches of death, almost, if not completely, oblivious in his delivery to what nearly happened to him. Pym embarks on the *Grampus*, as noted above, as if he had learned nothing from the previous experience. In fact, his former life and quotidian existence after the *Ariel* are symbolically forgotten in the denial of his grandfather. And once the narrator is saved by the *Jane Guy*, nothing more is said of the previous ordeal except to observe that Pym and Peters "were treated with all the kindness [their] distressed situation demanded" (p. 1114). Instead, the reader, who has been assured that *all* the events actually happened,[11] is plunged into the next hoax, in which life appears at first to be orderly but is ultimately macabre and meaningless. Each episode in *Pym* strives to outperform the previous one for horror until the climax, where Pym and Peters vanish into "the perfect whiteness" of the polar region—signifying Poe's subsequent pages and Pym's missing chapters.

In view of these wakes of blankness, it may be more profitable to ask what did not happen on the *Grampus*, or more broadly, what does not actually happen anywhere in the novel but only viscerally in self-destructing episodes.[12] On the *Jane Guy*, the slate is wiped clean again with more facts suggesting a deductive version of life—in this instance, details concerning the ship's mission and the natural sights encountered once the course is changed for the South Pole. Obviously, Poe was pushing himself to make his story long enough to qualify as a novel, cribbing from factual accounts of attempted polar expeditions in the hope that they would trigger not simply another episode but a narrative that was continuous. But as a short-story writer who would soon celebrate the "unity of impression" in his criticism, he found himself starting over again in his tale. It should be kept in mind, of course, that the lack of an international copyright agreement (till 1891) helped to create the practice of serializing novels by chapters or larger sections before total publication, and thus the invitation to plot episodically was one with the act of fiction in the nineteenth century. As a magazinist, Poe is one of America's early examples of how necessity shapes art—in this case, into the genre known as the modern short story. Irving's masterpiece not only consisted of "short stories" but was initially published by sections, perhaps accounting for its loose organization as a "book." In both the cases of *The Sketch Book* and *Pym*, the series of disparate "impressions" lends itself to a dream-text in which one tale is blanked out by the next. Poe's novel was not published seriatim, but it was introduced in this manner, the first two chapters actually appearing in *The Southern Literary Messenger* of 1837 at the time Poe was leaving its editorship over a disagreement with the proprietor, Thomas White. Thus, it was not only the circumstance of the literary market but Poe's own circumstance as a serialist without a journal that produced the rather dreamlike amalgamation of Poe and Pym in a hoax that fed the public appetite for "truthful" accounts of journeys to distant, unexplored, and perilous places.

With a title page typical of the era in fiction, Poe outlined an adventure intended to meet the interest created by the voyaging accounts of Benjamin Morell and Jeremiah N. Reynolds, whose "Mocha Dick" would appear a year after the publication of *Pym*. Earlier, Reynolds had popularized the Symmes Theory (concerning polar openings) and sailed to South America. Upon his return he called for a polar expedition but never managed, because of financial difficulties, to partici-

pate in one. Pym did—or does—of course: he lives in the past of Reynolds's supposed future, sailing literally on the uncharted seas of his
author's imagination. Poe not only invented the future but patently
invented its natural landscape as well (since it was not even proven
that Antarctica was a continent until 1838, and the Pole itself was not
reached until 1911). As a result, the physical reality through which
Pym moves is, in the words of Larzer Ziff, "one that ceases to exist
the moment he stops imagining it."[13] The observation sheds light on
the problem of *Pym*'s ending because, as Ziff also notes, the tale *stops*
rather than ends. But it also illuminates the episodical nature of the
tale because Poe's imagination stops with each sensation or horrifying
unit. Dreamlike, it merely ceases, and Pym gets out of each difficulty
before it is finished—or before it finishes him.

Actually, Poe had fabricated the "facts" as far as he could in each
story, and finally had to pull the plug with the Symmes Theory. The
hoax gave the sudden ending a credible close for the American reader
accustomed to the narrow escapes of captivity narratives and dream-
scapes then popular, but the British—as in the case of Melville's reviewers for *Moby-Dick*—were a little skeptical about Poe's possibly
posthumous narrator. As a result, in the English edition, published by
Wiley and Putnam in 1838, there appeared the following note, ap-
pended to the "Preface": "It will be seen by a note at the end of the
volume, that Mr. Pym's sudden death (of which we have no particu-
lars) occurred while these sheets were passing through the press; and
that the narrative consequently breaks off abruptly in *its most important part* [my italics]. But the exciting interest of the story, and the
intrinsic evidence of its truth and general accuracy, induce us to give
it to the public without further comment." By "most important part,"
the English publishers meant the climax of the tale, but to the American publishers and public, that was also the legitimate ending. The
narrator and Peters do not return home in the epic/English fashion of
a Tom Jones or a Pip but, like America's Tom or Huck, either live on
in the next story or "light out" for the fiction of a new one. Even
though we are told in the "Note" that Poe's voyagers got back home
safely, their return is retrospective in the context of the story in which
they are symbolically lost to its beginning in Edgartown.

Hence, nothing really happened on the *Grampus* or in the subpolar
village of Klock-Klock (whose name mocks the idea of *motion* or

forward movement) because the tale is all a drunken dream that ceases with the "Note" announcing the sudden disappearance of Pym. The story, it seems, is more realistic as the dreamlike projection of the drunk on the *Ariel* that begins the story and that takes place, in the words of Ziff again, "between sleep and breakfast, at dream time."[14] Poe's story exhibits the American need for the fantasy of the womb instead of the formality and finality of the tomb (or tome)—a recurring and reflexive desire to rebel from the parental authority of the human condition that was becoming as evident in the New World as it was in the Old. In the tradition of Rip, who won't work for a living; Hester, who won't weep for her sins; and Ahab, who won't wait for God to reveal Himself; Pym won't wait for the end of the story. He keeps waking up to yet another short story or dream of himself in which he will fall into the ancestral arms of Peters or slip into and through that polar opening at the bottom of the earth, surely another customhouse in which the American writer manages to regain control of his fiction.

Poe's last word in life was "Reynolds!"—which he shouted out from a four-day sleep or coma apparently induced by alcohol and laudanum. He "awoke" from this final drunk, as it were, to call out the name of the man whose publications may have inspired *The Narrative of Arthur Gordon Pym*. We can never know exactly why Reynolds was the last thing on Poe's mind, but the exclamation does suggest one final attempt at a beginning of sorts, when Poe, under the assumed name of Pym, began a new career with himself (quite literally as a novelist). It may have been the psychological projection of an earlier beginning, when in 1827 he had sailed from Richmond to Boston under the assumed name of "Henri Le Rennet," or the beginning when he had joined the U.S. Army under the pseudonym of "Edgar A. Perry." Poe's life was full of beginnings, or false starts, and indeed in his last years he tried to begin again after the death of Virginia with his engagement to Sarah Helen Whitman and, after that arrangement fell apart (because of drunkenness), with his betrothal to Elmira Royster Shelton. This final attempt at starting over brought him full circle to his youth, when he had first been engaged to Elmira.

One last time in the negative structures of the American *Dream* of beginning anew,[15] Poe dreamed of gaining financial stability through marriage and finally the chance to *begin* his own journal, to be called the *Stylus*, perhaps to signal a new literary beginning. But like Pym, who goes under in search of a better self, Poe *stopped*. Indeed, he drops out of American literary history in the same way Pym drops from his narrative. His premature disappearance from what we like to call the "American Renaissance" may account in part for his "oddity" as a major American writer. Poe seldom made use of the American scene and vernacular in his poems and stories, but in fact he (and Hawthorne) made the most dramatic use of its psychological landscape. This was the vista that kept disappearing. *Pym*, as the English caveat states, "breaks off abruptly in its most important part." It ceases like a dream because that was the discursive nature of Poe's sense of reality. In the preface to *Eureka*, his last literary beginning, he dedicated his treatise on the universe "to the dreamers and those who put faith in dreams as in the only realities." His argument ultimately rejects both the deductive and inductive methods of knowledge for intuition as the only capacity that can aid us (p. 1259). Yet this conclusion is but one step from the induction he championed in "The Imp of the Perverse" and demonstrated in *Pym*, for the heuristic of induction shares with the lesson of dreams the same sampling process in which a gathering of seemingly disparate incidents produces a principle. In both cases, their investigations must break off at the "most important part" and proceed on an informed but nevertheless "intuitive" basis.

In the "American Renaissance" one could not know anything for sure beyond the climax, could not go home again in the British sense of conclusion. In this context, Poe is surely as "American" as his longer-lived contemporaries who saw one civil war threaten to close out a literary flowering that an earlier civil war had ultimately inspired. Rip goes to sleep before the Revolutionary War and wakes up as Washington Irving the storyteller. Irving did not live to see the Civil War either, but he "sketched" out the beginning of the "Renaissance" in which Poe and others would wake up. They both woke up to the "climax" that was always at the beginning and never at the ending in the teleological sense of their forebears of the seventeenth and eighteenth centuries. Recent studies on the "origin" of the American self and its "jeremiad," namely Sacvan Bercovitch's, have taught us much about our historical or literal beginning as a nation of theological and ideological dreamers,[16] but they miss the mark when that argument is extended to America's *literary* beginning. For in the case of *Pym*, as well as the other major awakenings starting with Irving, the American ideology is inverted, its "motive" is reversed, and its motion is emotional. Personal rather than political, the narrator sleeps through the better part of the national sermon, or "jeremiad," and wakes up to the blankness of his own "short story."

The appeal of the American "jeremiad" was based on the burden of guilt about the future—that one might fail to meet the terms of his or her destiny as one of the saints of the Church. By the nineteenth century, this American destiny had become a secular dream of justification and sanctification as evinced by material success and political influence in the here and now. This meant the cultivation of such habits as industry and humility but also obedience to one's parents, whose example frequently pointed the way to wealth and respectability. In Pym's case, he is a descendant of a father and a grandfather who exemplify that good fortune. The latter has been successful "in stocks of the Edgartown New-Bank" (p. 1009), and Pym, the old man's favorite, stands to inherit most of his property—that is, if he conducts himself according to his destiny. Like many of Poe's men of the crowd in the American mass, this one is economically privileged but also perversely predictable. He disobeys his parents and risks disinheritance by his grandfather only to find himself prematurely buried in his attempt to escape his future, or the end of the ideological story. In short, he violates the conditions of his existence as a son (and a grandson) by entombing himself in the womb of the *Grampus* (colloquially, at least, a reference to a parentage that thrived before his birth). Rather than pursue his parental legacy as one of the saints of the "New-Bank," he recedes into the sea of the old one.

Although the result is calamitous and horrifying, the narrator expresses no feeling of guilt stemming from the knowledge that his life-threatening predicament could have been avoided if only he had listened to his elders. The most acute sense of failure comes from the squandering of an opportunity specifically reserved for oneself. It is the inverse of the Yankee adage "nothing ventured, nothing gained" because nothing has been ventured in the direction of the proper gain—or ending. Yet just as the narrator of "The Imp of the Perverse" can speak calmly about his inaction in the postnatal future, so Pym can relate the details of his ordeal without remorse. This is be-

[6 5]

cause it takes place before he was born, before he fell with the rest of humankind into a world that required ideology in order to survive. Poe's appeal, therefore, is anti-ideological, if not apolitical, in its implicit criticism of the American Dream from which Poe himself as a dispossessed foster child had been generally excluded. The voyage from Edgartown is away from North America's destiny of dollars and divines—and southward. For Melville in his anti-ideological excursions, it is the erotic South Seas; for Poe it is the South Pole, or the South Poe, whose existence is bathed in the coldly pristine and amniotic waters of his beginning.

Pym's "duty" was to his parents and their expectations for him in the commerce of America. His grandfather had been an attorney, or basically one who arranges for the legal transfer of property. "He had managed," Pym says, "to lay by a tolerable sum of money," which allowed the next generation to produce (through marriage in this case) "a respectable trader in sea-stores" (p. 1009). But like the writer lost in the customhouse of *The Scarlet Letter*, Pym becomes nothing more than "a writer of tolerably poor tales," or a trader in sea-*stories* that never end. In fact, it was Poe who never finished the story (as well as its episodes), but in his fiction of narration it is Pym's fault—especially when we consider the "many years" he had to provide those elusive "two or three final chapters" (p. 1180). Instead, Pym in the face of responsibility, whether pecuniary or literary, is drawn back to the sea, whose circulation "in the globe," Emerson observed in a lyceum lecture in Boston a few years prior to the publication of *Pym*, "is no less beautiful than the circulation of blood in the body."[17] In other words, Pym's perversity is "natural" but not "good" with regard to his society and his debt to it. That society, of course, would label his conduct *un*natural—if not perverse—because it does not conform with what is expected of its members. His failure to live up to the American Dream, however, gives him no sense of guilt because he has not intentionally attempted to subvert it. Rather, he has simply answered another call—one initiated by the exposed hoax about the destiny of death and the *beginning* of life.

Like Irving, Hawthorne, and Melville, Poe wakes up in the customhouse of the imagination, not at all sure whether he is coming or going. Pym sets out to sea, only to set out again repeatedly on another excursion or episode, but always returning to pay the custom or "duty" for his voyage backward in personal history rather than forward in public ideology. Poe's narrators are duty-bound to their creator. They are not permitted to work in the continuum of the novel but must die out after the sensation of the short story. They simply do not belong to the respectable society of the novel in which a (moral or commercial) destiny may be worked out; they are instead the products of the author's relentless hoaxes that scare them into life for what Poe called poetical effect. Their experiences are the records of his epiphanies in a life that otherwise gives no glimpse of the truth or reason for seeing life through to its dénouement. They are creatures not of conscience but of impulse. In one of his most famous literary hoaxes, "The Philosophy of Composition," Poe defined the long poem as "merely a succession of brief ones—that is to say, of brief poetical effects." [18] As we know, he chose Milton's *Paradise Lost* for his example, but what is interesting about the choice is that it allowed him to criticize a great work while also praising it. In this way, he remained both in and out of the literary game about life he hoaxed. More interesting, however, is that he chose a work whose theme reinforced (certainly more than most in the logocentric tradition of literature) the conventional *reasons* for living under the curse of Adam. And in calling it merely a series of poetic sensations, Poe was altering its message with regard to man outside paradise. Adam and Eve, one might say with Stanley Fish, are repeatedly "surprised by sin." [19] In other words, they are creations of the *moment* and not the *movement* toward a reasonable conclusion in life.

What Adam and Eve did only once in the Book of Genesis, they were "always occasionally doing" in what Poe viewed as a continual genesis. They were, in a phrase, always getting drunk on sensation instead of sense—or meaning in terms of the end of the story. In such a world, it made "sense," therefore, to pretend that "The Raven" was composed so rationally and systematically—where, in the reverse of Emerson's argument, form or worldly order precedes thought. It also made "sense" to employ a logician in the attempt to understand the enigma of the human condition, in this particular case a murder with a startling absence of motive. In "The Murders in the Rue Morgue," the world's first great "detective" story, Monsieur Dupin solves a mystery that completely baffles the Parisian authorities. It involves a human massacre whose gory details rival those in *Pym* for their shock value. And, as in the case of the shipboard mutilations, those of the two Parisian women are unemotionally related by the narrator. Although he does—like Pym—occasionally shriek at the horror of it all, he also poses as an objective witness to its intricate details. This detachment is heightened by the ratiocination of Dupin, who—as Cox observes—is indifferent to the law and who interests himself in the *affaire* for "the sheer satisfaction of solving the enigma."[20] It should be added that Dupin's aloofness from the law also indicates his rejection of its ideology: that its system of justice reflects a motive or sense of morality in society or in life. Dupin, an aristocrat reduced to poverty, has no illusions about his imperfect, often criminal world. Begun with the creation of Adam and Eve, it has no apparent principle from which a motive can be deductively ascertained. He is able, therefore, to imagine and thus solve a crime the police cannot (four thousand francs in gold and other valuables were left untouched by the murderer). Dupin solves it inductively by piecing together enough evidence to determine that the murders were committed by an animal.

In surely another of Poe's hoaxes, the murderer turns out to be an escaped orangutan who attempted to "shave" Madame L'Espanaye (one of the murder victims) with his master's razor. But this touch of grim humor is best left to the description of the hoaxer himself:

> Returning home from sailors' frolic on the night, or rather in the morning of the murder, he [a sailor who had captured the animal in the East Indies] found the beast occupying his own bed-room, into which it had broken from a closet adjoining, where it had been, as was thought, securely confined. Razor in hand, and fully lathered, it was sitting before a looking glass, attempting the operation of shaving, in which it had no doubt previously watched its master through the key-hole of the closet. Terrified at the sight of so dangerous a weapon in the possession of an animal so ferocious, and so well able to use it, the man, for some moments, was at a loss what to do. He had been accustomed, however, to quiet the creature, even in its fiercest moods, by the use of a whip, and to this he now resorted. Upon sight of it, the Ourang-Outang sprang at once through the door of the chamber, down the stairs, and thence, through a window, unfortunately open, into the street. (pp. 428–29)

The "murder," therefore, is relatively innocent or without motive, having been committed by a "fully lathered" orangutan fleeing from its master. Of course, the murders of the mother and daughter are tragic, but—aside from the gruesome details—only as much as any other fatal encounter with a wild animal. Yet in a more important context such deaths are more tragic than ones involving a cognitive killer because there is absolutely no sense to them, only sensation. Indeed, in the case of the daughter, it is the death of another (perhaps beautiful) woman who dies from an utterly motiveless crime—the same one which on a larger or cosmic scale took the lives of Poe's Ligeia, his "lost Lenore," and finally his beloved Virginia.

Premature death is a hoax, then, because there was never any sense for it to happen. Life has no sense but only sensation—those "scares" about the abrupt ending that shock us into life again and again. There is no other way to grasp it except through induction—Dupin's method, in which he associates one bizarre detail after another to discover a meaningless crime. The hoax is that the action was based on no first principle or movement toward a destiny, but rather it began in connection with another incident or sensation, that of the orangutan's being discovered and frightened by its master. With Poe in *Pym* (and throughout his fiction), the massacre does not end with the *Jane Gray* and its *National Geographic*–like details but (to employ another future Poe anticipated) on the *Zane Gray* and its sensational events. There is no discernible order, merely endless episodes, and thus there is no reason to feel guilty in the face of the inevitable end of the story. In Poe's fictional world—as in those of Irving, Hawthorne, and Melville—only the beginning matters. Life was simply one *affaire* after another. In discussing a newspaper account of the "frightful affair" in "The Murders in the Rue Morgue," the narrator notes in brackets that "the word '*affaire*' has not yet, in France, that levity of import which it conveys with us" (p. 406). Poe meant that the word, used by the French to denominate a most heinous event, connoted in nineteenth-century America something lacking proper seriousness or importance. The reader in the twentieth century, however, thinks of course of its meaning as a series of trysts between illicit lovers. The retrospection illuminates the point Poe was making before there was (literally) such a point—just as Dupin solves a crime by imagining one that in his experience had never happened. For the sensations of life *are* illicit "affairs" with the self. They are acts of disobedience in the face of a destiny.

Poe's identity-theme, as has been noted thousands of times in thousands of college classrooms, was the death of a beautiful woman. It began—or the catalyst appeared—in his boyhood when he became infatuated with the mother of a friend, Jane Stanard, and it was expressed some years later in "To Helen," a poem about a mother-woman who could never be found again:

> Helen, thy beauty is to me
> Like those Nicéan barks of yore,
> That gently, o'er a perfumed sea,
> The weary, way-worn wanderer bore
> To his own native shore.

Virtually motherless his entire life, Poe came a year after the publication of the poem to live with his cousin Virginia, a child of nine, and to marry her before she had reached her fourteenth birthday. It was not, of course, his first "affair"—that having occurred with a mother figure instead of a daughter figure. But it was his attempt to "father" motherhood, as it were. If not ever again a son, Poe became a father-lover in the *sensation* of returning to the "native shore" of his beginning.

It must have been something of a dream to marry the nearly pre-nubile Virginia—though one wonders how soon (or if ever) the marriage was consummated. The women in Poe's fiction, like the landscape in his stories, always seem to be vanishing as in a dream. Like Helen, whose sexual allure supposedly started the Trojan War, they tease their narrator into a turbulent voyage with himself. Indeed, Poe's marriage to his thirteen-year-old first cousin smacks of both child prostitution and incest (the latter not that uncommon in nineteenth-century American marriages). But by middle-class Victorian standards, Virginia was probably considered too young for sex (initially, at least), and so her narrator was hurled back in memory to an incestuous relationship with a mother figure, that is to say, Jane Stanard. While Virginia remained a virgin, Poe waited with her potential womanhood already on record in "To Helen."[21] It was all a dream and a drunk in which he had imagined the "crime" as already committed, and as such it could be told only in "the garb of fiction." Indeed, Poe solved the problem in the same manner he later had Pym tell his *true* story. We will remember the protagonist's reluctance, even embarrassment, to tell it initially and completely—allowing Poe to begin the story as fiction. That success frees Pym of his fear of not being believed, and he tells the rest of the story himself. Of course, he cannot finish it to Poe's satisfaction, and thus the reader is given the unlikely story that Pym died before turning in all the chapters to the printer. In other words, there *were* no other words to the story—just as there were no words in "To Helen" that would bring the wonder of Helen back from a past that had never quite existed.

It too had been "A True Story," a frequent and revealing subtitle in the fiction of nineteenth-century America, but only true in the face of the fiction about life's having "a proper ending"—a phrase I have used to open this chapter on the most representative and revealing chapter in Poe's fictional life. Poe was always waiting for the return of a Helen or a Virginia in his poems and tales—until he violently destroyed her in such stories as "The Murders in the Rue Morgue" or "Berenice." That was the only possible ending to a dream about such a joyous beginning—a nightmare of daybreak whose glare reminded one that Helen had been a "whore" and Virginia was no longer a virgin. It ends like *Pym*, in perfect polar whiteness and the drowning of all sensation in the sense of the human condition. Dupin, we remember, is "enamored of the Night": "At the first dawn of the morning [his new companion tells us] we closed all the massy shutters of our old building, lighting a couple of tapers which, strongly perfumed, threw out only the ghastliest and feeblest of rays. . . . reading, writing, or conversing, until warned by the clock of the advent of the true Darkness. Then we sallied forth into the streets, arm in arm, continuing the topics of the day, or roaming far and wide until a late hour, seeking, amid the wild lights and shadows of the populous city, that infinity of mental excitement which quiet observations can afford" (p. 401). Dupin, the fallen aristocrat, knows all too well the dangers of Day. *Duped* by its false sense of progress for so long, he remains back in the shadows of night where "that infinity of mental excitement" is possible. He stays back where the crime is motiveless and thus without a destiny or "proper ending." This is also why Poe did not finish *Pym* and why Pym could not finish with Poe. For their missing chapters belong to the beginning of yet another story.

5 : Emerson's Beautiful Estate

roper endings aside, Ralph Waldo Emerson is reported to have uttered on his deathbed, "Oh that beautiful boy."[1] The allusion, it is generally assumed, was to the poet's five-year-old son Waldo, who had succumbed to scarlet fever forty years earlier. Clearly, the child's early and swift departure helped to inspire "Experience," which, unlike the earlier (and later) essays, did not begin as a lecture. "In the death of my son, now more than two years ago, I seem to have lost a beautiful estate," he wrote in the essay, and added stoically, "no more."[2] Psychologists tell us that it normally takes three years to recover fully from the emotional trauma attending the loss of a loved one. In little more than one thousand days we come to accept the fact of the person's life as one more of our fictions in terms of the life that remains to be lived. Although Emerson's statement in "Experience" indicates a quicker recovery, his "deathbed confession" rings a little truer. It suggests that in writing the essay Emerson discovered that life's illusions were not so "caducous." "Dream delivers us to dream, and there is no end to illusion"—or allusion, he might have added. Following the death of his first wife, an event as painful as Waldo's disappearance, he had written in his journal: "There is one birth & one baptism & one first love and affections cannot keep their youth any more than men." In its fullest context, Emerson is anticipating his published response to Waldo's death in "Experience," that "grief too will make us idealists," but what stands in relief to this Transcendentalist pose is the fact of the "first love" and the problem of its lasting imprint on the experience which follows.[3]

In "Experience" Emerson appears to be arguing against himself, or his former position in *Nature* (1836). On the one hand, he continues to resist with Kant Hume's idea that since knowledge is based on perception, we can never know for sure that God exists;[4] but on the other hand, he now agrees that experience is not clearly emblematic of the Oversoul but the result of perception, whose source may be the subjective self.[5] Where he found himself in the middle of his life was between allusion and illusion: "We wake and find ourselves on a stair: there are stairs below us, which we seem to have ascended; there are stairs above us, many a one, which go upward and out of sight" (p. 27). What he had known more surely, that which had filtered his perception with delight, was gone: "I seem to have lost a beautiful estate,—no more." That which he was yet to know was sure to come: "There are always sunsets, and there is always genius" (pp. 29–30). This statement is different in tone, if not completely in meaning, from that in *Nature*, where "the sun shines to-day also."[6] There the focus was upon the developing present; here it is one of the interstices of life—between the seemingly concrete object and its subjective meaning in both the past and the future that would become the past almost before it had enjoyed a meaningful present and presence. In fact, "Experience" is the record of Emerson's most wakeful moment in life, his waking up from the Transcendentalist dream that was always a story about conclusion to face a present that was filled with allusions to the past.

God existed in such a present as nothing more than experience, that continuous transition from moment to memory. From ocular illusion to actual allusion, the pattern of experience allowed only the stability of temperament—what Emerson calls "a succession of moods or objects" (p. 32). Rather, they *were* moods of perception in which the past became a surrogate for the future. Like Hawthorne's "Actual and the Imaginary," they met and imbued each other on the neutral ground of the present. Life's symbiotic essence is most vividly conceptualized in "Experience," where the "loss of a beautiful estate" transforms the "property" of experience into the problem of living in the face of death. "Nothing is left us now but death," he writes. "We look to that with a grim satisfaction, saying, There at least is reality that will not dodge us" (p. 29). In an earlier study of Emerson,[7] I argued that "Experience" marks the sober point in the essays, where Emerson abandons romantic "vision" to adopt the more pragmatic "wisdom" of a man clearly in the second half of his life. Yet James M. Cox and others are right when they insist that Emerson's skepticism (if we can call it that exactly) is to be found in the "transparent eye-ball" metaphor of *Nature* and even earlier in the journal passage from which it grew. His faith in God depends more upon the metaphor than the vision it is supposed to reveal. It is, as Cox notes, "God acting as language," which like ocular perception reflects our own moods.[8] The only constant in the procession of visions is change, "the reality that will not dodge us."

The death of "that beautiful boy" dramatized the "property value" of experience. It shifted with the market or mood of the present and was ultimately no more (or less) tangible than a financial reverse: "If tomorrow I should be informed of the bankruptcy of my principal debtors," he writes in a sentence immediately following the allusion to his son's death, "the loss of my property would be a great inconvenience to me, perhaps, for many years; but it would leave me as it found me,—neither better nor worse" (p. 29). What remained was its record inscribed in language, the instrument of emotional economy that compressed experience into memory and revealed it as a "flitting state, a tent for the night" on a journey that moves inexorably forward. Dreamlike, experience never allowed more than what Robert Frost would call a "momentary stay against the confusion."

In "Experience," Emerson's most ambitiously philosophical essay in the modern sense of the word, he expresses one of those moments in which the question "To what end is nature?" ceases to be rhetorical. Instead of something, there is now the clear chance of nothing. "There is an optical illusion," he writes, "about every person we meet. In truth they are creatures of temperament"—which is to state that change is our only anchor in what we call reality. Emerson's "beautiful boy," now his "beautiful estate," existed only in the optical illusion of possession, a capitalistic exchange between the beholder and the beheld. But the ideology of owning things gave way to the dream of owning up to the Kantian idea that the noumenal source of reality will not allow phenomenal possession. The narrator of "Experience," despite his determination to reaffirm the practical application of Transcendentalism, keeps waking up to this philosophical "fact"—"Ghost-like we glide through nature, and should not know our place again" (p. 27). As Kenneth Marc Harris has demonstrated, Emerson had not misunderstood the distinction between Kant's Understanding and Reason when he wrote *Nature*, and similarly he did not confuse their relationship when he wrote "Experience."[9] "We wake," he says, "and find ourselves on a stair." The Understanding surveys the stairs below, and the Reason those "which go upward and out of sight." What was "out of sight" illuminated those "duly travel'd," as Whitman would say a decade later—and thus "I mount and mount."[10] In an 1838 journal entry, Emerson obliquely comments on the aspect of owner-ship in art which resists the idea that experience originates in the realm of Reason rather than Understanding. "My brave Henry Tho-reau," he wrote, "walked with me to Walden this P.M. and complained of proprietors who compelled him to whom as much as any the world belonged, to walk a strip of road & crowded him out of all the rest of God's earth. . . . Suppose, he said, some great proprietor, before he was born, had bought up the whole globe. So he had been hustled out of nature." Emerson the landowner—and the proprietor of the land on which Thoreau would conduct his experiment in *dis*possession seven years later—defended the "Institution" of ownership as a "scheme not good but the best that could be hit on for making the woods & waters & fields available to Wit & Worth, & for restraining the bold bad man." He encouraged Thoreau, however, to write his complaint "out into good poetry & so clear himself of it." In other words, Emerson urged the use of art—or writing—to transform a sense of alienation or loss into "literary property." Instead of viewing the artistic process as a quest for the Beautiful, he sees it as a means of Compensation. "The very recording of a thought," he conceded, "betrays a distrust that there is any more or much more as good for us. If we felt the Universe was ours, that we dwelled in eternity & advance into all wisdom[,] we should be less covetous of these sparks & cinders."[11]

In this context or definition, art saved us from being "hustled out of nature" by making—in the case of poetry—literary capital out of our sense of belatedness in every experience. It allowed us to wake up from those moments with "something" instead of the fear of nothingness, upon which aesthetics, or the desire for beauty, is founded. Art in Emerson's view by the late 1830s, therefore, was the ultimate artifice for dealing with loss, really the safest way to transcend the pain involved in the Neoplatonic gain, and yet in the death of his son Emerson appears to reject it as an unacceptable idealism. Even the artistically cultivated melancholy of the poem "Threnody" fractures occasionally into the sense of bewilderment that punctuates "Experience":

> And thoughtest thou such guest
> Would in thy hall take up his rest?
> Would rushing life forget her laws,
> Fate's glowing revolution pause? [12]

Waldo's death appears to have sorely tested Emerson's faith in transcendence. Earlier, in *Nature* and the lectures and essays that quickly followed, his focus had been on the potential present. But as he came under more pressure to find a place for evil in his theory, he turned to the principle of Compensation. In the essay he finally wrote on the subject, he said: "Beware of too much good staying in your hand." Yet while he was gathering in his journals the sobering Transcendentalist ideas for the message, he fell in love again. Thinking of Ellen, he had said that there was only one first love, but Waldo had been another. There *was* more than one "first love"—a second chance (at least in America) at an experience so wakeful as to reduce the rest of life to a dream that only Reason could explain. In "Compensation" he would say that "for every benefit . . . a tax is levied," [13] but Waldo, like Ellen, seemed a *gift* of nature, something so free that it would produce *happiness*—the only experience that art could not fully neutralize or purchase. Happiness, or its memory, was the worst kind of past, for it challenged the Transcendentalist principle extolling the present.

Waldo's existence could not be reclaimed by such a present. The "loss of a beautiful estate" supposedly transformed life into art, but in this case—as in the case of the loss of every truly ecstatic moment—life resisted the claim of its loss as part of the necessary continuum of experience. This restorative power of art was possible only if one believed, as Emerson claimed he did in "Compensation," that "there is a crack in everything God has made." But when Waldo died, it appeared that "the world and not the infant failed." [14] The converse was true, of course; beauty failed because truth prevailed. Art in

Emerson's application was supposed to celebrate Waldo's death as part of the larger life—this balance of nature that requires all experiences to be equally good because they constitute the change on which existence quite literally thrives. "Threnody," because it is a much more explicit expression of grief, probably fails as a traditional elegy because its lament never credibly transcends the personal or particular in nature to celebrate its balance. He could not cross "a bare common, in snow puddles, at twilight, under a clouded sky, without having in [his] thoughts any occurrence of special good fortune," as he had written in *Nature*, and enjoy "perfect exhilaration."[15] For this was the stuff of art that had made *something* instead of nothing out of the "sparks & cinders." Waldo was "no more" and thus simply the product of exchange, or inevitable change.

In "Religion," a lecture first given in 1840, Emerson said that "love is thaumaturgic." He was referring to the Transcendentalist vision, which found everything in nature miraculous, but it is strange that he used the condition of what is essentially infatuation as the basis for the metaphor. Love, he said, "converts a chair, a box, a scrap of paper, or a line carelessly drawn on it, a lock of hair, a faded weed, into amulets worth the world's fee."[16] Clearly then, Transcendentalist knowledge relies on perception, and infatuated perception at that. Its vision, as he also asserted in "Love" (written about the same time), beheld all things platonically. In the cases of both the lecture and the essay, love is spiritual rather than physical, general rather than particular with regard to the time zone of the heart. Yet the problem he grappled with in "Experience" was that life cast us again and again into the particular and never into the general. That was where we always "found ourselves." Only the most infatuated or inebriated observer could transcend those moments and enjoy what Emerson describes in *Nature* as "perfect exhilaration." The more *experienced* observer, Emerson of the 1840s, however, is not so easily gladdened by the ideology of Transcendentalism, and "Experience" is the best evidence of this resistance to the power of language to "exhilarate," uplift, or transcend. Indeed, the most *un*metaphorical sentence in the essay evokes the memory of his son, a happiness that he cannot get "nearer" to any longer. All he can do is compare it to a financial reverse and cash in his lost reality for the fiction of Transcendentalism.

In "Experience" Emerson insists—with a callousness that seems painfully necessary—that no personal calamity touches him. It might, as in the case of bankruptcy, "be a great inconvenience to me, perhaps for many years; but it would leave me as it found me,—neither better nor worse." Always being neither better nor worse, however, points up the crisis Emerson ultimately confronts in "Experience": being *nowhere* in this world. "I grieve," he says, "that grief can teach me nothing, *nor carry me one step into real nature*" (my italics). Grief, however, is an emotion much like love, which sees as "miraculous" a past moment instead of a present one. Both rivet the self to the personal and particular events of this world, and thus in using the language of desire to erase himself, Emerson corrupts the meaning of each word, applying "love" to Transcendentalist vision of the universal and "grief" to Transcendentalist rejection of the personal experience in nature. He *grieves* that the sense of loss cannot carry him "one step into real nature." In other words, he is lamenting instead of celebrating the human condition known as experience. It produces an "exhilaration" that takes him "to the brink of fear," but it is the fear of falling into the abyss of universal currents that consumes personal identity. To become "part or parcel of God," as Emerson had claimed in *Nature*, was to be apportioned out to eternity, to have one's personal force scattered throughout the universe. The "real nature" of "Experience," therefore, is alien to corporeal life, the very existence Emerson's Transcendentalism sought to justify. For in the lexicon in which "love" and "grief" are corrupted, life as we know it has no more meaning than Waldo's existence—which Emerson tries to dismiss as ultimately insignificant.

"The view taken of Transcendentalism in State Street," Emerson quipped in his journal of 1841, "is that it threatens to invalidate contracts."[17] The implication is that Transcendentalism honors the higher law that says that personal contracts are *made* to be invalidated. But this was before Waldo's death. Even then, Emerson borrowed from the quasi-legal language of business (as he would in "Experience" to deal with grief) to explain the true business of nature—or "real nature." Like Louis Daguerre, who became a subject in the Journals, Emerson "knew" that the picture was there before it became visible, the product of "spotless silver" before it was held over steaming mercury in Daguerre's experiment.[18] Nature was simply the "dial plate of the invisible," but it was nevertheless all we had on record as experience. Yet for whatever reasons—his Unitarian ministerial background, his New England Puritan legacy—Emerson continued, even in "Experience," to regard nature as nonexistent and hence untrustworthy in and of itself. Although he urged his readers in "Self-Reliance" and elsewhere to trust themselves, he meant the emblematic self and not the one that loved and grieved. He viewed marriage, for example, as a lifelong commitment despite its frequent failure to suppress male concupiscence. "For the romance of new love is so delicious, that [our] unfixed fancies would betray [us], and they would allow themselves to confound a whim with an instinct, the pleasure of the fancy with the dictates of the character."[19]

In Emerson's usage, "character" is another word for "calling" in the sense of the "Christian Calling" John Cotton enunciated. Yet Emerson's distrust of nature in cultivating character reminds us of another Puritan, John Winthrop, and his distinction between natural and civil liberty. The first was "common to man with beasts and other creatures," while the second was exercised "in a way of subjection to authority."[20] Under the authority of marriage, the husband shielded himself from "that certain light" found in all men's eyes that Emerson said "attaches them to the forms of many women, whilst their [formalized] affections fasten them to some one." Imagining this light in Emerson's eyes is probably as difficult as envisioning Arthur Dimmesdale making love to Hester—though Emerson's attention to Caroline Sturgis is not explained away by her mediocre poetry.[21] Nevertheless, the sexual metaphor is helpful in explaining Emerson's crisis in "Experience," for it was the *natural* attraction, or natural liberty, that sent him fleeing to the ivory tower of Transcendentalism. Nature was good and useful as an *end*, not as a *means* that took one nowhere but full circle with the memory of his fleeting happiness. In *Nature* he had asked about the "purpose" of nature, not the nature of nature. Because, as Emerson suspected, the physical aspect of nature lured us out of our faith in the Whole as opposed to the Part; it lured us like political promises, or western roads, which, Emerson observes in "Experience," "opened stately enough, with planted trees on either side, to tempt the traveller, but soon became narrow and narrower, and ended up in a squirrel-track and ran up a tree" (p. 34). Experience, then, simply could not be trusted on its own terms but had to be viewed only in its insignificance as the "Not-me."

What to do with that apparent insignificance is the central question in "Experience." Unlike the questions of *Nature* and the major addresses that have their own answers, or ends, the question in "Experience" *is* the answer. That is to say, we had better continue to ask who we are in the here and now and not blind ourselves with the ideology of Transcendentalism. This is perhaps not the ostensible or perorative message in "Experience," but it is the subtext that pushes Emerson from time to time to flirt with the possibility that language can create meaning as well as reflect it—can create ends as well as reflect means. After citing the metaphor of the kitten chasing its tail, he asks: "How long before our masquerade will end its noise of tambourines, laughter, and shouting, and we shall find it was a solitary performance?" (p. 46). Like the western road, experience finally trailed off to a reality that only ideology—and its tool, corrupted language—could broaden again. The American aspiration, especially it seemed, thrived on the belief that the traveler would always come upon a new horizon. Yet experience suggested a "trail of tears" that made Cherokees of every "native" American Transcendentalist. The actual "native Americans" had already been driven from their ancestral lands in Georgia by American ideology, despite Emerson's angry plea to President Van Buren in 1838. In that letter, Emerson, however briefly, put aside his Transcendentalist belief that reform should begin with the individual and not society to ask whether we would lie for our truth. "Will the American government steal? Will it lie? Will it kill?" He concluded his open letter by observing that "however feeble the sufferer and however great the oppressor, it is in the nature of things that the blow should recoil upon the aggressor."[22] More prescient than he ever could have guessed, the trail of American history more than a century later compelled Michael Herr to observe that "Vietnam was where the Trail of Tears was headed all along."[23]

That was where the American would finally find himself. In pursuit of the "slumbering giant" within and the Promised Land without, he would die in the ancestral land of another sufferer whose feebleness was but the latest American fable. He would hit the wall of experience, now inscribed (in the nation's capital) with the names of almost sixty thousand Transcendentalists, or heirs to the American Dream that land, or experience, could be bought and sold as "a beautiful estate." In "Experience" Emerson grappled with the past, attempting to cast it off for a present that is always better because it is closer to the future in the Whole, or mind of God. It was an ideological endeavor whose prolepsis not only confuses the present with the future but cancels out the past as "caducous." The native American Transcendentalist, however, could not so easily sell off the ancestral self as "a beautiful estate." As with the plight of the Cherokee Indians, this involuntary sense of destiny drove the "Not-me" across the Mississippi and westward to a land that could never—in the present, at least—measure up to the home he had left. On the surface of "Experience," Emerson advocates the idea that we are born to the Whole and not to the Part, but his desire for the past in Waldo—in Ellen—undermines the argument. It resists the capitalist exchange of Compensation, which barters away the past for the future, the Part for the Whole.

In other words, art—conceived not romantically but ideologically in the tradition of a European mixture of history and religion—converted every experience into a microcosm of the Whole. And thus Transcendentalism, as the first major American experiment in art, imposed a destiny on every present. In "Experience," however, Emerson struggles to resist this conversion. He reverses the aesthetic evolution, so to speak, and celebrates loss instead of teleological gain. The very title of the essay suggests Emerson's (only semiconscious) desire to remain outside the pale of Transcendentalism and its platitudinous ploys about the soul's being somehow separate from the body. It was the *experience* that counted, not simply its meaning in the cosmic context. And in the essay that strives to say this, therefore, we have one of our first pre-Modernist episodes or moments, the "near-miss" of American aesthetics and ideology. Emerson's desire for beauty, like that found in Keats's nightingale or Poe's moth, looked upward or forward, but the actual emotion was grounded in the "Not-me." Suddenly in the Emersonian canon, art clashes with the American ideology that said we were always just coming into nature, were always about to be. It was antinomianism of a new order—which is to say that whereas Emerson is generally perceived as doing for literature in America what Matthew Arnold had done in England (replacing religion with literature), in "Experience" he was, if only subliminally, challenging the logocentric aspect or function of art.

"Never mind the ridicule, never mind the defeat: up again old heart!—it [or the metaphysical argument] seems to say,—there is victory yet for all justice; and the true romance which the world exists to realize, will be the transformation of genius into practical power" (p. 49). This is Emerson's conclusion to "Experience," but it also concludes the author's unqualified participation in the ideology of Transcendentalism. He had always been skeptical, of course, and so initially exchanged Unitarianism for Transcendentalism. In fact, in *Nature* it *is* nature, and especially language, that keeps this post-eighteenth-century rationalist on the side of the yea-sayers. In "Experience," though, it is the "transformation" of literary genius into the "practical power" of being in the here and now. He *found* himself where he could *lose* "a beautiful estate." There might be "victory yet for all justice," but it—like our knowledge of God—would probably have to be linguistically conceived.[24] Language, however, also rooted the user in the "Not-me," for as Emerson had observed in *Nature*, "Words are signs of natural facts." Those facts, in turn, signified spiritual facts according to the Transcendentalist argument, but they also might signify spectral facts—"news" from the corporeal past as well as the Transcendentalist future. Emerson calls these specters, or their effect on the present, the "lords of life." "Illusion, Temperament, Succession, Surface, Surprise, Reality, Subjectiveness,—these are the threads," he says, because life by definition is incomplete. "I know better than to claim any completeness for my picture. I am a fragment, and this is a fragment of me" (p. 47).

These are the parts, however, that threaten in "Experience" to add up to a sum greater than the Whole. They are the dreams that deliver us—as Emerson suggests in his essay—to a reality whose point of interest is analeptic instead of proleptic. Emerson may grieve that he cannot grieve for the past and the Part, but the admission also confesses his desideration in the face (and ultimate facelessness) of the human condition, which mandates that "all mean egotism" must ultimately disappear. He grieves and loves in spite of temperament, which says that all things are relative—the result of perception and not prima facie evidence of anything but the invisible Whole. In "Experience," however, the Whole becomes the Black Hole that swallows up the self whose "estate" was always beautiful. Although the word Emerson used to describe the loss of his son denotes landed property or possessions, it also means the property of a deceased person viewed as an aggregate. It is one's property value, something a parent may leave to his or her children, but in the case of Waldo it was a presence—as Emerson noted in his journal—that lingered with the household items the child had touched. Waldo's "estate," therefore, was more than physical. It was this loss of something whose exchange value could not be measured that Emerson can neither hide nor assuage in "Experience." For the object of any genuine love and grief—as Emerson must have realized in the days of mourning that immediately preceded the first drafts of "Experience"—represented the human desire to spiritualize the physical. Waldo's estate could not be lost like a piece of property. If it could, there would have been no reason to write the essay that alludes to him, or any other essay about the human condition. That *was* the human condition: experience that threatened always to become "lost" in the telos of the Whole.

Considering that Emerson kept his emotional distance with most people, it is striking that he would tell the world about the death of one who, along with his first wife and brother Charles, had enjoyed his unqualified affection. The allusion in "Experience" contrasts dramatically with the lamentations he poured into his journal, prompting the editors of the Riverside Edition to use a portrait of little Waldo as a frontispiece to volume 6 and "The Lost Child" as the running title to open the 1842 entries. The "tribute" in "Experience" is almost Puritanical in its dust-to-dust dismissal, whereas the journal entries more nearly approach the mortuary themes of much popular American verse in the nineteenth century. "The plain, utilitarian, wedge-shaped coffin of the Puritans, meant to return man to the dust from which he came and so emblemize his mortal corruptibility," writes Barton Levi St. Armand, "was replaced by the shapely, luxurious casket, meant to frame, enhance, and show off its contents."[25] Which is to say that the popular response to death in Emerson's day was anything but Transcendentalist. It was an age, especially in the 1840s, of spiritualism in which the Fox sisters and other table-rappers held the attention of thousands of Americans who believed that the world held more spirits than bodies, and thus the "person" of a deceased inhabited inanimate objects such as tables. Curiously, in what we like to call the "Age of Transcendentalism," there was a tenacious regard for the body, for the emblem over the teleological existence it was supposed to signify; so much so—Emerson remarked in "New England

Reformers"—that "even the insect world was to be defended."[26] The times seemed to call out for the personal allusion in public writing, inspiring Walt Whitman in the next decade to celebrate himself in body as well as soul. Even Thoreau, as I shall argue in the next chapter, Emerson's heir apparent to the New England way to heaven, appeared to be often fixated on nature for its own sake. In this context, "Experience" seemed to be Emerson's valiant attempt to keep the faith.

But "The Lost Child"—"that beautiful boy"—was also "a beautiful estate" without an owner, another table rapping out the code of its occupant's disembodiment. Emerson's argument for the soul must be viewed as something of an anomaly, appearing as it does in the 1840s. American romanticism was already waning into the "practical" idealism of reform movements criticized by Emerson for their reductiveness in "New England Reformers." The final essay in *Essays: Second Series* (1844), it implies defeat simply by stating the problem. The individual might stand above the cacophony of voices advocating this or that social remedy, he might be persuaded that the present is greater than the past, but he would have to—as Emerson had told the Divinity School class of 1838—"go alone." Transcendentalism never became a movement per se because, as Emerson and Thoreau demonstrated by their refusal to join the utopian community of Brook Farm, it required a society of one—the solitary soul "singing in the west," as Whitman would put it, with his back to the past and the Part. Even the doctrine of Unitarianism insisted on the desire for the body (the sacrament of the Lord's Supper, the actual *words* of God in the Old Testament). At the end of his unqualified love affair with the soul, Emerson has to ask, "Where do we find *our*selves?" (my italics, of course). In fact, in using the first person, he chose the plural throughout all his essays up to and including "Experience."[27] The exceptions are for personal anecdotes, and in the most prominent exception in his oeuvre he has to confess: "*I* seem to have lost a beautiful estate." Again the italics are mine, but they should have been Emerson's because the statement exposes the delusion that the soul's destiny is anything but solitary. Here the "representative" voice becomes painfully biographical.

Emerson woke up in "Experience" to find himself alone in the prescient present of Transcendentalism. After extolling the Neoplatonic self in the American Scholar Address (his most stirring effort for the metaphysical), he went on in *Essays* (1841) and even in "The Poet" (which opens *Essays: Second Series*) to extend his vision to the various aspects or walks of life. Yet "The Poet" also hints at the doubt that threatened his faith in spirit over matter. Emerson's orphic voice, as I have noted elsewhere,[28] waned away in this essay. Emerson met his match, so to say, with the very subject that had installed him in the pulpit of Transcendentalism—namely, language. It was indeed a *transformational* grammar that had taken Emerson into a nature that seemed almost impossible by the 1840s. "If a man would be alone," he had said in *Nature*, "let him look at the stars. The rays that come from those heavenly worlds will separate between him and vulgar things."[29] Those rays, however, also come from heavenly *words* that led Emerson to say (in public) that he felt himself "a transparent eyeball." Bathed by "the blithe air" of language, Emerson was safe from the "ridicule" he confronts again in "Experience." The confrontation had been brought about not only by Waldo's death but by the composition of "The Poet," in which he attempted to define the effective version of the self described in the first chapter of *Nature*. Heavenly words might be wakeful, but they were also solipsistic because they were not necessarily those of a "Representative Man" speaking for all, but possibly the incantations of an exclusive self out there beyond the pale of humanity.

Ultimately, there was something selfish and self-destructing about transcending, thereby dismissing the beautiful estates of earthly life for the beauty of one's heavenly world—one that would "separate him and what he touches." "Was it Boscovitch," Emerson asks in "Experience," "who found out that bodies never come in contact?" "Well," he still insists, "souls never touch their objects" either. "An innavigable sea washes with silent waves between us and the things we aim at and converse with" (p. 29). It was, however, the same ocean—and life—where Melville would "find himself," a sea in which the silence was deafening. For its Transcendentalist logic drowns out all language and thus the senses from which it originates. It may have been true that bodies never come into complete molecular contact, but they did touch experientially. Although experience might always fall short of the Emersonian vision, the tragedy of that fact lay in nature's insistence on being rather than becoming. To *become* whole was to abandon the self in nature, to exchange one's "estate" for divine currency. It was God-reliance instead of self-reliance. We sold off our assets, mortgaged away our past (and hence our present) for a facile future. "This one fact the world hates, that the soul *becomes*," Emerson had said in "Self-Reliance."[30] Yet this was soul-reliance and self-*dis*trust.

Also distrustful, then, was the devastating grief for his son, not real because it was part of the drama of the "Not-me." Why then even write about it—as Emerson does in "Experience"? Perhaps he was taking his own advice, which he had given Thoreau, another "sun" that would rise to fall: to write out his grief "into good poetry & so clear himself of it." Such writing was the rhetoric of the right perspective, full of microcosms and incomplete points of view, fictions that awaited the ultimate facts of life. But another fact the world hated was that language *remembered*. It recalled, Emerson said in *Nature*, that "every rational creature has nature for his dowry and estate."[31] He means here that "world is nothing, the man is all" if he will only realize the micro-soul that slumbers within. But to wake up to that reality is to trade today for tomorrow. Nature in such a context is a dowry to be given away, not received; its estate is to be lost, not gained. Finally, it offered only the "grim satisfaction" that death is "a reality that will not dodge us." No wonder Emerson abandoned his Transcendentalist themes after "Experience." He continued to lecture as before, but the message rang a little hollow, especially in England in 1848, where the growing movement to emancipate the worker signaled, indirectly at least, a grass-roots quest for the body of today over the soul of tomorrow. He returned to America to write or publish his essays about *representative* men and English *traits* because the real things in his life had vanished. He had collided with them in "Experience" and would never again burden himself with a true sense of tragedy. In "Fate" of *The Conduct of Life* (1860), he urged his readers to "build altars to the Beautiful Necessity."[32] Now freedom is linked to divine limitation, and a sense of tragedy is possible only in *finding ourselves* outside this context.

To contend, however, that evil or adversity does not exist, to say that it is merely relative to the divine plan, is—as Thoreau suggested in his complaint about the ownership of nature—to allow oneself to be hustled "out of nature." It is to say that the Great Proprietor had bought up all the property of our nature before we came into it. And as "Fate" implies, we were destined "to walk a strip of road" whose divine boundaries were both invisible and unreliable. It was simply another western road that grew narrower and narrower. Ultimate adversity defined the physical, whose present was shaped by the disembodiment of the future. To call that "evil" was simply to manifest one's desire for identity for one's own sake, and not for the sake of tomorrow. Even the platonic past was preferable to the teleological future because it had—despite its similar claim for the Whole—at least produced our present, which was the Fall of Man. The other, or future, always threatened to take it back again by saying that grief "will make us idealists" or that Waldo was "a beautiful estate" instead of a "beautiful boy."

6 : Thoreau's Quarrel
with Emerson

O n *his* deathbed Henry David Thoreau is alleged to have said that he had no quarrel with God. The story is familiar to students of Thoreau, often quoted by professors to characterize Thoreau's sense of humor as levity to the last moment. When his aunt Louisa asked whether he was at peace with God, he told her that he did not know they had ever quarreled.[1] She might as well have asked her nephew whether he had made his peace with Emerson—with whom he had quarreled in the years immediately preceding the publication of *Walden* (1854). The nature of that argument is vague, but we know that it had to do with Thoreau's transition from literary apprenticeship to true authorship. By 1851 he was already insisting (though privately in his journal) that he seldom read Emerson's books anymore.[2] Attempting to ward off the same loss of faith Emerson had tried to dodge in "Experience," he came to view transcendence as only part of the transition he was experiencing. "I see details," he wrote in his journal, "not wholes nor the shadow of the whole."[3] *Walden* contains a good many of those details, what some students still consider digressions; but they probably come together more aesthetically here than elsewhere—in his other book, *A Week on the Concord and Merrimack Rivers* (1849), or in the posthumously published works and journals, where whole chapters on the "facts" of a region, in the Maine Woods or on Cape Cod, are sometimes inserted verbatim. Yet a literary appreciation of *Walden* is still problematic, prompting at least one critic to see the journal as Thoreau's magnum opus. Instead of his "Savings Bank" as it was for Emerson, the journal is viewed as the "whole text" that saves Thoreau from the "ideology" of literature. "We shall see," promises Sharon Cameron, "how the wholeness of nature and the wholeness of the *Journal* will come to be identical."[4] This retrospective canonization of Thoreau's interior life at the expense of his published thought in *Walden*, seen as a "prelude" to the journal, is perhaps as "deconstructive" as the nineteenth-century canonization of Thoreau's posthumous text(s) by Emerson and Channing was "reconstructive." Either effort denies his act of true authorship in *Walden* at the height of the American Renaissance, what I will call his waking up to and shaping the full meaning of his existence as one of the "details" of nature.

As Robert D. Richardson reminds us in the latest biography, the only books Thoreau published during his lifetime were begun at Walden Pond.[5] The others, as we know them today, were for one reason or another never brought to publication by Thoreau himself. Perhaps like Emily Dickinson, he required posthumous editors (and pre-emptive deconstructionists) to auction his mind according to the literary conventions of the day. Indeed, the two writers shared the same sense of agoraphobia when it came to the broad and often bland expanse of a literary establishment that did not necessarily welcome meter-making arguments. In Thoreau's case, however, the publication of his mind in *Walden* was less of a literary "auction" and more of an effort to price himself out of the metaphysical marketplace with statements that pounded beans instead of empires. For in *A Week* and *Walden*, he was reaching back down the evolutionary chain to where nature exists in a relatively unfallen state. "Who does not remember the interest with which when young he looked at shelving rocks, or any approach to a cave?" he asks in *Walden*. "It was the natural yearning of that portion of our most primitive ancestor which still survived in us."[6]

For Thoreau, such an awakening or approach to his original relation to that nature required the woods of Walden, which he records as his earliest reminiscence. Like Whitman's experience in "Out of the Cradle Endlessly Rocking," it was a childhood memory that released him from the literary memory of Emersonian ideology. "When I was four years old, as I well remember," he tells us in "The Bean-Field" chapter, "I was brought from Boston to this my native town, through these very woods and this field, to the pond. It is one of the oldest scenes stamped on my memory" (p. 155). A landscape instead of a seascape, it was the same shore of America that would allow Whitman after the exhausted euphoria of "Song of Myself" to resolve the recurring conflict between Emerson's—and literature's—idealistic version of the self in the ultimate Me and the corporeal version that never quite measured up to the soul's expectations. In Thoreau's case, this meant getting past the "meanness" of the present, not through any ideological flight into the future but through a genealogical descent into a past that always seemed to belittle the present. Thoreau went to the woods of Walden not only to re-order his life in the wake of Emerson's influence but to memorialize his relationship with another "older brother"—his brother John and indeed all the other Brother Jonathans whose teleological tendencies undercut his sense of belatedness in nature.

Thoreau's quarrel with God—if it can be termed that without evoking the ghost of Richard Bridgman's thesis[7]—was that God was the ultimate "elder brother" (to use Whitman's phrase for the deity) and never the benevolent father who abided our adolescence in the present. We were never allowed to grow *up*—only older in a life characterized by meanness, or what Emerson had called "mean egotism." The pattern of older brothers has a long tradition in America, beginning before its "Renaissance" with Franklin's brother James and currently manifested in the Big Brotherism in all sorts of social reform in the wake of the Vietnam debacle. Older brothers are "big brothers" in the sense that they watch *over* us, pre-empting our present with their view of the future. Yet their dominance in American life sometimes leads to the release of the native imagination that alerts the individual to a new reality. In Thoreau's case, the brother analogy profitably extends to his earthly "brothers" with the possibility that he found his literary voice in both John Thoreau's death in 1842 and in Emerson's "conversion," or loss of complete faith in experience after the death of his son the same year. In the aftermath of these two events, Thoreau found the courage to front—as he tells us—"the essential facts" not only of nature but of his own nature *in* nature. "However mean your life is," he would conclude in *Walden*, "meet it and live it" (p. 328). This is not to suggest any conscious quarrel between Thoreau and his older brother, but merely to allow for the sibling anxiety that Richard Lebeaux imaginatively surveys.[8] Nor is it to find acrimony in the angst Thoreau may have felt from Emerson's literary presence. Rather, it is simply to observe that Thoreau found himself—became more at home with himself as "part and parcel" of nature—somehow in the death of one brother and in the literary loss of another. It would be many more years before Thoreau would completely outgrow Emerson's influence, but by the time of the seventh draft of *Walden* in 1854 the break between them was fairly clean. In fact, one might conjecture that Thoreau wrote himself away from John in *A Week* (where he is never mentioned specifically) and away from Emerson in *Walden* (where he is seldom, if really ever, one of the "visitors").

As argued in chapter 5, Emerson was able to aestheticize his grief over young Waldo's passing almost immediately—in "Experience," an essay which also turned *his* transcendences into transitions. His grief was rather conventionally expressed in letters and journal entries, then resolved in the essay, where he wrote that he grieved because he could not grieve. With that admission, however, he also accepted the truth of Transcendentalism that Thoreau because of his early love of Walden and the woods in general would continue to resist: the idea that this life, or its corporeal version, is nothing but "mean egotism" without any worth beyond its correspondence with the Oversoul. The very idea of transcendence for its own sake belittled the importance of the transitions or changes in the Not-me, or nature. When John Thoreau died the same year, almost the same week, in 1842, his brother vented his grief in almost the opposite way of Emerson: he first assumed the stoical or Transcendentalist position, which grieved that grief made us idealists (about this world, not the next), and then fell into a stony silence that simulated the symptoms of lockjaw, the malady that had killed his brother. He took to his bed for six weeks or more, and—according to Walter Harding—it would be almost six months before he was strong enough again to work in the garden.[9] More than a few critics have commented on Thoreau's pathological reaction to his brother's death. It was not normal, even for a writer. But then, none of our great writers was ever "normal"—certainly not Emily Dickinson, who after thirty or so would receive no new visitors, including her doctor, who (legend has it) was forced to diagnose his poet-patient with glimpses of her movement back and forth across her bedroom doorway. Indeed, her reaction to sickness and death resembles Thoreau's in that they both sought to heal themselves through art.[10] Dickinson went within the confines of her bedroom, and Thoreau eventually went to Walden to mend his psychic wounds. John's death initially sent him there, back to the site—and sight—of his earliest reminiscence, but Emerson's "death" kept him there, long after he had left the woods in 1847 because, as he wrote, he had "several more lives to live, and could not spare any more time for that one" (p. 323).

He had, of course, a great deal more time to spare for it—six more drafts of *Walden*, in fact. Richardson notes that Thoreau experienced depression shortly after he left the woods, but that seems now a *normal* reaction to the ecstasy he had enjoyed by placing himself squarely among the details of nature as he had first experienced them. "Sometimes, in a summer morning, having taken my accustomed bath," he writes in "Sounds," "I sat in my sunny doorway from sunrise till noon, rapt in a revery, amidst the pines and hickories and sumachs, in undisturbed solitude and stillness, while the birds sang around or flitted noiseless through the house, until by the sun falling in at my west window, or the noise of some traveller's wagon on the distant highway, I was reminded of the lapse of time" (p. 111). Time stood still for Thoreau at Walden the way it sometimes appears to us that time in lower or vegetable nature stands still because it seems to know only the cycle of time and not its deadly sickle. There at Walden, he had learned to live without time's premonitions about the future. Emerson's "death," as I describe it, probably occurred with the death of his "beautiful boy"—which is to say that with the loss of Waldo he could no longer transcend with the abandon of *Nature* the "mean egotism" of his present for the future. He went instead into the present, yet only to focus there on English "traits" and "representative" men in his work, the "conduct of life" without the extravagance of art. But Thoreau began where Emerson left off: he stopped chanting the hymn of the Transcendentalist future and returned to his past at Walden, now not so much as a nature lover in the metaphysical sense but as a naturalist in the most primordial of senses.

It was not exactly the experience at Walden that loosened the grip of Emersonian—and Arnoldian—ideology for Thoreau and thus modified his sense of meanness about the present (as opposed to the more pristine life in lower nature) but the memory of the experience as he wrote and rewrote it in *Walden*. The book expanded with each draft as he gradually woke up to the significance of writing as an act of healing the belated self—the misbegotten self that had finally learned to become self-begotten. "I love Nature," he wrote in his journal for 1853, "partly *because* she is not man." [11] The naturalist in him found its catalyst, as Richardson notes, through recent readings of Darwin, Cato, Linnaeus, and Gilpin and their common focus on the earth and its productions: "Darwin on the distribution and differentiation of species; Cato, as good as a nineteenth-century farmer's handbook; Linnaeus on minute classification of plants and parts of plants; Gilpin on seeing and describing the larger arrangement of elements in landscape. These were Thoreau's great writers as he turned now to work on the second half of his man-in-nature theme." But the theme was also man-in-memory, for what also led up to the culminating drafts of *Walden* were his thoughts about what was—to quote Richardson again—Thoreau's "lost and largely unrecorded youth." [12] That was, in effect, the state of nature without humans (or society) in it, and to write about it only in retrospect was to become, as Thoreau described himself, "sadly scientific." [13]

In the chapter on "Reading," Thoreau calls the classics the "noblest recorded thoughts of man" (p. 100). He means specifically the Greek and Roman classics, but he is also alluding to any literature, which he defines as having "no cause of [its] own to plead." He describes this written word as "the choicest of relics . . . , something at once more intimate with us and more universal than any other work of art." While the description smacks of literature as "ideology," it also suggests the power of writing to bring out, as he says, "something at once more intimate with us" (pp. 102–3). It is writing as a revision of experience. In the actual revisions of *Walden*, Thoreau wrote himself out of nature and into its reminiscence. He drove life into a corner and discovered he could turn it into a living instead of a liability. In revising *Walden*, he was also reviving the myth of the Whole Person in matter as well as in the mind of God. Here he had no cause of his own to plead because he *had* no cause or ideological quest. In such a prelapsarian state, he also had no quarrel with God. This "relic" of an original self contained the seeds of a rebirth in nature, a reawakening to the whole of it. "I desire to speak," he says at the close of *Walden*, "somewhere *without* bounds; like a man in a waking moment, to men in their waking moments" (p. 324). The experience of Walden, as he remembered and misremembered it in the revisions of his manuscript, became dreamlike, and thus he left the pond with the alacrity of a man waking up to a new day. "I left the woods," he wrote, "for as good a reason as I went there [because] I had several more lives to live, and could not spare any more time for that one." He had learned in the interim between the first and final drafts of *Walden* that "if one advances confidently in the direction of his dreams . . . , he will meet with a success unexpected in common hours" (p. 323).

He had traveled, as he literally had, a good deal in Concord, preferring that to a "South-Sea Exploring Expedition." It was easier, he said, "to sail many thousand miles through cold and storm and cannibals . . . than it is to explore the private sea, the Atlantic and Pacific of one's being alone." But do even this, he counseled, "till you can do better, and you may find some 'Symmes' Hole'" (pp. 321–22). Poe's *Pym* had ended there, but Thoreau's quest never ventures out of the sight of land, or natural facts. Unlike Poe, Thoreau was *writing* nature rather than making up its facts, as he descended deeper into his psyche; yet in both cases, the imagination came full circle with its sense of a primordial past. He was—in this sense—writing his own "classic" or myth, which always contains the "noblest thoughts of man." Whereas *A Week* was two weeks and *Walden* two years and two months, their "reminiscences" were shaped, respectively, into the clean cycle of a biblical week and the natural cycle of the seasons. There life reflected the reality of the dream that promised to return us to the Garden again (to use Emerson's phrase). The reality recycled and cradled us in the silence of lower nature, where we always had "other lives" to live.

In the chapter on "Solitude," Thoreau talks obliquely of "occasional visits in the long winter evenings" from "an old settler and original proprietor, who is reported to have dug Walden Pond, and stoned it, and fringed it with pine woods." He told him "stories of old time and of new eternity, . . . and though he is thought to be dead, none can show where he is buried." Thoreau also speaks of an "elderly dame" who dwells in "my neighborhood, invisible to most persons, in whose odorous herb garden I love to stroll sometimes, gathering simples and listening to her fables; for she has a genius of unequalled fertility, and her memory runs back farther than mythology, and she can tell me the original of every fable" (pp. 137–38). These are the personifications of the original Father and Mother, and their visits conjure up what Thoreau calls the "indescribable innocence and beneficence of Nature,—of sun and wind and rain, of summer and winter,—such health, such cheer [which] they afford forever!" This conjuring up of the mythical past over the historical restores the cycle of renewal that a linear life denies.[14] In the presence of such storytellers (the parents of our *original* story), Thoreau is suggesting, everything is seasonal and cyclical and thus recoverable—even our "lost and largely unrecorded youth." To write about ourselves in *that* nature was about as close as language could take us with regard to an identity obscured by the vagaries of experience.

"Am I not partly leaves and vegetable mould myself?" Thoreau asks in the same chapter. It is that part of him that offers sanctuary from the perils of the ideological present, a condition in which death is the ultimate transcendence. For Thoreau, nature is not an emblem of the spirit exactly, but evidence that we are already perfected in the present as long as we locate ourselves in the solitude of our past in nature. There one has no "just cause [to] grieve," or if one did it would then be reflected in the *dis*harmony of nature: "all Nature would be affected, and the sun's brightness [would] fade, and the winds would sigh humanely, and the clouds [would] rain tears, and the woods [would] shed their leaves and put on mourning in midsummer" (p. 138). This is the confession of a nature lover who is also a reborn naturalist. While not refuting the Emersonian principle of amelioration, he tempers it with the concrete details of nature. "The sun is but a morning star" that wakes up Thoreau to the fact that he is as much "part and parcel" with the emblem as he is with that which it signifies. "Let me have a draught of undiluted morning air," he says, for Thoreau—unlike Emerson—does not wake up sad every day after the age of thirty.[15] That rather rude awakening was for the Transcendentalist, not the Transitionalist who woke up instead to the seasons of his original nature. Thoreau finds a symmetry in nature that valorizes its significance. "However mean your life is, meet it and live it. . . . It is not so bad as you are" (p. 328). The "you" is the present facing the future, that self which had to be transcended, but the "life" is one's existence in the presence of lower nature.

Such a life was possible in Concord as well as at Walden Pond, of course, because Thoreauvian solitude was as applicable as Emersonian self-reliance. "A man thinking or working is always alone," he says. "Solitude is not measured by the miles of space that intervene between a man and his fellows" (p. 135). In fact, it appears to be merely a hermit's version of Emersonian self-reliance in which "the great man is he who in the midst of the crowd keeps with perfect sweetness the independence of solitude." [16] The important difference is the source. When I argued earlier that Thoreau considers himself "part or parcel" with nature as well as with the Oversoul, I was echoing the famous "transparent eye-ball" statement of *Nature*. Yet the irony of the application belongs to Thoreau. In "Walking," he calls man "a part and parcel of Nature, rather than a member of society." [17] For all its emphasis on individuality, Transcendentalism is ultimately a *social* program, because its aim or hope is to draw all the parts back to the original Whole, in the Neoplatonic sense. In his present condition, man is fallen unless—the Transcendentalists say—he realizes his future. Indeed, the seeming harmony of lower nature mocks the existence of man in nature, that reluctant individual who is not at peace with himself unless he is heading out of the corporeal condition. In other words, he abhors his "mean egotism" and longs for the "society" of the whole in the mind of God. Thoreau, on the other hand, insists in "Walking" as well as in *Walden* that we are not fallen as long as we dwell in the solitude of our former—indeed, primordial—wildness. "I would have every man so much like a wild antelope," he announces in "Walking," which began as a lecture in 1852, as he wrote yet another, clearer draft of *Walden*, "so much a part and parcel of Nature, that his very person should thus advertise our senses of his presence, and remind us of those parts of Nature which he most haunts."

This was Thoreau's quarrel with Emerson—or God: that life had to be ultimately teleological instead of intimately analeptical. One had to discover his or her text or "subtext" in the details of nature, which was declared meaningless outside the teleological text that pressed those details like leaves in a book into static emblems of a more harmonious future. "Give me a wildness whose glance no civilization can endure," he declares in "Walking." Rather than accept completely an artificial order in life, Thoreau chose to drive its details into a corner and know their meanness—or, more correctly, their wildness." "Life consists with wildness," he says. "The most alive is the wildest." [18] That life resided in un*man*ned nature—an American frontier always west of Emerson and his Transcendentalist settlements. What Thoreau glimpsed in "Walking" and *Walden* was the essential contradiction of Emersonianism: that it betrayed its celebration of the present by living for the restoration of the Whole in the mind of God. In his relentless focus on details as details, Thoreau rediscovered the myth of humankind instead of its mission. "Where is the literature which gives expression to Nature?" he asks in "Walking." "He would be a poet who could impress the winds and streams into his service, to speak for him; who nailed words to their primitive senses, as farmers drive down stakes in the spring, which the frost has heaved; who derived his words as often as he used them,—transplanted them to his page with earth adhering to their roots; whose words were so true and fresh and natural that they would appear to expand like the buds at the approach of spring, though they lay half-smothered between two musty leaves in a library,—aye, to bloom and bear fruit there, after their kind, annually, for the faithful reader, in sympathy with surrounding Nature."

"You will perceive," he continues, "that I demand something which no Augustan nor Elizabethan age, which no *culture*, in short, can give. Mythology comes nearer to it than anything." Thoreau is referring to the myth of humans before the fall—out of nature and into society. "Mythology," he says, "is the crop which the Old World bore before its soil was exhausted, before the fancy and imagination were affected with blight; and which it still bears, wherever its pristine vigor is unabated." Whereas "all other literatures"—those characterized by Emersonian ideology—"endure only as the elms which overshadow our houses, . . . [myth] is like the great dragon-tree of the Western Isles," which is as old as humankind and which will outlast the other literatures because their decay "makes the soil in which it thrives." [19] The true "American mythology" is analeptic rather than proleptic— the tree in the forest that is never *fallen*. Once man was a god in nature; now he sought God in nature. He was called upon to transcend himself, to dismiss his wildness as meanness or "mean egotism."

In "Experience" Emerson had written: "It is very unhappy, but too late to be helped, the discovery we have made, that we exist. That discovery is called the Fall of Man."[20] This is the curse of knowledge that Thoreau seeks to counter with what he calls "Useful Ignorance . . . a knowledge useful in a higher sense." "My desire for knowledge," he insists, "is intermittent; but my desire to bathe my head in atmospheres unknown to my feet is perennial and constant. The highest that we can attain to is not Knowledge, but Sympathy with Intelligence." Emerson's—or the world's—knowledge is the discovery that we cannot know, but Thoreau's position is that we can learn much from that state of ignorance. This he calls "sympathy with surrounding Nature." The word is capitalized but also partly exorcized of its metaphysical connotation with the adjective—or present participle—"surrounding." For he wanted his words, as he said, "nailed . . . to their primitive senses" and not to their prescient expectations. He had other lives to live, not merely one to die for. The first sparrow of spring taught him more than Emerson's knowledge, or discovery, that he existed in order to transcend existence. "What at such a time," he asks in *Walden*, "are histories, chronologies, traditions, and all written revelations?"

> The brooks sing carols and glees to the spring. The marsh-hawk sailing low over the meadow is already seeking the first slimy life that awakes. The sinking sound of melting snow is heard in all dells, and the ice dissolves apace in the ponds. . . . the symbol of perpetual youth, the grass-blade, like a long green ribbon, streams from the sod into the summer, checked indeed by the frost, but anon pushing on again, lifting its spear of last year's hay with the fresh life below. It grows steadily as the rill oozes out of the ground. It is almost identical with that, for in the growing days of June, when the rills are dry, the grass blades are their channels, and from year to year the herds drink at this perennial green stream, and the mower draws from it betimes their winter supply. So our human life but dies down to its root, and still puts forth its green blade to eternity. (pp. 310–11)

This knowledge of nature involves the dialectic of the nature lover and the naturalist. Nature is an emblem that is not simply emblematic but evidence of our *current* worth, which we ought to be waking up to with the regularity of the seasons: "As every season seems best to us in its turn, so the coming in of spring is like the creation of Cosmos out of Chaos and the realization of the Golden Age" (p. 313). Thoreau's "Life in the Woods"—the subtitle to *Walden*—consisted not so much of building a cabin and demonstrating economy in the face of a greedy, consumer-oriented society, but a romp in the forest in which the saunterer—like Irving's sojourner—made "something" out of the nothingness of his existence. Like Shakespeare's characters in *A Midsummer Night's Dream*, Thoreau's persona renews his vigor (and his vision of himself as born again with every breath he takes) by moving away from Emerson's notion of existence and toward *life* in the woods. It was ultimately not a question of the Me or the Not-me, not so much the experience of the woods but its literary reminiscence that saved Thoreau, as it saves us, from—and perhaps for—eternity. Through the medium of art, Thoreau validated his experience and existence in nature. He exists every time we read him because he wakes up our sense of nature as a series of transitions instead of transcendences, endless cycles that began before time was merely a stream to "go a-fishing in" (p. 98).

In the famous *Walden* passage about time, which concludes "Where I Lived, and What I Lived For," Thoreau seems to boast that he "would drink deeper; fish in the sky, whose bottom is pebbly with stars." In other words, he would transcend nature; but this Transcendentalist reading ignores the basic metaphor in which the vehicle controls—as it ought to control in all *unmixed* metaphors—the tenor. That is to say, the eternity that remains is not represented by the stars above, but by their reflection below in nature. It is a sky whose "*bottom* is pebbly with stars" (my italics). The focus in Thoreau is always on nature as evidence of prelapsarian innocence. Thoreau would, as he states, "drink deeper; fish in the sky, whose bottom is pebbly with stars." Yet it is important to read the paragraph through to the end. "I cannot count one [star]," he says. "I know not the first letter of the alphabet. I have always been regretting I was not as wise as the day I was born." Thoreau's interest in pre-Columbian America merely reflects the *direction* of his literary quest in *Walden*; his instinct tells him that intellect "is an organ for burrowing, as some creatures use their snout and fore-paws, and with it [he says] I would mine and burrow my way through these hills. I think that the richest vein is somewhere hereabouts" (p. 98). Just as the screech owls in "Sounds" appear to sing out *"Oh-o-o-o-o that I never had been bor-r-r-r-n!"* Thoreau laments that part of humanity that was born for the future instead of the past, and hence the present (pp. 124–25).

In *Walden* Thoreau expresses the American desire to be restored to a state of prelapsarian, pre-Puritan (in terms of *their* spiritual quest) innocence. "Not till we are lost, in other words, not till we have lost the world," he states in "The Village," "do we begin to find ourselves, and realize the infinite extent of our relations" (p. 171). Those relations, he asserts in the next chapter, "The Ponds," extend back before "that spring morning when Adam and Eve were driven out of Eden." Even then, he adds, Walden Pond, the scene of his literary nativity, was already in existence, "breaking up in a gentle spring rain accompanied with mist and a southerly wind, and covered with myriads of ducks and geese, which had not heard of the fall" (p. 179). They never would, of course. Lower nature would continue in the harmony that always eluded humans, who were condemned as a consequence to brood about the present. In this context, it is easy to understand Thoreau's fascination with Whitman's 1856 edition of *Leaves of Grass*. "I think I could turn and live with animals," the poet confesses in section 32 of "Song of Myself," "they are so placid and self-contain'd":

> They do not sweat and whine about their condition;
> They do not lie awake in the dark and weep for their sins;
> They do not make me sick discussing their duty to God.

Thoreau found Whitman, as he told Harrison Blake, "the most interesting fact to me at present." Though somewhat repelled by the poems that would grow into the "Children of Adam" sequence of 1860 because they "do not celebrate love at all" and thus threaten moral identity, he thought even here that Whitman had "spoken more truth than any American or modern that I know of." Indeed, Whitman's sensuality, he said, "may turn out to be less sensual than it appeared." It was not sex that troubled Thoreau but the fallen state of humans with regard to it: "I do not so much wish that those parts were not written, as that men & women were so pure that they could read them without harm, that is, without understanding them."[21] Whitman was "classical" in that he could celebrate sex without guilt—or indeed "love." By the same token, Thoreau may have pondered the "love" requirement in matters of human sex: that humans in the ideological present were condemned to mistrust their lower nature, to purge it with notions of human nobility when it came to the sex act. While the animals did not have to "sweat and whine about their condition," or "their duty to God," humans did. They had to worry about the future with its emphasis on "true love," when—as Shakespeare defines it in Sonnet 116—

> Love is not love
> Which alters when it alteration finds,
> Or bends with the remover to remove.

Love was not "Time's fool," but humans were, for by ignoring time they were also abiding it.

True love, in Shakespeare's definition, welcomed the ameliorative movement away from the self in nature to an ultimate state of nature without that (particular) self. It was "the star to every wandering bark,/Whose worth's unknown, although his height be taken." Shakespeare's reference to celestial navigation—the method by which sailors plot their course out of the sight of land—reveals the ideology Thoreau was questioning in *Walden*. Whereas the star's worth was always "unknown," the land, or nature, that Thoreau always kept in sight was clear evidence of the beginning, if not the destination, of one's voyage through life. And that beginning, or its reminiscence, was the source of his "literary" awakening—that is to say, Thoreau's aesthetic rendering of time into seasons instead of sermons about the future. In *Walden* Thoreau's life is shaped into the self-renewing cycle of nature, where love is always "Time's fool" and sex is always its master. "Urge and urge and urge/Always the procreant urge of the world," Whitman had written and Thoreau had read with at least quiet approval, for he had already secretly celebrated the cycle of sex in *Walden*. It was the rhythm of (our) lower nature, which insisted on life as repeated awakenings to nature—insisted on our falling in love repeatedly instead of bending "with the remover to remove." Thoreau had fallen "in love" publicly only once as far as the record shows, to Ellen Sewall—whose physical beauty could outlast even the mandatory five-minute pose for the daguerreotype. He had *fallen* in the sense that he proposed (primarily) "a marriage of true minds" instead of (more primarily) a mating of two natures in the act of sexual renewal. And yet the possibility of even a sexual *beginning* with the beautiful Ellen Sewall must have excited the homely Thoreau out of all Transcendentalist composure.

Of course, it is difficult to imagine Thoreau in such a libidinous circumstance. Like Poe's Helen, Thoreau's Ellen was probably better left in "yon brilliant window-niche"—statue-*like* and thus safely beyond the demands of "true love." In nineteenth-century America, of course, all women, or at least those considered worthy of marriage, were regarded as statue-like, on the pedestal of maidenhood and (then rather miraculously) motherhood. Thoreau's quick recovery from Ellen Sewall's ultimate refusal of marriage suggests that he finally preferred the loss of her to the ideological reality a marriage would have mandated. The point is that nature—for its own sake and significance—was the only way out of the quarrel with God, the only release from the demands of His—and Emerson's—jeremiad. He had, as he told his aunt, never really quarreled with God, but if so, it was because he had survived the transformation from nature lover, or Transcendentalist, to naturalist, or Transitionalist—that is to say, not only one absorbed by the transitions of life but one always in transition between the two points of view. As Frederick Garber observes, "Thoreau's most obvious quarrel with Emerson's *Nature* came from his awareness that the hard stubbornness of [natural] facts implies the resistance of nature to the mind."[22] At the same time, he desired that nature's meanness be somehow sublime. The transition, therefore, was the perpetual state of ambiguity, of never knowing for sure, and thus retaining one's humanity.

In a sense, Thoreau had also survived literature. He had survived its nineteenth-century "culture," or the romantic idea that nature is exclusively an emblem of the future instead of the ever-recurring past. Recent attacks on literature as ideology suggest that it is the post-eighteenth-century, or "modern," equivalent of religion ("secular humanism," as it were), but literature in Thoreau's hand—as in those of every other important American writer—evokes our sense of the past in the present. It does not seek to "transcend" nature, or anybody or thing in it. The stoic who would do that resides in Emerson's essay on Thoreau. The real Thoreau simply had too many lives to wake up to, and he lived them one at a time in the American literary present. *Walden* is the product and proof of those existences, which always begin in the psychological if not physical vicinity of one's earliest reminiscence. By the time Emerson had written "Thoreau" (and long before, going back to "Experience"), he had given up on the natural origins of the self and focused on its mythical future. Thoreau gave up in a way, too, after *Walden*, no longer able to balance the needs of the nature lover with the facts of the naturalist. But in *Walden* we have that most delicate balance, which we call art. Nature's details are friendly, even after Thoreau's experience at Katahdin in 1847.

Much has been said of his discovery in Maine of a nature less receptive than the one of Massachusetts and Walden Pond: "Here was no man's garden, but the unhandselled globe. It was not lawn, nor pasture, nor mead, nor woodland, nor lea, nor arable, nor waste-land. It was the fresh and natural surface of the planet Earth, as it was made forever and ever. . . . Man was not to be associated with it. It was Matter, vast, terrific,—not his Mother Earth that we have heard of, not for him to tread on, or be buried in,—no, it were being too familiar even to let his bones lie there—the home this of Necessity and Fate. There was there felt the presence of a force not bound to be kind to man."[23] He goes on to say that it was "a place for heathenism and superstitious rites,—to be inhabited by men nearer of kin to the rocks and to the wild animals than we." Yet it is also in "Kataadn" that Thoreau began to develop his ideas about lower nature and our proper relation to it. We were not to be the culmination of nature but rather "part and parcel" with it. Believing that, Thoreau was free to express himself without regard to the prevailing logocentric tradition in literature. This was the insight that gradually reshaped *Walden* over the next seven years—the belief that nature could support more than "one order of understandings, could . . . sustain birds as well as quad-rapeds." "I fear," he says in the concluding chapter of *Walden*, "lest my expression may not be *extra-vagant* enough, may not wander far enough beyond the narrow limits of my daily experience, so as to be adequate to the truth of which I have been convinced" (p. 324). In the Maine woods, he had first been shocked at the sight of nature without humans in it, or controlling it, but he came to realize the cathartic value of that conspicuous absence. It indicated that we had to insist on the importance of the Not-me and not rely merely on nature's emblematic signature for our existence. Nature's details were possibly all we had, and it was no *extravagance* to study them for their own sake.

When Thoreau complained in his journal of 1851 of seeing the details of nature at the expense of its whole (meaning), he acknowledged his becoming more "scientific; that, in exchange for views as wide as heaven's cope, I am being narrowed down to the field of the microscope."[24] Yet he had always been scientific, though for a time influenced by the metaphysics of Emerson and the creationism (but never the social Darwinism) of Louis Agassiz. *A Week on the Concord and Merrimack Rivers*, with its division between Thoreau's sojourn through nature and his philosophical "asides," strongly suggests the struggle he had with "literature" in nineteenth-century America. His contribution to it is essentially the "travel narrative" in which the pilgrim saunters through lower nature. Often the recorded details conjure up a sermon on friendship or economy, but the larger theme is nature itself and its resistance to being called something else. Like the artist in the fictional city of Kouroo, this narrator makes little or no compromise with Time, or Emersonian ideology. It was not an "ingredient" in his works of art, but it was in the life that made the art. The story of the artist of Kouroo, therefore, alludes to nothing factual and everything fictional. Thoreau of Concord had to confront Time, but the saunterer in him returns to the source of time—that beginning clearly implied by the ending, or death. In "Walking" Thoreau provides the etymology of *saunterer*. It derives from the example of "'idle people who roved about the country, in the Middle Ages, and asked for charity, under the pretense of going *à la Sainte Terre*,' to the Holy Land, till the children exclaimed, 'There goes a *Sainte-Terrer*,' a Saunterer, a Holy-Lander." The art of walking, therefore, is the act of waking to the imagination's uncanny relationship to lower nature and its apparent wildness. "He who sits still in a house all the time," Thoreau wrote, perhaps with Emerson in mind, "may be the greatest vagrant of all; but the saunterer . . . is no more vagrant than the meandering river, which is all the while sedulously seeking the shortest course to the sea."[25]

Thoreau's first important literary excursion had also begun on a river, but he found his literary métier at a pond in *Walden*. There the ideological pilgrim became the saunterer. Speaking further about the derivation of the term in "Walking," Thoreau wrote that some "would derive the word from *sans terre*, without land or a home." But the "successful" saunterer is one who is "equally at home everywhere."

The idea resembles Emerson's in "Self-Reliance" and the lectures that led up to it: one is "at home" whenever following the urgings of the soul. Yet there is an important difference in that Emerson is guided by emblematic nature, whereas Thoreau is ultimately—in *Walden*—led as much (or more) by "lower" nature as he is by its emblem. Both quests were simulated by language, but natural facts were less remote and illusive than spiritual ones.[26] In *Nature* the Concord Philosopher had said that "the sun shines to-day also," meaning that every day promised a new opportunity for discovering the correspondence between nature and the Oversoul, but for the Concord Saunterer the sun was also a "morning star" that woke us up to the equality of that correspondence—indeed, of its inverse Transcendentalism that took us backward in time as well as forward. Thus, Thoreau's quarrel with Emerson was a family feud in which the younger brother, like Franklin, became ultimately an inventer instead of a printer, a naturalist instead of exclusively a nature lover and Transcendentalist. Thoreau re-invented the American self in society (whether at Walden Pond or in Concord or Boston); he fleshed it out again and—in anticipation of Whitman—tried to make it whole again in the here and now.

The American Renaissance
PART TWO

7 : Whitman's Idea of Women

n an age when physicians rejoiced that neither the "emancipated" woman nor the prostitute "propagates her kind," Walt Whitman claimed that *Leaves of Grass* was "essentially a woman's book."[1] He said so in 1888 about a book first published in 1855, but he undoubtedly alluded to the whole of *Leaves*, which took final shape in the early 1880s, in the sixth edition. By this time the doctors, who exerted at least as much influence as the ministers on society (perhaps more), had coined the term "neurasthenia" to describe the state of nervous exhaustion middle-class women suffered from being (we would conclude today) depicted as "creatures inferior to men yet somehow akin to angels."[2] The woman's place was in the home, maintaining the values or "moral affections" of her society, while also providing it with what Whitman called in "Song of Myself" "bigger and nimbler babes."[3] Whitman's mother had stayed at home and given that society six boys and two girls. His sister Mary had five children and his sister-in-law Mattie two. Only his sister Hannah failed in the propagation effort, probably because she had married a landscape artist and developed "neurasthenia"; today Whitman's biographers diagnose it as hypochondria in view of the fact that she outlived all her brothers and sisters. None of the Whitman women had been "emancipated" in the sense of working outside the home, and yet they were, with the possible exception of Hannah, the models for the women in "A Woman Waits for Me," who know "how to swim, row, ride, wrestle, shoot, run, strike, retreat, advance, resist, defend themselves" (p. 102). In other words, they were "working women" who—given an equal chance in society—could have performed equally well in most male-dominated pursuits. "The idea of the women of America," he wrote in *Democratic Vistas* (1871), was to be "extricated" from the "daze, [from] this fossil and unhealthy air which hangs about the word *lady*." Such women were to be "develop'd, raised to become robust equals, workers, and it may be, even practical and political deciders with men."[4]

Whitman sounds like a feminist of the first order (in the nineteenth century, at least), but the rest of his sentence suggests that he is at best advocating what Harold Aspiz calls "a positive feminism."[5] Not only are women potentially as great as men, Whitman says, but they are "greater" because of "their divine maternity, always their towering, emblematical attribute." This superiority may not detract or distract from their equal qualifications with men in all other "departments," but it does add an important dimension to the woman's role in the future of America. For in using the West as a metaphor for America's development, he called not only for "vigorous, yet unsuspected Literatures, perfect personalities and sociologies," but also "perfect Women, indispensable to endow the birth-stock of a New World."[6] In an era when there *were* no female athletes, he welcomed athletic women who would develop their own identities in society, but he also valued this unprecedented athleticism in terms of female fecundity. As Aspiz notes, "The women who are depicted in the poems exhibit healthy sexuality *and* the capacity for excellent motherhood."[7] I emphasize the conjunction here because it points up Whitman's dilemma with the "Woman Question": that of the woman's unresolved division of labor with regard to the burden of her sexuality. At a time when medical theorists discouraged all but the most infrequent sexual intercourse between married parties (mainly because "recreational" sex with spouses drained the male of vital fluids—one ejaculation thought to equal the loss of forty ounces of blood), it must be said that Whitman called not only for a liberated view of human sexuality but for the "complete" woman—that is, a life that included the female's "animal want" as well as the male's, her "eager physical hunger"; yet it was the purpose to which that passion was to be ultimately directed that may have brought him full circle in his argument for female emancipation.

Whitman sought to free the American female, as he did the male, from the same Victorian ideology about sex that had led to the threatened expurgation of *Leaves of Grass* in 1881, but in the woman's case the idealistic context of his argument always brought him back to celebrating her role as a mother. The occasion for the poet's remarks about the female's "eager physical hunger," for example, came in a conversation with Horace Traubel in 1889, upon the birth of Traubel's nephew, also the son of Thomas Harned, another of Whitman's literary executors. "Your sister," he told Traubel, "has done the proudest of proud things: . . . she submitted her woman's body to its noblest office. I look at the girls—at the childless women—at the old maids, as you speak of them: they lack something." He went on to say that these women without the full exercise of their sexuality, and of course its resulting childbirth, "are not quite full—not quite entire: the woman who has denied the best of herself—the woman who has discredited the animal want, the eager physical hunger, the wish of that which though we will not allow it to be freely spoken of is still the basis of all that makes life worthwhile and advances the horizon of discovery. . . . Sex is the root of it all: sex—the coming together of men and women: sex, sex." At this point, Whitman stopped, but Traubel was so enthralled by the old man's outburst that he urged him to continue. An Emersonian social "progressive," Traubel shared Whitman's belief in the amelioration of the race through a realization of nature's laws. "Oh! how gloriously beautiful motherhood is," Whitman told Traubel in reference to his sister. "She went through that business of having a baby like the sun comes up in the morning: no cross, no shock, no shame, no apology."[8] In accepting, however, the natural state of sex and childbirth, they were also accepting the woman's "natural" disposition to remain at home and raise children. It is especially interesting to note, for example, that the child whose birth provided the occasion for Whitman's praise of nature's eugenic character was named for Herbert Spencer, the nineteenth-century English philosopher whose evolutionary writings reinforced the age's conservative estimate of the woman's place in society. The determinist argued that the woman's physical development had concluded earlier than the male's in order to preserve "those vital powers necessary for reproduction." That indeed being the "weaker sex," she had to rely upon her maternal instincts to survive during the early stages of human evolution. "A woman who could from a movement, tone of voice, or expression of face, instantly detect in her savage husband the passion that was rising," Spencer wrote, "would be likely to escape the dangers run into by a woman less skillful in interpreting the natural language of feeling."[9] Although the physical danger the woman faced with the male had largely disappeared as a result of the development of civilized man, she nevertheless retained her capacity for survival, which also led to the propagation of modern society.

Hence, in calling for the liberation of the impassioned woman, Whitman was also calling for perfect mothers whose full sexual response (including orgasm, it was thought by eugenicists in the nineteenth century) was necessary for healthy offspring. "There are millions of suns left," he had proclaimed in "Song of Myself," intending no pun; but the fact is that the "healthiest" birth in Victorian America was thought to be that of a male, possibly a philosopher or a poet whose prophetic powers would lead the new nation to its great destiny, and daughters were sometimes thought to be the product of a conception involving an unimpassioned female, if indeed any issue at all were to result from the woman's suppression of natural inclinations. This idea flew in the face of the more conservative theories of the Victorian era, such as Sylvester Graham's, that encouraged women to lie still during sex so that the male could perform his part of the act without losing any more "vital fluid" than necessary. It may have been "sex, sex" that Whitman was advocating to Traubel, in *Democratic Vistas*, and as far back as "A Woman Waits for Me" (1856) and section 11 of "Song of Myself," but it appears to be sex with a purpose that threatened to pre-empt the woman's competition in those other "departments" of professional life which the male had thus far dominated. We have to ask, therefore, how *Leaves of Grass* was "essentially a woman's book."

In making that declaration, Whitman admitted that women were "by no means" always on his side, but when they were "they were." What seemed to attract such female readers as Sara Willis Parton and Anne Gilchrist, for example, was the poet's lifting of the veil to reveal their feminine vitality, their desire to be co-equal lovers instead of objects of male sexual (and social) utility. "Walt Whitman, the effeminate world needed thee," wrote Parton, better known to the literary world as Fanny Fern. "I confess that I extract no poison from these 'Leaves'—to me they have brought only healing. Let him who can do so shroud the eyes of the nursing babe lest it should see its mother's breast."[10] Such reviews sound more like love letters addressed to the poet directly. "O dear Walt, did you not feel in every word the breath of a woman's love?" Gilchrist asked in reference to her 1870 essay entitled "An English-woman's Estimate of Walt Whitman."[11] Parton, Gilchrist, and others were not responding to a call to give up their femininity in exchange for male equality; they were answering one to validate it as an equal part of what Whitman called in "Song of Myself" the "procreant urge" that animated everything else—inside the home or out. The world was sexually charged, whether or not the Victorian Age would admit it, and women were both subject and object of its "body electric." "Finally and decisively," Gilchrist told Whitman, "only a woman can judge a man, only a man a woman, on the subject of their relations."[12] If this sounds too heterosexual for what many now view as the Good *Gay* Poet, it must be remembered that Gilchrist's love letter was rejected by Whitman the man and accepted only by the poet he had invented in *Leaves of Grass*. "My book is my best letter," he told her, "my response, my truest explanation of all. In it I have put my body & spirit."[13]

Here may lie the key not only to Whitman's idea of women but to the source of his literary awakening in the 1850s. There are many such "keys" or theories which explain Whitman's extraordinary development as a poet during his "foreground" and focus on the original aspects of his "language experiment," but one innovation that made his poetry most clearly different from the competition in the nineteenth century was his open and "fraternal" treatment of women. He still encouraged them to bear children, of course, and to raise them—though today he would perhaps agree with the behaviorists who argue that "nature" stops with childbirth and that offspring can be "mothered" by either parent, depending on which one occupies the primary domestic role. Yet in sorting out emotional priorities in the late 1840s and 1850s, Whitman must have been at a loss, given his emerging homosexual tendencies (which may or may not have been ever fully acted upon), as to his attitude toward the so-called weaker sex. His earliest-known (and only recently discovered) letters indicate a conventionally thinking male between the ages of twenty and twenty-one, if not a young man clearly interested in the opposite sex, at least one who was interested in becoming involved in the social mix of men and women.[14] As his bachelor life became more pronounced in the 1840s, however, he apparently became a "bachelor" in the literary sense as well and began to study poetically the women he may have never known sexually. His clearly unrealistic engagement of them in the poetry suggests the seduction of a god rather than the lovemaking of a man. As a "free companion" to all, including women, he boasts:

> I turn the bridegroom out of bed and stay with the bride myself,
> I tighten her all night to my thighs and lips. (p. 65)

Such assignations are as farfetched as Whitman's description in section 5 of "Song of Myself" of the libidinous embrace of Body and Soul. "Unscrew the locks from the doors!" he announces later in the poem. "Unscrew the doors themselves from their jambs!" (p. 52). In this vicarious encounter with women, anything is possible.

Heterosexual intercourse is exaggerated beyond all sense of reality—as in the case of the nymphomaniacal "lady" in section 11 of "Song of Myself" whose desire requires a month of male sex all at once. It has been argued that she is inserted in the poem as an aristocratic contrast to the healthy working-class woman who gives herself willingly to motherhood.[15] A "lady" instead of a woman, "the twenty-ninth bather" represses her sexual desire, only to realize it in her fantasy. Yet it is important to note that her descent upon the twenty-eight male swimmers is as bizarre as the poet's rape of the bride in section 33 of the poem. There is nothing "natural" about either encounter, nothing so "healthy" as the sex that was supposed to produce a Herbert Spencer Harned or a Walt Whitman Whoever. These were males named for males. Three of Whitman's brothers carried the namesake of American patriots (George Washington, Thomas Jefferson, Andrew Jackson), and Walt had been named for his father. It was the "natural" extension of the stock for Walter Whitman, Jr., if not the poet "Walt," who required no progeny from his sexual acts. The poet is so sufficient unto himself, so autoerotic as it were, that he can enter the bridal chamber unseen and unencumbered, and by the same token his female persona can caress twenty-eight young men at once without their knowledge:

> The young men float on their backs, their white bellies bulge to
>   the sun, they do not ask who seizes fast to them,
> They do not know who puffs and declines with pendant and
>   bending arch,
> They do not think whom they souse with spray. (p. 39)

Leaves of Grass may be a woman's book because it celebrates sex in the subjunctive, which frees the female *as well as the male* from the burden of her fecundity.

Whitman cherished motherhood, as does also his persona in "Song of Myself," who states that "there is nothing greater than the mother of men," but in praising the mother he also calls out the woman in her own right as the lover of men. Perhaps only an individual with homosexual tendencies could celebrate that capacity so *unpossessively*. In any case, Whitman consciously suppresses the male tradition in western civilization that tends to celebrate wars instead of the "female" virtue of peace. "Let the age and wars of other nations be chanted . . . ," he states in the 1855 Preface. "Not so the great psalm of the republic. Here the theme is creative" (p. 712), not destructive, and his heroics include the man *and* the woman.

The inclusion of the female in his democratic chants is best exemplified in "A Woman Waits for Me," an evangelical call for sexual partners in the democracy of the future. The final version of the poem is somewhat misleading with regard to Whitman's androgynous purpose, for in saying in the title (and first line) that a woman waits for *him*, he is imposing the traditional male paradigm upon a theme that calls for sexual equality. Originally, the opening line read, "A woman America knows (or shall yet know)—she contains all, nothing is lacking" (pp. 100–1 n.). This is quite different from "A woman waits for me, she contains all, nothing is lacking." The woman waits not for the particular male but for a time when her sexual equality in America is fully recognized. Just as in "Song of Myself" the body is not complete without the soul ("lack one lacks both," p. 31), in "A Woman Waits for Me" "all were lacking if sex were lacking." This is not a description of dominant male sexual activity but one of communion between genders. It is not a question of subject and object in the Petrarchan love tradition but one of balance and reciprocity:

> Without shame the man I like knows and avows the deliciousness
>   of his sex,
> Without shame the woman I like knows and avows hers. (p. 102)

The division of sexual labor and satisfaction is underscored by the
point of view in the poem, but without its original opening lines the
poem celebrates the role of the man from the vantage point, again, of
a god. As the poet had entered the bridal chamber in "Song of Myself," he becomes "the robust husband" of *all* impassioned women in
"A Woman Waits for Me."

"I draw you close to me, you women," he says, using the plural. Is
this not as unrealistic and thus godlike as the action of the twenty-
ninth bather? She passes her unseen hand over the bodies of the
twenty-eight young men, and he draws close to legions of impassioned women. Such carnal omniscience produces the safest sex in
America. "I dare not withdraw till I deposit what has so long accumulated within me," the narrator of "A Woman" announces. "Through
you I drain the pent-up rivers of myself." He describes here not the
individual sexual encounter (or its expectation) of the "me" of the
original first line of the poem but the eroticism of America. "For these
States," he admits, "I press with slow rude muscle" (p. 102). If Dreiser
or Hemingway or any other male author whose completely heterosexual activity is a matter of record had written the poem, it would be
interpreted (today) as vulgar and sexist. But the biographical facts suggest that Whitman was clearly not a flesh-and-blood player in the
libidinous game he describes. He said, of course, that he was "both in
and out of the game," yet his view of the game—like Emily Dickinson's—is essentially an androgynous, outsider's view. Neither poet
becomes exclusively the heterosexual subject or object. What they re-
count is not their personal ecstasy but the ecstasy of the game, which
involves two consenting adults. And what they consent to is mutuality,
which is to say that women are just as (sexually) robust as men. "They
are not one jot less than I am," the poet announces as the composite
American male. "They are tann'd in the face . . . ultimate in their own
right . . . [and] calm, clear, well-possess'd of themselves" (p. 102).

The key passage in "Song of Myself," it is almost unanimously
agreed, is section 5 because it celebrates through sexual imagery the
co-equal status of Body and Soul—and by implication the mutuality

of the male and the female. The emphasis, however, is on mating without the thought or possibility of offspring, though one critic has suggested that the section describes Whitman's "birth as a poet." [16] In the words of another critic, the union is "mystical in kind" and "sexual [only] in idiom." [17] Indeed, even the physical aspect Whitman describes here is flawed with regard to offspring because the process of conception involves fellatio rather than copulation.[18] With the tongue as the agent of insemination, the offspring brought forth is a voice that transcends "all the argument of the earth" (p. 33). That includes not just philosophical and religious questions but society's expectations for the impassioned and orgiastic sexual encounter, which is the transformation of the woman from active sexual partner to passive loving mother. Rather, Whitman's heterosexual encounters never reach closure but (especially in this instance) become abstracted into quasi-mystical states that preserve the ecstasy of the past. In the words of James M. Cox, "The famous description is a pastoral memory into which the present tense of the poem dissolves. . . . The act of conception and creation in which the disembodied tongue or soul of the poet weds the body is a complete fusion which in turn democratizes and articulates the body." [19] It also frees the body—the female body— from the earthly burden of its gender. For this is no "cold pastoral" Whitman carves on his urn but a warm and passionate scene that allows the woman to retain not only her existence as a woman but her equality as one.

That equality, as Whitman knew, derived from her sexuality, which in Henry Adams's symbology is equated with strength. It was Adams who first articulated this central point in Whitman's poetic vision. He began to ponder, as he wrote in *The Education*, "asking himself whether he knew of any American artist who had ever insisted on the power of sex, as every classic had always done; but he could think only of Walt Whitman." Through Whitman's "procreant urge" is always to be born the word of life in *love* rather than in *labor*. Here the woman, like Adams's Old World dynamo, is always fecund and never forgotten, always perceived as force instead of sentiment. "Why was she unknown in America?" Adams asked. "When she was a true force, she was ignorant of fig-leaves, but the monthly-magazine-made American female had not a feature that would have been recognized by Adam." [20] Nor by Whitman, it should be added, who uses the "valvèd voice" of poetry to re-enact the equality of Adam and Eve in the Garden. In Whitman, remarks R. W. B. Lewis, "we must cope with the remarkable blend . . . whereby this Adam, who had already grown to the stature of his own maker, was not less and at the same time his own Eve, breeding the human race out of his love affair with himself."[21]

In celebrating female sexuality, therefore, the poet of *Leaves of Grass* becomes not only Adam the Namer but the namer of the Namer who has created Adam and Eve in the poem. Beyond gender, as it were, he can, from his lofty position, risk even the appeal of the common prostitute. He can speak to her as "Walt Whitman, liberal and lusty as Nature" (p. 387) and yet wait until she has put away her sex before accepting her as a lover. What he awaits is her passion and not her sex as a marketable commodity. In other words, she is a *common* prostitute. The adjective has always struck me as redundant until we consider that "prostitution" is common to all women who barter their sex for social reasons instead of *using* it for selfish reasons. He appoints "an appointment" with her when she will be "worthy" to meet him—or rather to re-encounter herself as a woman instead of a "lady" and a whore. The poet refuses to recognize her until she recognizes herself as an unpaid and impassioned lover, who will, by preparing to meet him on his terms, come to him on her *own* terms.

This brings us back to the matter of motherhood and Whitman's development as a poet. Motherhood was perhaps the only female role he knew firsthand. It was real, whereas female sexuality was not, except as a prerequisite to motherhood. Whitman had "unfolded" (p. 391) out of the folds, as he wrote, but he never became a male "unfolder" or father (despite his old-age claim for six illegitimate children)[22]—only a son who could celebrate the mother. Her past in sex was as remote to him as the sex in *The Scarlet Letter*, which concludes before the story begins. Hence, without direct involvement with the woman's sexuality, he could romanticize it as much as Hawthorne initially romanticized the past of Arthur and Hester. In Hawthorne's case (as I have argued in chapter 2), the author confused himself with his "Arthur." Yet in Whitman's case, it was the most disinterested literary voice in America that celebrated the woman's sexuality. This is why we have no totally persuasive feminist study of this writer, or even a credible attack upon him as a "male chauvinist."[23]

It is probably true that as a person Whitman was—in his argument for women—"trapped by his own rhetoric." This is the conclusion of Myrth Jimmie Killingsworth, who sees the poet as never quite escaping a Victorian culture that mystified and glorified the mother-son bond.[24] Its ideology rendered the female politically inferior by proclaiming her superior as a mother and thus the keeper of social mores and religious principles. As a poet, however, Whitman could speak of the "perfect equality of the female with the male," as he does in "By Blue Ontario's Shores," one of the poems based on the 1855 Preface. In celebrating her sexual capacity in his poems, he focuses more on the act than on its teleology. As a good Transcendentalist, he celebrates her present as much as he does the male's. In other words, the female is equal *now* if "superior" and hence inferior physically and intellectually later. Her future as a mother is more often the subject of the prose. This is not to say that mothers are absent from "Song of Myself" and the other great poems of the first three editions of *Leaves of Grass*; they are not. Rather, it is to argue that the women, mothers included, generally escape the sentiment ascribed to them by Victorian consensus. This includes even the "red girl" of section 10 of "Song of Myself," who is probably already pregnant and will no doubt become subservient to her husband, the white male trapper. "She had long eyelashes, her head was bare," the poet writes, "her coarse straight locks descended upon her voluptuous limbs and reach'd to her feet." The unmarried "lady" in the next section can be seen "dancing and laughing along the beach," her ladyhood completely abandoned for the womanhood of the moment (pp. 37–38). Even the prostitute in section 15 is deemed as worthy as the president. The point is that Whitman's rendering of women is a poetical fantasy that ignores the reality of their future, which has already come true in the present—ignores the fact that since women *will* in most cases become mothers, their identities as women instead of ladies is already preempted. His vision is no more viable than his concept of a "divine average" in a nation where everyone is encouraged to become the best. More precisely, it is the male fantasy of a son who never became a father and husband, of the latent homosexual who becomes heterosexual and indeed omnisexual in poetry. *Leaves of Grass* is "essentially a woman's book" because the males in it are instructed and excited by women instead of mothers and wives, partners instead of propagators. "Before

I was born out of my mother," Whitman insists in section 44, "generations guided me" (p. 81). He was, in other words, the product of the "procreant urge" that made men and women equal in the creation of life, and not the son whose adult life often made them unequal.

It was, in fact, *as* a son that Whitman responded to most if not all real-life overtures from women. "Walt," wrote Fanny Fern upon reading *Leaves of Grass* in 1856, "what I assume, *you* shall assume."[25] Whitman's reply (if any) is not known, but the thirty-seven-year-old poet did become friendly with the forty-five-year-old Fern, to the extent that her thirty-four-year-old husband, James Parton, lent the poet $200.[26] Apparently, Whitman never repaid the debt to Parton's satisfaction, but Whitman may have blamed Fern for her husband's threatened lawsuit to collect the money. A year later, in the *Brooklyn Daily Times* of 9 July, he wrote that "one genuine woman is worth a dozen Fanny Ferns."[27] The unsatisfied loan has been cited as the cause of the rupture in the Fern-Whitman relationship, one that had been as professional as it had been personal, given the similarity in cover designs of *Fern Leaves from Fanny's Port-Folio* (1853) and *Leaves of Grass* (1855). Obviously, Fern had been pleased not only by Whitman's celebration of women but also by Whitman himself, whom she had described earlier (before reading his book) as having a "muscular throat" and shoulders "thrown back as if even in that fine ample chest of his, his lungs had not sufficient play-room." "Mark his voice!" she continued, "rich—deep—and clear, as a clarion note. In the most crowded thoroughfare, one would turn instinctively on hearing it, to seek out its owner."[28] The thrice-married, middle-aged Fern was clearly taken with Whitman the man as well as Whitman the poet.[29] It was a confusion of big Walt with little Walter (whose oratorical voice was allegedly slightly high-pitched rather than "deep"),[30] but the attraction apparently displeased James Parton, who married Fern in 1856. Otherwise, why would Parton never have forgiven Whitman the debt, which was satisfied with goods whose value exceeded the amount of the loan? As late as 1878, years after Fern's death, he still bore the poet ill will.[31]

Just as a woman (and a wife) may have been the principal cause for Whitman's 1872 quarrel with his old friend and literary ally William Douglas O'Connor,[32] one was also at the center of the Whitman-Parton controversy. In both cases, Whitman failed to respond to the advances of a married woman. No ménage à trois, the Whitman-Parton-Fern triangle was twisted in ways that made all parties losers. Yet the record indicates that Fern did not share her husband's antipathy for the poet, even after his assault on her in the *Brooklyn Daily Times*. One has only to read *Ruth Hall* (1855) to understand why. A lachrymose tale in which the only "friendly" males are dead, avuncular, or otherwise uncompetitive, its plot allows the female room to grow beyond the traditional limits of her sex without also abandoning the same liberated female identity that Whitman validates in *Leaves of Grass*. Overcoming a series of male exploitations (from her father, father-in-law, and brother) as well as the condemnation of females that advances that exploitation, this widowed mother of two surviving children becomes the famous writer of witticisms and common sense that Sara Willis Parton became as Fanny Fern after the publication of her first book in 1853. *Ruth Hall* is sentimental not because it necessarily dwells in part on the domestic problems of householding and child rearing, but because it is a fantasy-come-true. Not only does Ruth succeed in the male literary world, but she retains her eligibility for the storybook possibilities of connubial bliss.

Like the women in *Leaves of Grass*, Fern's character has it both ways: she caps her worldly success by remaining available for a successful marriage. Fern did the same by marrying the prototype of the "gentlemanly, slender, scholar-like looking" male in *Ruth Hall* (James Parton), but she endured, unlike the fictional Ruth, a stormy marriage from the very outset.[33] It seems to be the rule in female fiction of the nineteenth century that the woman's unconventional activity never disqualifies her (as it does Hawthorne's Hester, James's Isabel, or even Chopin's Edna, for example) from personal or domestic happiness. Indeed, the heroine of Lydia Maria Child's *Hobomok* (set in Colonial times, no less) wins back her white male suitor after marrying and having a child with an American Indian.[34] In both Whitman's and Fern's case for women, the success in exercising their freedom is unrealistic for the times (indeed, for all times in Whitman's vision). Yet the work of Fern and most of her compatriots has been dismissed as sentimental, whereas Whitman's has been celebrated as romantic. The difference is that Fern's fantasy in *Ruth Hall* sets up the woman independently in society, while Whitman's vision reinforces the frontier ideal in which the woman—though "equal"—stands *behind* her male counterpart in the making of American society. Furthermore, while Fern's tale is linear because its drama, like most utopian plots or social visions, is based on wishful thinking about the future, Whitman's presentation is at least two-dimensional because it also reflects the ideology about the present.

That ideology depicted the woman as a mother-lover who nurtured the genius of the American male. She nurtured him in order to mate with him in the making of the American future. We encounter the downside of this New World relationship in the prose of *The Scarlet Letter, The Portrait of a Lady*, and *The Awakening*, but in the poetry of *Leaves of Grass* the American male is always being created to create—or procreate:

> Unfolded out of the folds of the woman man comes unfolded, and
> is always to come unfolded,
> Unfolded only out of the superbest woman of the earth is to come
> the superbest man of the earth,
> Unfolded out of the friendliest woman is to come the friendliest
> man,
> Unfolded out of the perfect body of a woman can a man be form'd
> of perfect body,
> Unfolded only out of the inimitable poems of woman can come the
> poems of man, (only thence have my poems come;)
> Unfolded out of the strong and arrogant woman I love, only thence
> can appear the strong and arrogant man I love.
>
> .   .   .   .
>
> First the man is shaped in the woman, he can then be shaped in
> himself. (p. 391)

The celebration in this poem is ultimately about the nativity of the son *and* the poet who will reinscribe the mother as a lover.

This is precisely Whitman's accomplishment in *Leaves of Grass* and why it is "essentially a woman's book." By focusing on her fecundity—that is, the woman's *becoming* a mother—he temporarily liberates the female body from its future motherhood. In "Unfolded Out of the Folds," Whitman calls the woman's sexuality the poem from which his own poems come. In a word, the woman is nature, the wellspring (Whitman had learned from Emerson) of all poetry. With her exclusive ability to conceive life, she was Whitman's symbol of human growth, her sexuality the means to it. His book is a "woman's book" because its strength and vision come from the belief in nature as always creating us anew, always waking us up to life's passion—its "procreant urge" to be unfolded out of the folds of our existence. What the woman did afterwards *as* a mother was also worthy of inclusion in his poems, but her primary claim to his attention lay in the passionate act of creativity. She might even, like Ruth Hall if not Fanny Fern (who had no children), compete in a man's world and be included in the older poet's admiration of her, if not so clearly in the 1855 poet's depictions. For the younger Whitman, it was in nature and not society that the woman first flourished, in a state of innocence before the fall into intellect and the news that we existed as fathers and mothers instead of as sons and daughters, mortal instead of immortal. Whitman never became a father himself, except to his younger siblings and the series of "sons" he collected in his old age. In his strong poetry, he wrote as a son who never commits himself to a female lover. He might "turn the bridegroom out of bed and stay with the bride" himself, but the other self remained back with the woman "aft the blinds of the window." Ever the voyeur (and perhaps not even a voyager when it came to heterosexual intimacies), Walter sent Walt into a world of women that had existed—like Emerson's idea of poetry—"before time was."

Probably the best indication of the poet's hesitation in such matters is depicted in "The Sleepers," where the poet's nocturnal emission is achieved only by identifying with another's passion and that of the female gender ("she who adorn'd herself and folded her hair expectantly," p. 426). Furthermore, in this strictly voyeuristic survey of the sleepers, he does not, for example, "turn the bridegroom out" but merely watches "the married couple sleep calmly in their bed, he with his palm [the husband's, not the poet's] on the hip of the wife" (p. 425). Even more revealing is that the object of this sexual "voyage" is the mother, symbolized by the night in which the dreams (and the best sex) take place. She is the night "in whom I lay so long" (p. 433). Her embryonic realm is contrasted with the day where lovers go unrequited. In the night, in the darkness of her womb, "The Soul is always beautiful,/The universe is duly in order, every thing is in its place" (p. 432). All come back to life after their sleep, which is simulated death in the poem, even the swimmer whose "beautiful gigan-

tic" body had been "bruis'd on rocks" and borne away a "corpse."
Indeed, this dream is so imagined in consciousness that it even fails
to end inconclusively.[35] Rather, it concludes with the poet coming tri-
umphantly home to the mother:

> I too pass from the night,
> I stay a while away O night, but I return to you again and love you.
>
> . . . .
>
> I will duly pass the day O my mother, and duly return to you
> (p. 433)

Whitman's idea of women, dramatized as a pageant of Oedipal love
in "The Sleepers," was just as poetical and just as impractical as Poe's
idea of Helen, Hawthorne's vision of Hester, or even Irving's revised
memory, or mis-memory, of Matilda Hoffman. It was in all American
cases that of the mother who rendered the sons "journeymen divine"
(p. 426).

8 : Twain's Cigar-Store Indians

By the time Whitman's idea of women had become a memory instead of a dream, on the occasion of the poet's seventieth birthday party organized by his Camden disciples, Mark Twain wrote him: "You have lived just seventy years which are the greatest in the world's history & the richest in benefit and advancement to its people." Twain's letter was one of thirty invited responses, many of which were read at the banquet in Morgan's Hall in Camden. Like the other literary lights solicited, Twain sent a letter instead of attending, having heard Whitman deliver his final Lincoln lecture in New York City in 1887. Even the guest of honor, too sick to leave his home on nearby Mickle Street, missed the dinner and had to be carried to the hall afterwards to hear the eulogistic speeches. The year was 1889, and the closest Twain got to Morgan's Hall was to invent Hank Morgan, the narrator of *A Connecticut Yankee in King Arthur's Court* (1889) who brings deadly efficiency to Camelot. Indeed, Twain's optimism in his letter matches the mechanic's for its blinding pride in the triumph of the industrial age in America. "What great births you have witnessed!" he told Whitman. "The steam press, the steamship, the steel ship, the railroad, the perfected cotton-gin, the telegraph, the telephone, the phonograph, the photogravure, the electrotype, the gaslight, the electric light, the sewing machine." The author who had reached back to the romance of his antebellum youth in *Tom Sawyer* (1876), *Life on the Mississippi* (1883), and *Huckleberry Finn* (1884), was turning in *A Connecticut*

Yankee to the future in order to declare war on that past. In his letter he urged Whitman to "wait thirty years, & *then* look out over the earth! You shall see marvels upon marvels added to these whose nativity you have witnessed. . . . Abide, & see these things! Thirty of us who honor & love you, offer the opportunity. We have among us 600 years, good & sound, left in the bank of life. Take 30 of them . . . & sit down & wait."[1]

In a birthday greeting better suited for Andrew Carnegie, Twain was perhaps revealing his anxiety about a world whose salvation was now to be found in technology instead of poetry, in the drama of future expectations instead of the dream of the past. Then at work on *A Connecticut Yankee*, which imposes an ingenious mechanic on the superstitions of a Church-driven ideology, he would ultimately feel compelled to conclude that dream-vision with one of the instruments of its own technological advancement. The future could not reform the past any more than technology could save the present with "science," another ideology whose time had come—and had been coming since the days of magicians who inhabit Twain's book. Under its spell every enigma supposedly had a solution, and in *Pudd'nhead Wilson* (1894) it is fingerprinting. It cannot, of course, solve the mystery of even one *human* condition. It merely restores the order of masters and slaves—with Tom back in his place as Chambers (and sold down the river) and Chambers out of the "nigger gallery" (in body if not spirit). David Wilson, one of Twain's "mysterious magicians" spanning from "The Celebrated Jumping Frog of Calavaras County" (1865) to *The Mysterious Stranger* (1916), really fails to sort out the identities which history has miscegenated. Twain's success in reflecting America's racial confusion is certainly measured by the fact that the reader of *Pudd'nhead Wilson* can hardly ever again think of Thomas à Beckett Driscoll as anyone other than Chambers, and Valet de Chambre as anyone other than Tom. Yet just as Twain in *Huckleberry Finn* had morally entrapped his readers (and perhaps himself) by having them identify with Huck's postwar conscience instead of his antebellum practicality,[2] so he mixed black and white in *Pudd'nhead Wilson* to produce an off-white narrative that was really all white in its endeavor to appropriate and understand the black world. Almost a century later in American race relations, John Howard Griffin in *Black Like Me* (1961) would—more literally—try the same experiment, but in both cases the point of view remained stubbornly white. Chilled as modern readers were by Griffin's account (and later by his early death, possibly brought on by the chemicals he had consumed to darken his pigmentation), they were still blocked by the author's white point of view. Similarly, modern readers of Twain hesitate to applaud his treatment of Jim in *Huckleberry Finn* or his resolution of plot in *Pudd'nhead Wilson* because they suspect that they have been invited into a territory of the white conscience that the author himself was not adequately prepared to explore.

By the time Twain completed these novels, blacks had already begun to disappear into the twentieth century of economic slavery and Jim Crow laws. Reconstruction had officially ended in 1877 with the withdrawal of federal troops, versions of social Darwinism were reinforcing the notion of black inferiority, and African Americans were increasingly advised to compete in a white world without government help. "The late 1870s and 1880s," writes George M. Frederickson, "constituted a transitional period in the history of Negro voting between full suffrage of the Reconstruction era and total disenfranchisement of the end of the century."[3] By 1900, the antebellum condescension to blacks had hardened into a white consensus of Negrophobia. This rise and fall of Reconstruction rights is presciently limned in *Huckleberry Finn*, where Jim begins as Miss Watson's slave, develops as Huck's equal on the river, and concludes as a "nigger" at the Phelpses. At the end of the novel, it is—as Roxy tells her son in *Pudd'nhead Wilson*—the "nigger" in Jim that dictates his situation. Only in the middle of the book is Jim a memorable character in American literature. In other words, the Jim that Twain and most readers celebrate is the one on the river, and they do so because he is there manifestly—as Huck tells us—"white inside."[4]

The fact that Jim is forgotten in his freedom at the end of the book does not tarnish his *literary* image because it is the white Jim who inhabits this fictionalized reminiscence that is not only Twain's but the property of every reader of *Huckleberry Finn*. Jim, as it were, is "enslaved" by literature, recruited by the white conscience to evoke our sense of pathos but nevertheless allow us to exit under the sign of a "happy ending." The dénouement is slightly different in *Pudd'nhead Wilson*, probably because Twain's boyhood memory of Hannibal was increasingly beclouded by the more apparent failure of Reconstruction. Like Jim, Roxy disappears at the end of the tale, but she is also remembered as much as a culprit (of the "tragedy" of the switched babies) as she is a victim. Twain's ambiguous treatment of Roxy, who is literally white *outside*, reflects as well the white fear of miscegenation at the end of the century. The word, incidentally, derives from an 1863 pamphlet entitled *Miscegenation*, which was a hoax supposedly representing the position of the Republican Party during the 1864 presidential election; it claimed that Republicans viewed the breeding of blacks and whites as both inevitable and desirable.[5] The ploy was intended to play on the growing belief that any products of racial "pollution" were genetically destined for degeneracy and extinction. This white dread of miscegenation (a pejorative until a few years ago) seems to have dissipated somewhat today. Which is to say that lighter-skinned African Americans are probably finding it easier to "integrate" socially as well as professionally. Yet it is also true that a person with even the slightest amount of "black blood" is designated a black instead of a white. It would be hopeful to see the distinction as the result of black pride, but in fact it is upheld by the white establishment as well. The *New York Times*, for example, still refers to persons of white and black parentage as "black."

It is difficult to understand how this practice is different from that in Dawson's Landing, which brands Roxy a slave because she is one-sixteenth black and the rest white. The distinction reveals the same white hesitation toward the black that Twain was not only writing about but acting out in the novel. The plot, in fact, is based upon the unfairness of Roxy's social position to the extent that its resolution returns her son (who is even "whiter") to slavery. In other words, the dénouement of the tale implicitly argues against miscegenation and for a time in the mythical past when there was white "purity." Apathy toward black human rights is condemned and even ridiculed in the book, but the basic scenario nevertheless suggests Twain's (white) reticence toward any kind of amalgamation. It was, as Griffin writes in *Black Like Me*, a "complex matter to get from the white world into the Negro world."[6] Forrest Robinson has pointed out that *Tom Sawyer* is almost a totally white world (with only one half-breed who is the villain), whereas *Huckleberry Finn* introduces the realities of slavery and race relations.[7] Yet even here Twain was reluctant to make the story anything more than Huck's "adventure." Jim as a runaway slave has been, as we discover at the end, free throughout most of the book. In retrospect, this fact renders Huck's involvement in freeing Jim almost as meaningless as Tom's prank during the last eleven chapters of the book. In other words, in spite of his good (racial) intentions, Mark Twain was playing Tom Sawyer's game in *Huckleberry Finn* by having us believe that this white boy was actually helping to free a black slave. Huck *thinks* he is helping Jim escape just as Twain surely intended a condemnation of slavery, if not altogether of racism, in his story, but it all turns out to be a "boy's book" and a prank after all. No wonder, then, that we generally dislike the ending of *Huckleberry Finn*, because it mirrors the whole story in which Mark Twain turns out to have been Tom instead of Huck. With the white romance of the river ruined by the ending, we find ourselves at the same old American beginning with regard to racial relations—left with the truth that the story was never successful in its intention to violate the traditional relationship between masters and slaves.

This is the "joke" in *Huckleberry Finn*, not only on the reader but on the author, Mark Twain, the socially reconstructed Southerner from Hannibal, Missouri, the son-in-law of an abolitionist, a writer who set out to correct the racial errors of his past but ended up producing a fiction that was all too factual.[8] His expiation went further in *Pudd'nhead Wilson*, but it could never go far enough in either book. The problem was not only Southern but American, because it lay with the white reluctance—indeed, inability—to reconcile the awful blackness of slavery with the dream of American New-Worldness. The predicament is poignantly described by W. E. B. Du Bois in *The Souls of Black Folk* (1903). He speaks of a white "kingdom of culture" that produces in the black a most "peculiar sensation, this double-consciousness, this sense of always looking at one's self through the eyes of others. . . . One feels his twoness,—an American, a Negro."[9] Du Bois's complaint identifies the white ideology that withheld a full sense of American citizenship to non-whites, especially ex-slaves. Rather than explore the possibilities of an Americanization of blacks, it sought to colonize them in another country, to get them out of the American story. This had been the most attractive solution prior to the Civil War and even before the abolition movement had begun to gather momentum in the 1830s. It was the solution of the Great Emancipator, who told Horace Greeley in his letter of 1862 to the

New York Tribune that he "would save the Union" first and abolish slavery second. It was a priority of Lincoln's enthusiastic admirer, Walt Whitman, who—though he despised slavery, black *and* white—considered the integrity of the Union as the "good cause" above all others, even abolition. This Emersonian love of the Whole in politics led to the consensus in the history books (even today) that the Civil War was fought over "States' Rights" instead of White Rights or Black Slavery. In Twain's case, blacks were also expendable for the sake of the American story. Whereas the author allows Huck the possibility of lighting out for the Territory and David Wilson the chance to prove he is not a "pudd'nhead," he can only free Jim to become another "Free Joe" and sell Tom down the river. Like Lincoln, he first had to save the Union—the integrity of his story, or the fiction about the essential whiteness of America. It was a tale in which African Americans never fit into the dénouement, the "happy ending" that there exists an American "territory" whose social problems are "black and white" instead of hopelessly miscegenated.

Twain was writing—it seems clearer today, if also fashionable to say—*American* literature, white male literature for a white male audience he knew well how to entertain as well as educate. Even now an adjective seems necessary, if also anachronistic, to describe "minority" American literature as black or female. In our discussions of *Huckleberry Finn*, we resurrect Jim as "Nigger Jim" in order to make an issue of his race and—in historical retrospect—to make him one of the two major characters in this white bildungsroman. The actual appellation does not appear anywhere in the book, but the lowercase "nigger" does hundreds of times to signal that Jim is a minor player in the tale until he invades Huck's white conscience. Even then, he is merely white on the inside, his exterior blackness still the sign of his minority status in American literature. In modern interpretations of the book, we observe the tragic implications of Jim's situation. Twain, on the other hand, saw the situation as primarily a white tragedy. He crossed the Color Line in fiction for us, but he did so by whitening the color of blacks instead of shading their place in American society. The latter endeavor might have satisfied the modern desire for realism (if not truth), but it would have put Twain into the category of his Nook Farm neighbor, Harriet Beecher Stowe. It is precisely Twain's failure to write "reform literature" that makes *Huckleberry Finn* so interesting with regard to the enigma of (white) American culture.

It is important to remember that *Huckleberry Finn* and *Pudd'nhead Wilson* are named for their white characters. Jim and Roxy (as well as her son) are "whitened up" for their roles but finally swept away by Tom Sawyer endings in which we discover that they are black after all. Jim may have seemed "white inside" to Huck, but he is all black to Tom and thus the convenient target of his chicanery at the end of the book. Roxy might look white on the outside, but it takes only a "pudd'nhead" to discover otherwise. If there was a "happy ending"—or even a meaningful middle—for Twain's black characters, it remained beyond any social view he could sell as literature, somewhere in the fantastic future to which Twain beckoned Whitman in his birthday greeting. By that time they would both be dead, but in the meantime Tom Sawyer would prevail.

Twain could never end his stories any other way. In a sense, they never end at all but start over in another episode of relative innocence, often with Hannibal in mind. Yet when Twain took what Justin Kaplan calls "his last long look at America"[10] in *Pudd'nhead Wilson*, he must have realized that his Tom Sawyerism reflected the larger fiction of American life and law with regard to non-whites both at home and abroad. Clearly, the romantic delusions of the citizens of Dawson's Landing, especially Judge Driscoll's self-activating adherence to the code of "honor," reflect the imperialistic policies of the United States under William McKinley and anticipate the braggadocio of his successor in the White House, Theodore Roosevelt. More than a decade after the publication of *Pudd'nhead Wilson*, and almost simultaneous with his deterministic arguments in *What Is Man?* (1906), Twain thought Roosevelt "far and away the worst President we have ever had, and also"—he added significantly—"the most admired and the most satisfactory."[11] He was the worst, Twain thought in dictating his autobiography, because he had reinscribed America as a Tom Sawyer "adventure." "He was in a skirmish once at San Juan Hill," he said, "and he got so much moonshine glory out of it that he has never been able to stop talking about it since."[12] Or *living* it as President of the United States, we should add, for Roosevelt envisioned a simplified version of America (not unlike the one imagined by a later actor-

president) in which everybody could "stand tall" and tell the difference between black and white. Roosevelt was the worst president because he was the best at pleasing the great majority of voters with his
evocation of frontier individualism—what Twain called his "dime-
novel heroics." Like the Tom Sawyer who wrote the conclusions to
Huckleberry Finn and *Pudd'nhead Wilson*, however, Roosevelt got into
trouble when he tried to extend his romantic fiction to black America.
"He invited a negro to lunch with him at the White House," Twain
said in his autobiography, "and the negro did it." The guest who came
to dinner was Booker T. Washington, and the reaction from the South
was "furious." To get back into Southern favor, Roosevelt dismissed
"without honor" an entire regiment of black soldiers falsely accused
of rioting in Brownsville, Texas, in 1906.[13] The racial incident had
been created when the War Department dispatched the 25th Colored
Infantry to Brownsville over the objections of local leaders, who feared
"that the sight of a nigger soldier could not be endured by Texans and
disaster must certainly follow if the colored soldiers came there."[14]
When the self-fulfilling prophecy came true, Roosevelt—whom
Twain thought the "Tom Sawyer of American Politics"—changed the
ending of the "story" to align it with the white fiction about most
blacks.

Roosevelt had stretched the fiction about American equality too far
when he invited a black American to the White House, and his response to the Brownsville incident may underscore his own white in-
sincerity on the racial issue. Black "advancement," as he had said
more candidly in 1905, had to be compatible with the Southern ban
on "social intermingling of the races."[15] Twain had nothing good to
say about Roosevelt in 1908 when he continued dictating materials
for his autobiography. Yet he must have suspected that there was
something of a "Teddy" Roosevelt in Mark Twain, as popular a writer
by then as Roosevelt the politician, who that year practically hand-
picked Taft as his successor as president. Both Roosevelt and Twain
were American showmen, creating tales out of the fabric of the nation's ideology. Twain's great value as a writer is that he realized that
the American Dream was a "funny story" whose punch line had curiously tragic dimensions. This can be seen not only in the pretensions
of Judge Driscoll and his highbrow relations but also at the lower level
of American society in Pap Finn's tirade against the freedman from

Ohio—"a mulatter, most as white as a white man." Discovering that the black, a college professor, can also vote in his home state, Pap says, "Well, that let me out." The professor cannot be "put up at auction and sold," Pap learns, until he has been in Missouri for at least six months (*HF*, pp. 33–34). Here Twain not only ridicules the white American voter who supports slavery by having him impersonated by a drunk, but he underscores the hypocrisy of a nation that would obscure its essentially racist policies with petty and meaningless distinctions that only further denigrate blacks. America meant well—or dreamt well—but its system of social equality was nevertheless a fiction that required a Tom Sawyer ending. And thus Mark Twain, who along with Walt Whitman is considered one of America's most "native" writers, was obliged to strike out for the "territory" in his endings rather than face the social reality that animated his novels. Twain's problem with endings extended beyond "race," of course, to the human race, and this is seen most dramatically in the various versions of *The Mysterious Stranger*. Here again Twain's best effort is to have Tom rush in one last time to declare it was all a game—that there is "no God, no universe, no human race, no earthly life, no heaven, no hell." [16]

This was the ultimate fate of his fiction, that life was a "joke" and nothing finally mattered except thought itself. Yet the nihilism that marks the last stage of Twain's literary career likewise shaped the first in the joke about the jumping frog. In every case, the unexpected is funny because it is all too familiar. The joke is always on the believer whose pride sets the stage for the comic incongruity. Twain generally played it safe with this kind of "human comedy," but when he ventured into the area of American race relations he risked the very ridicule his characters so justly deserve. It was—and is today—deucedly difficult for a white person to write about blacks unless the writer, like Twain's friend George Washington Cable, was prepared to condemn American racism and not simply the slavery which had most profoundly manifested it. Probably no other story in American literature, with the exception of Melville's "Benito Cereno" (1856), evokes our sense of white (liberal) guilt more than *Huckleberry Finn*. And no other book in the nineteenth century mocks the guilty better than *Pudd'nhead Wilson*. Yet both books are implicitly "racist" in the sense that the blacks are not "white." As much as Twain may have wished to include blacks as full-fledged characters in his fiction, he could not avoid the white truth that African Americans could be "equal" only when they were "separate." As they approached whiteness, as Roxy and her son Tom do, they stirred up white guilt in the guise of Negro-philia. This was the American paradox about race: that blacks should have been "white" in the first place and not because of miscegenation, a legacy of slavery that underscored its double cruelty because the hegemony had been sexual as well as "practical" in the operation of large farms and plantations.[17] Religionists of the antebellum South might conjure up sanctions for slavery from the Bible, and certain intellectuals in the North might resort to arguments in the pseudosci-ence that defined blacks as less than human and thus legitimate chat-tel, but neither group could find an excuse for the white lust that was evidenced everywhere by the existence of light-skinned blacks.

This is the South of Dawson's Landing to which Twain returned in 1894. Nostalgia had kept St. Petersburg clearly black and white in *Huckleberry Finn*, but the failure of Reconstruction was all too appar-ent by the 1890s when Twain re-imagined his hometown. In Daw-son's Landing the blacks are approaching whiteness as the result of miscegenation. Roxy and her son are "black" now only in the ideology of whites, and yet they are just as much slaves as the blackest of their ancestors. Like the equator, the Color Line is imaginary, but it still reshapes the facts for Roxy and her son. Blacks cannot cross the Color Line because Twain cannot in his engagement of the racial question. Roxy is indeed, as many critics have noted, Twain's most realistically depicted female. "She was of majestic form and stature, her attitudes were imposing and statuesque, and her gestures and movements dis-tinguished by a noble and stately grace."[18] This is the description of a "lady," a white woman who yet must become "meek and humble" in the presence of white people. "By fiction of law and custom a negro" in the book, Roxy is not allowed to express any "white" emotions. It is realistic, of course, that Twain have her talk like a slave and act like one in the face of white oppression. Yet we never see the dilemma from her point of view, only through the voyeuristic eyes of the white author, who observes only her crafty ways and calloused emotions. *Her* view, if Twain could have ever truly known it, would undermine the humor as well as distract from what is a most subtle white confes-sion, one whose delicacy required an ending to match the tone of the beginning. Framed like *Huckleberry Finn* in the tradition of a white anecdote, the story investigates the dark theme of American racism but finally only as a white issue. Its heart of darkness always sent the author in search of his childhood and Tom Sawyer. No doubt, Twain woke up to the fact that Tom had written *Huckleberry Finn* and would have to finish *Pudd'nhead Wilson* by making it a detective story. It was an artistic dilemma that Twain must have brooded over for many years, until the end of his life. In order to educate white readers, he finally had to entertain them. Not long after his death, the Mark Twain estate rushed to sell his personal books in the expectation that nothing of Twain's would be worth much money in four or five years.[19] The decision was probably in response to Twain's own belief that as a humorist he would very likely be quickly forgotten by the American public. Twain's posthumous reputation as a writer grew almost immediately, of course, because his "jokes" expose human hypocrisy as well as the general folly of humankind. Few critics, however, paid that much attention to his treatment of race until the 1950s and 1960s, when the American consciousness was raised by the civil-rights movement. Yet even today as its motion is fueled by the post-Vietnam era of "political correctness," we face the same disturbing contradictions about race in reading Twain that he faced in writing about it.

Readers of *Huckleberry Finn* have come to accept more than to reject Hemingway's caveat in *The Green Hills of Africa* (1935) that "if you read it you must stop where the Nigger Jim is stolen from the boys. That is the real end." This was the starting point at the height of the Vietnam protests for John Seelye, whose tragic version of Twain's novel kills off Jim. He drowns in flight from slave catchers led by the originally avuncular Silas Phelps, now a Simon Legree type that would have never been allowed in Twain's antebellum story. Indeed, Seelye's *True Adventures of Huckleberry Finn* (1971) is more "realistic" all around—from giving Jim and Huck a libido to suggesting (as Jim tells Huck) that Tom Sawyer is "gonna be a mean man someday."[20] As the bloodied Jim bobs up and down in the water at the end of the book and finally goes under for good, we hope along with Huck that his black companion will make it back to the raft for yet another "adventure." We long for one more reprieve from the racism that dooms Jim—and continues to haunt Twain's American readers. Because Seelye's is a twentieth-century view of that dilemma, Tom Sawyer is not allowed back in the book. Instead, in the epilogue (chapter 32) we are left with "the sight of that lonely raft, all shadows and emptiness." Huck mourns that it "sent a dern lump into my throat like somebody had hit me there. I got into the canoe and never once looked back."[21] Unlike *The Adventures of Huckleberry Finn*, *The True Adventures* does not end as a letter (with Twain's "YOURS TRULY, HUCK FINN") because there can be no further letters from Seelye's narrator, no more adventures to tell, because Jim is dead. There is no reason to compare the two versions, to say which is "better," because they are different stories from different centuries about the same problem. While each deplores racism—Twain in depicting Huck as the dupe of organized religion and Seelye as having him more openly racist—neither can resolve this white dilemma. Neither can overcome the white self-consciousness that influences the narrative.

Aside from adding more realistic touches expected by the modern reader, Seelye's version dramatizes our dissatisfaction with Twain's Tom Sawyer ending. T. S. Eliot, like Twain another Missourian who did not want to be *shown* the consequences of Jim's flight, argues that "it is right that the mood of the book should bring us back to that of the beginning. Or, if this was not the right ending for the book, what ending would have been right?" In other words, "Huck Finn must come from nowhere and be bound for nowhere."[22] He must never be allowed to wake (us) up completely to the racial violence that dictates Jim's fate in Seelye's version. Rather, as Eliot suggests, Huck must remain a *literary* character "not unworthy to take his place with Ulysses, Faust, Don Quixote, Hamlet and other great discoveries that man has made about himself."[23] He is no agent of social reform but an agent of conscience, which despises a person's helplessness to help anybody else. "The pessimism which Mark Twain discharged into *The Man That Corrupted Hadleyburg* and *What Is Man?*"—argues Eliot—"springs less from observation of society, than from his hatred of himself for allowing society to tempt and corrupt him and give him what he wanted."[24] Whereas Seelye's version focuses, especially with its tragic ending, more on the social injustice than the isolation of the individual, Twain's story does exactly the opposite because it is *not* a "true" adventure about a boy and a slave but the fabrication of their creator on the lam from society. In *Huckleberry Finn* Tom and Huck end up back together again in boyhood, ready for their next adventure. In *Pudd'nhead Wilson* Dawson's Landing survives the chicanery of *another* Tom—as well as the racial problems the plot raises—and falls back into the drowsy routine of settled adulthood. Indeed, Twain's novels follow the pattern of American fiction in general by waking up to the boring routine that compelled their telling. They follow the somnambulistic design established by Charles Brockden Brown's *Edgar Huntly* (1799) and polished into a functional prototype in Washington Irving's *The Sketch Book*, namely in "Rip Van Winkle," but also—as I have argued in chapter 1—throughout Irving's volume. In the words of Leslie Fiedler, "The figure of Rip Van Winkle presides over the birth of the American imagination; and it is fitting that our first successful homegrown legend should memorialize, however playfully, the flight of a dreamer from the drab duties of home and town. . . . Ever since, the typical male protagonist of our fiction has been a man on the run, harried into the forest and out to sea, down the river or into combat—anywhere to avoid 'civilization.' "[25] It is true that the American male figure is always running away from society, but like Irving's original he also runs back to it rather than face the consequences of the enigma he had investigated. Jim has to survive in Twain's story because, as W. H. Auden once remarked, "poetry makes nothing happen."[26] I would extend the meaning of poetry to include all *literature*, which deals with experience rather than events. For experience, after all, can only be talked about and never resolved into political questions of black and white.

"Rip Van Winkle" is our prototype because the protagonist returns home to *tell* the story rather than resolve it with the realism of Seelye and every other critic who searches for a social theme in experience. Seelye wants to acknowledge the facts about slavery and so has Jim die for our sins. He has reshaped a fiction to satisfy modern complaints about Twain's treatment of the racial questions, but *The True Adventures*, good as it is on its own literary merit, also represents our fiction about Twain's true authorial intention. With Hemingway, we want the story to end with Jim *on* the river, not in it. The opposite is our reality, but Twain's fiction, *his* reshaping of reality, concludes the story where it began: with Huck and Tom together again and Jim out of harm's way. Twain was writing out the American legacy of rebirth in which we are all "reborn" as free—even "Nigger Jim." In the

American *Renaissance*, just about everybody gets home safely to tell about the adventure, from Rip to Huck; even Ishmael survives his ordeal—in the American version, of course. Dimmesdale makes it back to the regeneracy of the church. Pym survives through the pseudoscience of a Symmes Hole. Emerson finally denies the perils of experience in an essay called, ironically, "Fate." Thoreau forgets much of the harshness of the Maine woods in *Walden*, and Whitman ultimately discovers that imaginary passage to India. Twain was bowing to the American fact that fiction always ends with the beginning of the story and never with a conclusion as final as Seelye's—not in the "American Renaissance" and its succeeding decades, at least.

This era of literature, the nineteenth century beginning with Irving, which I am labeling the American Renaissance, extends beyond the crisis poems of Whitman in 1860 to the suicide of Hurstwood in *Sister Carrie* (1900), the original ending of the novel. Afterwards, American literature with a few notable exceptions may be said to conclude, or to dissolve into "modernist" and "postmodernist" literature, which, like Colonial "American" literature, reaches back to Europe or other cultures for its example. American literature, on the other hand, is replete with native awakenings to the dream that experience is cyclical. Twain's age demanded a reborn Jim after all the fun was over, whereas our far less romantic age requires a sacrifice for freedom. This difference explains Twain's inablity to cross the Color Line with regard to Jim's plight as well as the twentieth-century dissatisfaction with his literary treatment of Jim. It also accounts for Twain's more evident pessimism in *Pudd'nhead Wilson*, where the conclusion enslaves a black rather than frees him. Reflecting the racial polarization of America in the 1890s as well as the 1830s, the citizens of Dawson's Landing are utterly insensitive to the plight of blacks. Nobody in *this* visit to Twain's antebellum hometown is willing to "go to hell" for them. That kind of retrospection was possible only in a "boy's book." [27]

In the "truer" adventure of *Huckleberry Finn*, that is to say Seelye's version, it is Jim who "goes to hell" as far as any happy ending or new beginning is concerned. Yet we dwell in the same "kingdom of culture" that Du Bois lamented at the end of the nineteenth century—one that extended into the latter half of the twentieth to prompt another writer on the black soul, Eldridge Cleaver, to declare that he hated "everything in America, including baseball and hot dogs." [28] Although we live in the age that Twain's promise to Whitman of technological advancement has more than fulfilled, the same degree of racial polarity remains, however subtle. The "South" that Twain wrote about may have shifted to South Africa, but the "North" that obscured the problem remains in North America. We might regret today Twain's "humorous" treatment of the problem the way Twain deplored Cooper's treatment of reality in "Fenimore Cooper's Literary Offenses" (1895), particularly in his depiction of Indians whose wooden stereotypes, by Twain's day, suggested the cigar-store versions. Yet our ulterior objection is that literature can rarely serve reality so directly. It does not solve problems but merely remembers them anew—so that in *Huckleberry Finn* we encounter the same white guilt that Twain appears to evade. This reading of Twain, as sound as it might be, is also our evasion in the twentieth century of what is the same issue recycled—the charade that the slaves have been freed in America. In other words, Jim is "free" throughout most of Huck's story but treated like a slave, and Roxy is "free" for most of Pudd'nhead's story but treated like a "nigger." This discrepancy between fact and fiction is probably what motivated Seelye to rewrite *Huckleberry Finn* and what compels us to reread it as a book about slavery instead of a tale about a boy, a raft, and a river.

There is no twentieth-century revision of *Pudd'nhead Wilson*, probably because here Twain better accords with the "reborn" American conscience with regard to race. To bring the story completely in line with the racially troubled conscience of this century, however, a revision would surely dispense with the beginning as Seelye's does the Tom Sawyer ending of *Huckleberry Finn*. Pudd'nhead, or David Wilson, would go the way of Tom Sawyer, and the "black" Tom, Roxy's son, would die in the end, probably in his "white" mother's arms. I leave the rest of this second story to the reader's imagination because the first story belongs to Twain and can never be changed, only retold. We can rewrite it, or we can interpret it and thus misread it as our own story, but we cannot avoid the truth either version tells about humanity: that we serve ourselves, or our anxieties, first and then rewrite the story. This is the risk of any second story: it strives for conclusion where none exists. A century later we can see Twain's stories in a different, more conclusive historical context, but all *he* wrote was the story. Twain left the social and moral conclusions to writers like

Charles W. Chesnutt, Joel Chandler Harris, George Washington Cable, and Harriet Beecher Stowe, and to the critics of *Huckleberry Finn* lured in by the "NOTICE" to stay out: "Persons attempting to find a motive in this narrative will be prosecuted; persons attempting to find a moral in it will be banished; persons attempting to find a plot will be shot." Without a motive, moral, or plot, all we have is Mark Twain remembering, or dreaming aloud, what we would like to forget.

Criticism, therefore, attempts to recover the dream—or the theme of the work—but in doing so it also creates a new fiction by reshaping a reality already reshaped or experienced. This fiction (the one you are reading now) has argued that Twain's blacks are not "native" enough to satisfy the standards of the late twentieth century. His "Indians," as it were, are not Native Americans, the designation today of another minority whose history is unsettling to many Americans. Since the Indians preceded the whites on the North American continent, the logic goes, they are the natives and the whites are the "foreigners." Yet this retrospective, really "New Historicist," view is but another second story, or revision of the undeniable fact that there was no "America" until white Europeans arrived and invented it. When we call the Indians "Native Americans," we rewrite or make retroactive the story. We do so to avoid the truth that the Indians were merely the first racial minority to suffer for the American Dream of white prosperity—from the Trail of Tears and before to the Mylai Massacre and after. We also rewrite or misinterpret the story when we search for black heroes and heroines in *Huckleberry Finn* and *Pudd'nhead Wilson*.

9 : Dickinson's Unpublished Canon

*J*ust as we have endeavored to bring Twain's view of black Americans into line with the utopian consciousness of our twentieth-century desires, so have we sought to update Emily Dickinson with regard to the most recent engagement of American middle-class anxiety, the gender debate. Cynthia Griffin Wolff's biography of the poet culminates with impressive historical detail the effort in the last decade to see the poet as chafing under the social constraints of womanhood (or "ladyhood") in the nineteenth century. We want now a poet—a female—who had already inscribed this view of women before history demanded it. In an attempt to characterize almost a score of books on Dickinson between 1980 and 1985, I wrote that she has been viewed as a modernist, feminist, symbolist, linguist, philosopher, crypto-politico, cultural inebriate, unrequited lover, aging adolescent, inverted astronaut, and ravished romantic.[1] Yet the underlying theme of most of these (otherwise mutually exclusive) categories is feminism: the desire to revise the ideology that is said to have privileged the male since the misogynistic mythmaking of biblical times and before. Because Dickinson is America's greatest female poet, it is imperative that her work be enlisted in the contemporary debate or cause.

The "cause," of course, has been vocalized in the United States ever since the first national women's convention in Seneca Falls, New York, in 1848—

when Dickinson was eighteen. It was the only year (1847–48) that she lived for any significant length of time outside Amherst and outside the home of her father. Her other absences—in Washington, D.C., and in Cambridge, Massachusetts—were clearly temporary, but this one could have led to her independence from her family because it was for the purposes of a formal education, the very solution for women that Mary Wollstonecraft argues for in her *Vindication of the Rights of Woman* (1792). Of course, Dickinson was not attending Yale College, the alma mater of her father, or even Amherst College, the school her grandfather had helped to found, but Mount Holyoke Female Seminary, begun and tightly controlled by Mary Lyon, described by Wolff and others as intense, earnest, and deeply religious.[2] Although the curriculum was theoretically "academic" or secular, it was in fact preponderately religious. Lyon's campaign to persuade the young women to declare their commitment to Christ clearly set the educational agenda and defined the tone of how the students' education might liberate them. The daily schedule, as Dickinson described it to her friend Abiah Root, consisted of an hour of "devotions" in the morning and "advice from Miss. Lyon in the form of a lecture" in the afternoon for at least another hour.[3] As the school year progressed, the headmistress divided the school into "Hopers" and "No-hopers" in terms of their Christian status. She met with each group separately once a week, and by the end of Dickinson's time at Mount Holyoke had reduced the ranks of "No-hopers" by 85 souls. That 30 (out of a class of 230) remained uncommitted Christians, however, suggests—as Richard B. Sewall reminds us—that Dickinson was not alone in her rebellion.[4] It also implies that the long-brooding spirit behind the Seneca Falls Convention had already begun to filter down to the population, to the extent that some women of Dickinson's age were not so readily persuaded by the myth whose icon was corporeally male.

As Dickinson told her friend shortly after returning from Thanksgiving vacation, "I have not yet given up to the claims of Christ, but trust I am not thoughtless on so important & serious a subject."[5] In the very next (and last) sentence, however, she turned to the subject of the weather. If the spiritual "marriage" to Christ was not simply a boring prospect, it was at least less interesting than the spring-like winter she described. Dickinson did, of course, fret about not converting, but it may have been a pose to dramatize the sense of loneliness that would become memorialized in her poetry. By the close of the school year she told Root that she still regretted missing the "golden opportunity" of becoming a Christian, "but it is hard for me to give up the world."[6] She did not return to the challenge the next year, but it is not entirely clear as to why. One of the legends about this legendary recluse is that her father insisted she return home, but the more likely reason is that he silently encouraged her to do what she was destined to do—recover her "Father's ground" and hardly ever cross it again "to any House or town."[7]

Dickinson's love of home or sense of place was all-consuming throughout her life: "Never did Amherst look more lovely to me & gratitude rose in my heart to God, for granting me such a safe return to my *own* dear HOME," she wrote after returning from her school vacation.[8] "Home" for Dickinson was her childhood, a past that animates the present of her poetry. The irony here is that her literary success had its origin in a flight from one patriarchal situation back to another—from Christ to the Christian ideology that made her brother the apple of her father's eye.

Dickinson told Thomas Wentworth Higginson in 1870 that she "never had a mother"[9] (a statement that has evoked its share of feminist theorizing), but she may have also meant that she *always* had a father. Edward Dickinson's frequent absences from home (as an attorney twice elected to the Massachusetts State Senate, one-term U.S. Congressman, delegate to the National Whig Convention, and a politico serious enough to be considered for both governor and lieutenant governor of his state) merely intensified his influence on his daughter. He was the elusive "Master" that undermined the continual presence of the mother. The man belonged outside the home in the nineteenth century, and the woman belonged inside it. This was the ideology, and hence the typical wife (or daughter) could not have felt as deprived or as alienated as Wolff suggests of Dickinson's mother upon her arrival in Amherst as a new bride.[10] More important, however, than the isolation of the woman we would like to see from our twentieth-century retrospective was the effect of the externality of the male on the female's sense of identity and indeed of Edward Dickinson's impact on his daughter's poetry. The cycle of the father's comings and goings turned house into home—the other family members mere tenants without his shaping presence. Dickinson stayed home from Mount Holyoke, as she told her friend, because her father de-sired it, [11] but she also went home to the father. It was largely this sense of logocentrism, which in Dickinson locates the prelapsarian in child-hood, that defines her best poetry. Beginning with her own father and culminating with God the Father (if not Christ the lover), this obses-sion with home also provided the stimulus for an artistic voice that simultaneously accepted and rejected its limitations imposed on fe-male authorship.

Dickinson's voice of rebellion in the poetry is essentially the same one we hear in *Moby-Dick* and throughout the nineteenth century in America: at its clearest pitch it calls into question the motives of God and his frequent absences from home, and comes away with an an-swer that is full of irony. Her protest, however, can also be under-stood in terms of gender because while Melville and others, who also grappled with the problem of God's absence, were her literary precur-sors (if not "fathers"), they were not exclusively this poet's source of artistic anxiety. As a woman writer, Dickinson probably felt more acutely than her male counterparts what Harold Bloom has called the "anxiety of influence"—must have felt what Sandra M. Gilbert and Susan Gubar have called the "anxiety of authorship." [12] Yet the seat of her "anxiety" was deeper (as it was also with her American precur-sors) than either of the artistic or political concerns suggested in these latest theories of authorship. The anxiety that made Dickinson one of the world's most original poets (male or female) cannot be reduced to a theory at all—unless it be a theory which highlights the artistic in-dependence of mind that in fact characterizes the creativity of all great writers, Homer and Sappho included. Yet part of the reason for Dick-inson's great talent is that she was writing outside the male literary establishment because her womanhood distanced her from the (albeit tortured) logocentrism of a Melville. As a literary nonentity (indeed, not even part of the tradition of what has been called "the feminist fifties" [13]) in the struggle between Man and God, she thus acquired her own original view of the human condition. This was Dickinson's "slant" view of creation and its consequences. Her sense of gender served as a ploy, as it were, to trick her persona into looking at the human drama from an outsider's or (often) posthumous observer's point of view. It was from this vantage point that Dickinson produced in poem after poem a poetic vision that was startlingly original for its time (and ours). Nevertheless, it is something of a (New Historicist) mistake to view the poet's art as mainly a reaction to gender oppression. This is not to say that she did not sometimes regret the social restrictions of her gender. Those regrets, however, merely served to hasten her discovery of the woman's voice in an essentially male literary world.

It was "natural" in such a world—in the eyes of the "father"—that her brother Austin would be the future "poet." Yet Austin, who was his father's proper son, became a lawyer instead because American writers are always, in some way or another, outsiders to what is deemed "natural" and thus part of the social order. Even Emerson, the most "respectable" of writers covered thus far in this study, was a self-made outsider when he finally argued that nature was superior to the "nature" of society, more reliable than its bible. But unlike Whitman or Poe, he was also an insider, and so was Dickinson as a member of the middle class of Christian idealists. What so shocked Andrews Norton and the theological establishment at Harvard and Boston about Emerson's Divinity School Address was not merely its antinomian content (which had previously been articulated by Emerson and others) but the fact that the anti-authoritarian advice to the Class of 1838 came from one of the Unitarians' best products—a former minister with ancestral roots reaching back to the Puritans. And what "shocked" Higginson and other readers of Dickinson's poems was that such a typically sheltered, middle-class female could hold such a bold, almost Melvillian view of the world. Indeed, it went beyond most of Melville to achieve his Ishmaelian/posthumous height in *Moby-Dick*. Not only was her identity-theme out of sync with the religious fortunes of her theological (and teleological) establishment, it also took her beyond the "moral sentiment" of even the most cynical Transcendentalists (hardly an oxymoron when applied to Melville).

With the entry of Emily Dickinson into the panoply of American Renaissance writers, what F. O. Matthiessen called a "renaissance" truly became one again—a reawakening of the antinomian spirit that characterizes the writers named in Matthiessen's study as well as the boldest moments of such Puritan writers as Anne Bradstreet, Roger Williams, and Jonathan Edwards. What had cooled in the Franklinism of the eighteenth century found its re-ignition in the first half of the nineteenth, most notably with Emerson's literary declaration of independence and Poe's critical declaration of independence. It would take the Civil War to make the country culturally dependent (and deficient) again—as America turned from national (and "native") themes to those of local color and regional humor for its identity. Fractured by the war, it looked to its parts instead of the whole, ignoring Emerson's caveat in the American Scholar Address. Yet as the nation broke in half, it also doubled its literary wager by sending the best writers of the war generation underground. Even the popular Mark Twain had to hide himself in "lowbrow" writing, his most important themes only emerging in the twentieth century. In order to return as a canonized writer in the next century, Henry James had to rediscover the "native" American in Europe. And Kate Chopin's and Theodore Dreiser's best works were killed off in their own times by bad reviews.[14]

Only Dickinson survived the immediate malaise of our literary reconstruction—by refusing to publish in it. No matter how many poems of hers we ultimately discover as published during her lifetime (the number now standing at eleven[15]), the case is clear that she chose not to publish her work. The "renaissance" that she led (into the twentieth century) was more subversive than even the one that David S. Reynolds describes,[16] for it subverted the present to the future. With the prescience of Henry Adams (who also chose not to publish his most important work in 1905), Emily Dickinson prepared her work for a posthumous debut. Indeed, Mary Lyon had succeeded where Dickinson probably thought she had failed because the poet *lived* for the canonization only dead people (and saints, of course) can hope to achieve. Her "letter to the World" was postdated in order to insure its delivery and readability in the twentieth century when an American literary canon based more on aesthetic than theological/conventionally logocentric premises would finally be established. There was simply no reason to publish oneself till then—till the country and the culture had been refocused upon the solitary voice of the American experience. Even the most readable works of Melville and Hawthorne were lost in a sea of domestic dramas self-consciously crafted for an emerging market that favored the themes of self in society and "society" in the cosmos. Walt Whitman, who had published *himself* over and over again in the latter half of the nineteenth century, finally sensed the futility of waking up America after the Emersonian era. In "A Backward Glance O'er Travel'd Roads," the last word in his last book, the 1891–92 edition of *Leaves of Grass*, he expressed some astonishment that he and his book had weathered more than thirty years of cultural reconstruction. "Proud, proud indeed may we be, if we have cull'd enough of that period in its own spirit to worthily waft a few live breaths of it to the future!"[17] With his "Death-bed" edition, Whitman may have suspected what Dickinson had known all along— that it was "disgraceful"[18] to publish until the "renaissance" happened again. One's state of grace had to be posthumous. Dickinson would not "stop for Death," but neither would she "start" before it. Her writing, a fairly well kept secret with regard to its great bulk, became literature in the next life, just as Whitman's nineteenth-century free verse or "prose" became American poetry in the twentieth. Dickinson's maidenhood as a writer is lost only in the twentieth century, when the speaker in "Because I Could Not Stop for Death" is released, as the final stanza suggests, from her corporeal limitations. She looks back on that dead present with the reader, much in the way Whitman looks back in "Crossing Brooklyn Ferry." Dickinson refused to be published in her century, and her work as relentlessly rejects a political canonization in our time. It is as stubborn as Dickinson herself in the face of Mary Lyon's campaign to get her to accept Christ as her spiritual master. She sang, as she told her nieces in 1863, because she could not pray,[19] and there is no way to reform this literary antinomian—no way to re-form the poetry to meet the political demands of today—right *or* left. Its universe is just as ragged as Melville's, yet just as metaphysical as Emerson's in its chants to a master-listener.

The single overt effort Emily Dickinson made to have her poems published came in her 1862 letter to Higginson, and even on this occasion she ultimately decided against publication. This reluctance may have been due, as critics have wisely conjectured, to the fact that Higginson advised the poet to "dress" her works in conventional literary garb. Indeed, if Dickinson *could* have written to the Higginson of 1890, the co-editor of her *Poems* that year, she would have found a literary market better prepared for her verse. In his brief introduction he concluded that "a lesson on grammar seems an impertinence" when the "thought takes one's breath away."[20] Higginson had apparently learned much about poetry in the twenty-eight years since he had first written to his "Young Contributor." Or had he? His introduction, while admittedly apologetic about Dickinson's literary unorthodoxy, also reflects the changing expectations about poetry. It was not so much that the poet's "thought" compensated for grammatical and orthographic irregularities (which in any case were silently edited out of the 1890 edition), but because it better suited the psychological and philosophical needs of the end of the nineteenth century. Whitman's so-called "Death-bed" edition of *Leaves of Grass*, published about the same time as Dickinson's literary debut, also found its proper era—after so many commercial and critical false starts going back to 1855. In Whitman's case, it was the first time his work enjoyed the protection of an international copyright agreement (bogus copies of the 1860 edition had been selling since 1879), but its "thought" also enjoyed the protection of the emerging twentieth century. Whitman and Dickinson, then, came to life after death as the two most important poets of the modern-day canon. In Dickinson's case, much of the acclaim that surrounded her first book was due to her reclusive, nun-like (posthumous) reputation as well as to the charm and seeming simplicity of her verse. Yet it was also created by an array of established critics beginning with William Dean Howells, who had previously served literary criticism as a Higginson to Mark Twain. "The strange *Poems of Emily Dickinson*," Howells wrote in 1891 in *Harper's*, "we think will form something like an intrinsic experience with the understanding reader of them."[21] Long before the emergence of reader-response approaches, Howells seized upon the universality of Dickinson's theme—uncontainable by the traditional story line found in the other New England ("Fireside") poets he had admired along with Emerson and Hawthorne. He found in the *Poems* the fantasy of Blake and the philosophy of Emerson, yet he declared that "the utterance of this most singular and authentic spirit would have been the same if there had never been an Emerson or a Blake in the world."[22] He counted "I Like a Look of Agony" (awkwardly entitled "Real" by editors Higginson and Mabel Loomis Todd) among Dickinson's "mortuary pieces," but he nevertheless credited this group as having "a fascination above any others." "I Like a Look of Agony," in other words, was a "mortuary" poem (in the vein that Barton Levi St. Armand so skillfully identifies[23]) in the year, or era, of its composition (around 1861), but "fascinating" in 1891. Howells here is waking up to the "renaissance" Dickinson began in the 1860s—when the one of Emerson had crumbled with the Civil War and its technology that changed forever how wars would be fought. The poem captures the "modern warfare" of the twentieth century, where the nagging absence of God the Father is somehow uplifting. He found the same startling level of modernism in Dickinson's so-called "Love" poems. "In them," he wrote, "love walks on heights he seldom treads, and it is the heart of full womanhood that speaks in the words of this nun-like New England life."[24]

That life, of course, devoted the woman to the poetry of prolepsis. It was not, however, the "corporeal friend" that was to be fulfilled, or even its spirit, but the message itself:

> The Martyr Poets—did not tell—
> But wrought their Pang in syllable—
> That when their mortal name be numb—
> Their mortal fate—encourage Some—
> The Martyr Painters—never spoke—
> Bequeathing—rather—to their Work—
> That when their conscious fingers cease—
> Some seek in Art—the Art of Peace— (Poem 544)[25]

Much like Whitman at the end of "Song of Myself" or in "Crossing Brooklyn Ferry," Dickinson throughout her poetry bequeaths her life to the art of tomorrow. Which is to say that what was prayer in its state of composition has become poetry today. The "Martyr" poets and painters, as Poem 544 affirms, *died* for their art. Dickinson wrote what Emerson dubbed "the Poetry of the Portfolio," defined as a verse too private and technically unfinished for publication.[26] As St. Armand notes, the portfolio tradition "was a means of preserving the secret self in the face of . . . growing technological exposure" found in Dickinson's new age of popular journalism—a print technology that "rapidly transformed the private and the domestic into common public property."[27] Yet Dickinson's unpublished canon contained much more than private jottings whose sentimentality would have been exposed by the light of publication. Her literary thoughts were not private and domestic but public and universal. It was the private *made* public, transformed not merely by the technology of print but most surely by the genius of the artist, who knew the truly representative value of her art. Such artists lived for their art—"did not tell—But wrought their Pang in syllable." Such martyrs "never spoke—Bequeathing—rather—to their Work." Like Whitman's dreamer or Poe's drunk, the "supposed person" in Dickinson is not merely autobiographical but metabiographical. And as such, her poems were not ready for the "prime time" of immediate publication. Contemporary publication exposed the writer to the present, where one's corporeality limited the impression, localized it in the flesh of political considerations; whereas the metavoice of the posthumous writer articulated impersonally the universal themes of love and death. Probably because it never happened, there is no record of Whitman's ever giving a public reading of "Song of Myself" or "The Sleepers." Nor is there any evidence of Poe's public reading from *The Narrative of Arthur Gordon Pym* or from the other stories in which the protagonist is engaged in (symbolic) necrophilia and other sorts of pre-posthumous activity found in the literary awakenings of the American Renaissance from Irving to Chopin. For Dickinson as well, the "private-made-public" was too private to be told directly, or publicly. For the other artists who were willing to have their dreams published, such as Whitman and Poe, they counted on the persona to protect them from the biographical witch-hunting of literary criticism. The twentieth century, if not the nineteenth with its disapproval of their personal and psychological visions, has proved them wrong, of course, with its attempted emphasis on Whitman's alleged homosexuality and Poe's assumed alcoholism. Dickinson, too, depended on her "supposed person" when Higginson's response to her poems became uncomfortably intrusive. And she doubled that effort to conceal the life or separate it from the work by instructing her sister to burn her letters. As we know, Lavinia did not burn (all) the extant letters, and we use them today to explicate the poems. Those efforts, especially in Dickinson's example, are rarely successful because her persona lives more in our present than in her past, having finally waked up a "saint" to our canonization of the poems. Her poems, like all great literature, appeal to our time and all times, except possibly to the time in which they were written. This is because the writer is still a player and at best—as Whitman wrote—"both in and out of the game" of life. Much more of an outsider,

Dickinson published only in personal letters in which the persona was still the poet herself, and only *it*self after her death.

In Dickinson's case, this "proleptic" devotion to art also stemmed from her post-Puritan ideology about duty and God- (if not self-) reliance. A posthumous literary debut was appropriate for this "New England Nun" dedicated to daily "prayer" about a present experience that is too private for contemporary publication. In using this appellation for the first time in 1895, another critic of much less stature than Howells but almost as perceptive described the "conscience of New England a half century ago" as sternly aware of its limitations as well as spiritually uplifted by them. "To those who could acquiesce in its demands, it opened avenues to spiritual heights whence the outlook was large and superb, though the air might be somewhat thin for the health of daily life." [28] To appreciate, however, that New England legacy of conscience and conflict in the most telling circumstances, one need go no further than the courtship letters of the poet's father Edward and the love letters of her brother Austin to his mistress. In 1827, a year before his marriage to Emily Norcross, Edward—though erotically anxious about his fiancée—nevertheless cautioned her to help him "put on the shield of conscious virtue—let us look down [on] every thing which may attempt to excite our passions, & thus lead us to ruin." [29] By contrast, Austin expressed his erotic feelings in 1882 to a woman not his wife at the beginning of their yet-to-be-consummated affair by asking, "When will that tomorrow be today? Days & weeks go by when it would be wine to me to see even the hem of your dress, not so much as that permitted me." [30] His desire for Mabel Loomis Todd, a married woman, was satisfied the next year in the dining room of his father's house, next door to his own. Whereas Edward's disciplined sense of eros is predicated on desire that can never be fully satisfied, Austin's desire goes well beyond language of denial to seize the day. Yet neither father nor son ever surrendered totally to the sense of physical abandonment that beckoned them. Although Edward sired three children, he apparently maintained his emotional distance from his wife, if not all his children. And despite Austin's ecstatic declarations (usually after sexual intercourse with Mabel), he exercised caution about ever advancing their affair beyond the stage of illicitness. Austin never formally abandoned his marriage, and the letters of the two lovers suggest that neither one really expected the relationship to go beyond what it already was.

The paradoxical patterns of Edward and Austin in love demonstrate the same conflict between Puritan identity and the romantic loss of it that characterizes the poetry of Emily Dickinson. The poet of "I Like a Look of Agony" wrote out of the same tradition, wrote as the daughter of one who could conceal his eroticism in a tirade against prostitution (the ultimate subject of the letter quoted by Edward) and the sister of one who—though he could not even conceal his extramarital affair—was outwardly every bit as self-righteous as his father. In Dickinson's case, we have the reclusive, "old-maid" daughter of the father who is capable of his son's sexual ecstasy in a poem like "Wild Nights—Wild Nights!" (Poem 249). She is capable of much more than that, of course, but the poem, like the love letters of the two most important men in her life, symbolizes the sense of longing to sear one's very initials (or "letters") into the most intense experiences without losing wholly the name those initials stand for in the experience. To write about that desire is by its very nature to make a public confession, unless one is either pretending he or she is a "supposed person" or that the experience is long past by the time its manifestations are "auctioned" off, in an age of rapidly expanding print technology, to the lowest bidder. In a real sense, Dickinson's poetry is "illicit"—a form of secret writing in which the poet conjures up her muse and surrenders about as much of herself as is safely possible. The three so-called "Master" letters suggest the pathological extremes of this practice, but the poetry is where we find the same balance between dignity of the self and erotic desire for the Other that her father and brother also sought to maintain.

We could take this formula into a reading of practically any poem in her canon, but it is best exemplified in her best-known poem, "Because I Could Not Stop for Death" (Poem 712):

> Because I could not stop for Death—
> He kindly stopped for me—
> The Carriage held but just Ourselves—
> And Immortality.
>
> We slowly drove—He knew no haste
> And I had put away

My labor and my leisure too,
For His Civility—

We passed the School, where Children strove
At Recess—in the Ring—
We passed the Fields of Gazing Grain—
We passed the Setting Sun—

Or rather—He passed Us—
The Dews drew quivering and chill—
For only Gossamer, my Gown—
My Tippet—only Tulle—

We paused before a House that seemed
A Swelling of the Ground—
The Roof was scarcely visible—
The Cornice—in the Ground—

Since then—'tis Centuries—and yet
Feels shorter than the Day
I first surmised the Horses Heads
Were toward Eternity—

In this poem death is the ultimate experience, its characterization here certainly the most powerful example of metonymy in Dickinson's unpublished canon. Death is the illicit lover that we dare not stop for, because he will surely stop us. For Dickinson he is the gentleman caller who crosses her "Father's ground" because she will not cross it herself. He is the ultimate invader (and the sexual imagery of penetration should not be overlooked) who will take her for a carriage ride *away* from the ancestral Homestead of life—from Home to a "House that seemed/A Swelling of the Ground." Generally, the narrator's bedroom attire ("For only Gossamer, my Gown") has been read as the state of her unreadiness for a visitor, but it is also the dress for sexual activity, the last vestment and vestige of the unconsummated life of the virgin. For this is not one of those "Wild Nights" that Austin repeatedly experienced with Mabel but the day on which the Suitor comes to take his bride away, much in the way Edward Dickinson arrived in Monson, Massachusetts, on 6 May 1828 to take Emily Norcross back to Amherst and to the life of a wife and mother (of two daughters who also stayed at home with this father figure). Though not as "reclusive" as her daughter Emily, she too clung to the father—twice postponing her marriage day and finally consenting to a ceremony with as little fanfare as possible (and no attendants). Death is the ultimate release, and as such its inevitable arrival is symbolic of the simultaneous desire and dread of giving oneself to a totally fulfilling experience such as sexual passion. Better to hold back and to write about it—as Edward Dickinson did, as Austin Dickinson did, too, after a fashion, and as Emily Dickinson probably did throughout her life. In the same manner, she held that writing back from the public consumption that results in canons instead of in the canonization of the self in the here and now of experience.

Much has been written in the last decade about the difficulty of defining the author and the reader (or their exclusive roles), based on the assumptions from Saussure to Derrida about the power of culture to create texts that can only be *shared* by the writer and reader. Yet the argument for the circularity of language merely serves to underscore the compelling sense of irony in literature (as opposed to writing on the quotidian level). In this poem of Dickinson's, we find the ultimate statement about desire. What we seek at our hungriest moments for life is not ahead of us but behind—that missed opportunity with God "before time was." Poem 712 reports a dream, a deep sleep in which the figure that fathered the poet returns to make the house a home again. I intend the sense of home that Dickinson the child acquired and never forgot—the one with "the School, where Children strove/At Recess—in the Ring." It is the necessary circularity of desire that language records in its self-reflexive tropes. All language is metaphorical because the self is imprisoned in a reality that will not yield significant change. It is a prison, but not a prism, which requires a select society, that audience of one(self) who must—certainly in Dickinson's case—perish before publishing. Her work is predicated upon perishing—into "Centuries" that feel "shorter than the Day" she "first surmised" the true nature of experience. It was at once too personal and too universal to be auctioned off in a literary world of resolutions instead of dissolution. Dickinson's "surmise" made poetry necessary. Higginson's expectations merely trivialized it as melodramatic musings about "Time and Eternity," the title of the section that contained "Because I Could Not Stop for Death" in her *Poems* (1890). As editor of the volume along with Mabel Todd, he called the poem "The Chariot," as if to imply a glorious journey to *somewhere* instead of a carriage ride to nowhere except to the heart of desire. It was death in the subjunctive that put life into the imperative.

Of the literary awakenings discussed thus far in this study, Dickinson's is one of the most interesting because her persona is consistently dazzled by (human) nature. Dickinson's awakening, like her work, cannot be mapped out on a graph because the entire canon, or most of it, remained hidden and thus safe from critical demarcation. Just as such works as *Moby-Dick* or *Leaves of Grass* were initially misunderstood and dismissed, her poems under the harsh light of contemporary publication would have formed a mosaic of misapprehensions—until they were viewed posthumously. In the cases of Melville, Whitman, and the others, the problem lay in the fact that their best works really had no literary foreground—in terms of their previous work. *Moby-Dick* is a compendium of everything Melville wrote up to 1850, yet it marks the beginning of books that cannot be conventionally concluded. As Ishmael exclaims, "God keep me from ever completing anything. This whole book is but a draught—nay, but the draught of a draught."[31] *Leaves of Grass* for Whitman *was* his life in all its social and philosophical complexity: "Who touches this touches a man," he confidently concluded in the poem "So Long!" Without the critics, Dickinson was free to spread her great work over a *life*time, from "Success Is Counted Sweetest" (Poem 67) to "A Route of Evanescence" (Poem 1463). Indeed, Dickinson was the "freest" writer in nineteenth-century America: she did not have to worry about either making a living or living to make the critics happy. Mark Twain, of course, made a living by warning off the critics (as he does in *Huckleberry Finn*), yet I agree with Van Wyck Brooks that he paid a higher price (psychologically) for being a "lowbrow" writer than Bernard DeVoto allowed.[32] These writers knew, as Dickinson knew, the value of their work as a surrogate for the life to which they had awakened. It was to be "literature" only after the life was over. If Dickinson had published, her life as a poet would have vanished in the "dazzle" that was anything but gradual. For many of the writers covered thus far in this study, the great work was probably the exception not only to previous work but to the life that afterwards went on publishing more conventional works—such as Irving's travel books, Hawthorne's gothic novels, Poe's short(er) stories, Thoreau's incomplete works, and Emerson's post-"Experience" essays on "Power," "Wealth," and "Culture." Indeed, the act of publishing was essentially post-experiential, the experience given over utterly to the reader. No wonder Whitman continued to write *Leaves of Grass*, expanding it, revising it, appending to it almost to the last year of his life. He held on as tenaciously as Dickinson to the work that had created the life. He surely would have agreed with her that "This was a Poet." The work *was* the life, and to publish it was to perish with it by universalizing one's most anguished and private moments. Whitman probably realized this ultimate value of his book when he called one of its last issues the "Death-bed" edition. His book was finished only when he was. Dickinson was finished, too, when her work was finished—and ready for publication.

It seems to me no accident that the fascicles were in the poet's room ready to be found by her sister Lavinia, no accident that there *were* those booklets as well as fair copies of many of the poems Dickinson had sent to friends over the years. It was also no accident that the poems were left to be found by the poet's closest ally, who proved her sisterly allegiance many times over by getting the poems published in the face of strong resistance. She first went to Susan Dickinson, next door; and when, after almost a year Susan had done little or nothing to advance the cause,[33] Lavinia turned to Mabel Todd, who laboriously typed out the poems for the three editions in the 1890s. It is as if Dickinson knew her poems would be in the best hands possible. What she could not have imagined is that the poetry would be fought over with competing editions throughout the first half of this century, first by Susan Dickinson and Mabel Todd and then by their daughters. Several times readers were told that they now had the "complete" poems (and poet), only to see "newly discovered poems" come into print. It was not until 1955 that the world finally had a variorum edition of Dickinson's works. Yet even this monumental work has been challenged by R. W. Franklin, first in *The Editing of Emily Dickinson* (1967) and then—indirectly—with the two-volume edition of *The Manuscript Books of Emily Dickinson* (1981). The latter work ironically *un*published Dickinson almost one hundred years after her death, returning the poems to the approximate state in which her sister found them. One of Franklin's goals was to argue for the fascicle arrangement over the Johnson ordering, which is "chronological" according to changes in the poet's handwriting. At this writing, Franklin is at work on a printed edition based on the fascicles, yet by having already returned the printed poems to manuscript, he raises the possibility that a definitive edition of Dickinson's work may never be possible. Many of the poems have alternate endings, for example. (Johnson "solved" this problem by printing different endings in the 1955 variorum and the 1960 one-volume complete works.) We might imagine that Dickinson struggles even now against final publication and canonization. Traditional criticism, of course, attempts the same for other great authors by finding endless interpretations for their work. The authors continue to *live* for us every time we read—or more properly, write about—their work. The recent feminist interest in Dickinson is but another form of this desire. Yet Dickinson poses her own special problem by having refused to release a final text. We have no definitive "text" and thus cannot reduce her *work* to this bloodless term. Calling a literary work a "text" with all the linguistic assumptions the term carries finally kills off the author—takes him or her out of the affair and makes it completely ours. New Criticism's emphasis on the "work" exclusive of its historical and biographical context curiously opened the way for today's New Historicism in which a writer's work is re-immersed in historical facts to reveal it as an unconscious construct of ideology. Yet Dickinson and the other canonized writers of the nineteenth century did have a point of view, one formed out of their own age to confront the problem of all ages. Its focus, of course, is on the human condition, and more precisely on the problem of identity. In other words, Dickinson was "Nobody," so who are we? This question as well as the one in the next line ("Are you—Nobody—too?") may anticipate in the late twentieth century the theory of linguistic deconstruction (of which New Historicism is the "social" agency). Yet imbedded in this word is "destruction," of the author's meaning by invoking the metaphorical dependence of language. It seeks to destroy the author by reducing his—or her—message to the status of unanchored signifiers. Taken to this extreme, even the phrase "human condition" is rendered meaningless, a mere construct of "culture." Dickinson's point of view throughout her work is that we are nobody only until we say we are somebody, until we identify ourselves as individuals in spite of evolutionary and cultural evidence to the contrary. Life begins, therefore, not at birth but with the process of humanizing ourselves, creating ourselves culturally and aesthetically out of raw nature, which *naturally* begins at our conception. (It ends, of course, with death—which is a reality that not only gives meaning to life but is also a "fact" that cannot be deconstructed.)

Life has to be mothered after it has been fathered. Art, and specifically literature, reminds us subtly and over a lifetime that we are more than creatures who eat and sleep, more than the sum of even our political needs. Even literature's most pessimistic renditions of life— for example, the stark naturalism of Chopin, Crane, or Dreiser—suggest the crucial importance of personal identity and of its connection with the rest of humanity. Emily Dickinson's poetry is finally an antidote for the loneliness of being human and of longing for that time of universal childhood. As she told her brother not long after becoming a poet, "I wish we were children now. I wish we were *always* children."[34] Probably no other writer spent more of her adult life "alone." Her poetry is the record of that loneliness as it is transformed into a vision of the self as a "simple separate person." The phrase is Whitman's, of course, but it is also Dickinson's, as it is Hawthorne's for Hester, Poe's for Pym, and so on. Their point of view is that life is replete with contradictions which form a splendid irony that wakes us up again and again from the numbing routine of our solitary existence. We are defined by losses which provide insights that cannot be conveyed except through the supposed version of life called art. Probably no better example of art's ability to awaken us to these insights exists than the following poem:

> A Route of Evanescence
> With a revolving Wheel—
> A Resonance of Emerald—
> A Rush of Cochineal—
> And every Blossom on the Bush
> Adjusts it's tumbled Head—
> The mail from Tunis, probably
> An easy Morning's Ride (Poem 1463)

The sensation of the hummingbird's rapid movements suggests the elusive nature of the life whose rhythms stun us into a consciousness of its beauty. The observer in the poem takes the departure of the bird (and thus life's beauty) for granted, yet nevertheless feels the emptiness left behind ("And every Blossom on the Bush/Adjusts it's tumbled Head"). The whimsical comment of the observer in the last two lines suggests how easy life might be if that beauty were capable of total possession. This complex observation on life's simplicity suggests also the need to be a part of that beauty and at the same time to be apart from it as a knowing observer. "A Route of Evanescence" is one of Dickinson's great poems of "occasion" because it gave the world in eight short lines a point of view instead of a view that is ultimately pointless. Dickinson's point is that "life" or beauty is always anterior to the present unless we write about it. That she did not require publication of her vision only serves to underscore its timeless ubiquity.

10 : Henry James's Pearl at a Great Price

*T*n *The Portrait of a Lady* (1881) Henry James compares Gilbert Osmond's daughter Pansy to a "sheet of blank paper—the ideal *jeune fille* of foreign fiction."[1] Having recently published his study of Hawthorne in the English Men of Letters series, he would use Pansy much in the way Hawthorne had used Pearl in *The Scarlet Letter*—as a "living symbol" of the failed American quest of becoming reborn through the power of love, and sex. Indeed, in his remarks on the novel in the 1879 study, James calls it the "sequel" to the history of "passion."[2] Like Pearl, Pansy is what remains of the female American quest that characterizes what I am calling the "second" American Renaissance, or its logical extension of male authorship in the nineteenth century. If not the author in most cases of canonized American literature of the nineteenth century, the woman clearly becomes the object of this authorship—the Eve-figure who succeeds the male protagonists of Irving, Poe, Melville, Emerson, and Thoreau in their quests for a "new world." This is Isabel Archer, whose precursors are probably Hester Prynne, the intellectual (ex-)virgin, and Whitman's athletic and active mother(-to-be), two figures who accept the limitations of their female status but nevertheless have the capacity to rebel against it. Dickinson's "supposed person" may also possess the energy of the "New Woman," but she fails to "publish" it; rather, her encounters with experience remain personal. James's characterization of Isabel is also personal to the extent that she is based in part on the memory of his late cousin Minnie Temple, but the portrait is not, as I have argued for *The Scarlet Letter*, a self-portrait of the writer's desire as much as it is a celibate's empathic portrait of the heterosexual in the fashion of *The American* (1877). Like Christopher Newman, the inverted Columbus who returns to the Old World in search of the psychological freedom and fulfillment the New World had promised, Isabel is the prototypical postwar heroine that launches the female conclusion to this American drama of the nineteenth century. Whereas Christopher seeks a "queen" in his pursuit of Claire de Cintré, Isabel seeks a "subject" in her marriage to Osmond. Anticipating such representative literary women as Kate Chopin's Edna and Theodore Dreiser's Carrie, each of whom carries female independence increasingly farther than Isabel, she represents the first of three stages of American womanhood that will be acted out in the second part of the American Renaissance, in which the literary quester wakes up, like her earlier male counterparts, in the New World of nothingness instead of something.

In this regard, Pansy's situation is almost a parody of what happens to Isabel once she marries Osmond. The product of the same double moral negative as Pearl—both are the illegitimate children of illicit relationships—Pansy will also be the only "issue" of the marriage when Isabel discovers that Madame Merle has made a "convenience" of her. Like Pearl's beginnings, hers are also in medias res. Pansy, James tells us, was already "formed and finished for her tiny place in the world" (p. 238), and Isabel, who, unlike Hester, never even participates in what Hawthorne's heroine will remember as a passion that had "a consecration of its own," is eventually expected to fill Serena Merle's motherly role with regard to the daughter she never had. She is asked to assist Osmond in arranging (as Merle had for Osmond) another marriage of money, in this case between Pansy and Lord Warburton. That Pansy obviously has not only no chance at happiness, but much less of a chance than Isabel herself had of fulfilling a romantic sense of destiny, merely underscores her function as a haunting symbol of female failure in an American world in which neither gender ever succeeds in the romantic quest of rebegetting the self, of starting over endlessly. Warburton is never seriously interested in her, and Ned Rosier, who cannot possibly win Pansy anyway because of Osmond's objections, is as much of an art collector as the man who "collects" Isabel. In fact, everybody in this next-generational telling of *The Scarlet Letter* is a collector who seeks to exploit Isabel— from Ralph's mother, who needs a daughter to renew her sense of lost youth, to Osmond's daughter, who requires a mother to help her find a future. But it is Isabel herself who is the arch-quester, if not the most successful collector in the novel.

To see her as a victim finally of anything other than the American sense of belatedness that motivates the males in Melville and other antebellum literature is to continue to focus on the male as the more ambitious or powerful or interesting character in this period of the American Renaissance. In fact, in this book Osmond and the other males are at best catalysts in a tale of relative monomania. Isabel is not exactly Ishmael (certainly not Ahab), but she approaches the daring of the standard American hero in defying or—as James puts it in his New York preface—"affronting her destiny" (p. 8) as a mortal. Whereas there are no women, to speak of, in *Moby-Dick*, and *The Scarlet Letter* is mainly about a minister in a maze with the woman as the catalyst, *The Portrait of a Lady* is about an American lady who seeks to become a woman again in Europe—in the sense of realizing or experimenting with the full *im*possibilities of her freedom as an individual. For Goodwood tells the Jamesian truth, which emerges much more clearly in the wake of the Civil War and the accompanying influence of the women's movement, when he tells Isabel that "an unmarried woman—a girl of your age—isn't independent" (p. 143). Symbolically, Isabel seeks a romantic return to the status of Venus or the Virgin, who in medieval Europe—at Chartres and Amiens, as Henry Adams astutely observed[3]—had reigned supreme. On the quotidian level, she seeks not even a marriage of equals but one in which she will retain the psychological advantage of the maiden with an endless store of possibility. This becomes with her legacy of seventy thousand pounds the desire to be a financial benefactor to Osmond in an inversion of the relationship she would have (without her inheritance) experienced with either Warburton or Goodwood. She ultimately discovers that money, especially American money, is no match for the mythological power of the European past.

The Portrait of a Lady continues Washington Irving's paradigm of looking in Europe or elsewhere for something lacking in America—

the search, as noted in previous chapters, for something on what he calls in *The Sketch Book* the "blank page in existence." As Jeffrey Rubin-Dorsky has observed, "Escaping from the pressures and demands and drudgeries of their own New World existence, Americans immersed themselves in an idealized Old World."⁴ After the War of 1812, Europe (with the possible exception of the European revolutions of 1848) posed no serious economic or military threat and could thus be poeticized into a quaint and archaic land that had never really existed (the image of Merry Old England in Irving's book, for example). Following the Civil War and the renewed military fear posed by the threat of intervention by foreign countries, however, Europe lost some of its romance for Americans, or American males, lost its place as the "neutral territory" of their imagination. Its antiquity became at best something to be exploited by American business. James's "New Man" of postwar America goes there to find a wife to crown his commercial success, and Lambert Strether of *The Ambassadors* (1903) initially returns there to bring another male American back to his mercantile responsibilities. It became after the Civil War the American woman's turn to immerse herself in the timelessness of Europe. The war, which had marked off for the American woman the Age of Innocence from the Age of Experience,⁵ beckoned her to search for the same thing the male of Irving's era in literature had sought. As a prototype of the American female who demands more out of life (and marriage), who verges on the point of acting out her life instead of waiting for it to be defined through marriage, Isabel books passage, as it were, on the *Washington Irving*—the name, incidentally, of one of the ships that took Ralph Waldo Emerson to Europe.⁶ Yet all she ultimately finds there is Pansy, another "sheet of blank paper" that Irving had begun with in his "grand tour"—"the ideal *jeune fille*" instead of the fulfilled woman she dreamed of becoming in Europe.

The "germ" of James's idea for the novel, at least as he recalled in its New York preface, came not from any idea of "plot" in the traditional sense but altogether from "the sense of a single character, the character and aspect of a particular engaging young woman" (p. 4). It might appear odd to hear that character takes precedence over plot in the work of the first American author to write the kind of comedy of manners fiction often identified with British literature. Yet even in

James's complex plots involving Americans and Europeans, the relatively simple American idea of character or the errant individual emerges, the romantic self-begotten self that awakes every morning in the Emersonian schema to retest its vision of itself and the world. Following the Civil War, this figure becomes, beginning with James, the *jeune fille*—the new American girl whose image populated the essays that appeared in the *Atlantic Monthly*, where *The Portrait of a Lady* was first published between November 1880 and December 1881.[7] James sent at least two other notable female characters to Europe, but Isabel's story is more significant than either Daisy Miller's or Milly Theale's because she is not an innocent victim whose quest can finally be dismissed as a mistake, but rather, like her male counterparts in the American quest, an individual whose intellect is as powerful as her emotions. Instead of literally dying there as the despoiled virgin (socially, if not sexually) or succumbing there as the American maiden still waiting to be defined, she survives the drama to view the specter of her death in the life cycle that begins again in the illegitimate child who has become her "daughter." Like Ishmael, she wakes up from "a long pernicious dream" (p. 428) to tell the story, or in her case to *hear* (from the Countess Gemini) the story of Pansy's beginnings and her ending as a New World quester. She wakes up to Pansy in the same way Hester wakes up to Pearl. The latter goes to Europe after the spell of her parents' bliss is broken; in James's story it is Pansy's mother, Madame Merle, who goes abroad—to America because, in the words of Mrs. Touchett, she has "done something very bad" (p. 475). Pansy remains in Europe, thus symbolizing the curse Isabel now lives under for trying to "affront" her destiny as a woman and a human being.

Because Isabel's character developed through the serialization of the novel for the *Atlantic Monthly*, a process in which James often stayed only a couple of chapters ahead of the next installment, she fools not only her author and her reader but herself as well regarding the nobility of her intentions. All three learn in chapter 42 what finally Osmond regrettably discovers after his marriage—that "she was not what he had believed" precisely because she had hidden herself. "She had," as she now admits, "effaced herself when [Osmond] first knew her; she had made herself small, pretending there was less of her than there really was." She attributes this to Osmond's "extraordinary charm," but the following statement indicates another reason: "That he was poor and lonely and yet that somehow he was noble—that was what had interested her and seemed to give her *opportunity*. There had been an indefinable beauty about him—in his situation, in his mind, in his face. *She had felt at the same time that he was helpless and ineffectual*, but the feeling had taken the form of a tenderness which was the very flower of respect. He was like a sceptical voyager strolling on the beach while he waited for the tide, looking seaward yet not putting to sea. It was in all this she had found her occasion. *She would launch his boat for him; she would be his providence; it would be a good thing to love him*" (pp. 357–58; my italics).

We have in this admission—clearly a historical echo of Queen Isabella and Columbus—possibly the first reversal of the Petrarchan paradigm of possession so common to that of the male questers in works from Irving's sketch of "The Wife" to Whitman's poem "A Woman Waits for Me." In creating the character of Isabel Archer, James sensed not only the necessary shift of the gender focus but also the fact that the emerging American woman would be tempted by the same idealism, the same egotism of her male counterpart. James—apparently sexually abstinent himself (indeed his "portrait" of Isabel is almost as androgynous as Dickinson's depictions of the female mind)—was probably better suited as a genius than most to succeed with such a characterization. The true Ralph Touchett in the book, James is both in love with his heroine and jealous of her youthful illusion of freedom. He is both within and without his Isabel, and the literary result is a female point of view touched by the male history of her oppression.

Leon Edel remarks upon a lifetime immersed in James that the writer, throughout his life, avoided any kind of physical or emotional consummation—with either sex. The biographer of James finds "no affairs, no mistresses, no shy avowals, only touches of infatuation." Ever the observer of life, James adhered to the belief that "one renounced love, or was deprived of it. Accepted," Edel remarks, "it represented ruin."[8] Like Emily Dickinson, who once asked whether God was "Love's Adversary,"[9] Henry James knew that the American story at least—the one in which infatuation with the self or another was still confused with love, or truth—always concluded where it had begun. It was the story of the solitary self-reliant self, seeking its identity in another and finding it only in the fact of the quest itself. For the American male, the life objective became more practical—as it took him into war, business, or crime. For the female it became practical in the sense that it involved the search for a marriage or mating in which her identity as a woman was not flattened out into the status of merely "wife" or "mistress." The woman's story is the story of "Daisy"—from Dickinson, who often referred to herself (in two "Master" letters and sixteen poems) by the term, to F. Scott Fitzgerald's Daisy Buchanan, whose quest becomes as brutal and businesslike as the robber barons of the Gilded Age. In both cases "Daisy" is assertive, but Dickinson's Daisy sets the mood, if not the stage, for the American woman James presents in *The Portrait of a Lady*. He began, of course, with "Daisy Miller" (1878), which was first rejected by *Lippincott's Magazine* in Philadelphia, no doubt, James suspected, for being "an outrage on American womanhood," and accepted by the *Cornhill Magazine* of London, where it ironically enlarged James's reputation as a novelist in America.[10]

Though initially cast in the role of Daisy, Isabel is no flirt longing for the fantasy of postadolescent love but a young lady intent upon becoming a woman with an identity distinct from whomever she marries. The opposition she faces in this quest is formidable and finally overwhelming. Virtually plucked by Mrs. Touchett from inevitable marriage to Goodwood in America, she finds herself in a matter of weeks the matrimonial target of Warburton, Goodwood's English counterpart in the quest for Isabel. She also becomes the apple of her uncle's eye as well as the love of his son's languishing life. All the men are in love with her, it seems. The possible exception is Osmond, but his relative passivity in pursuit of Isabel is not exactly the reason he succeeds where the others do not. Rather, the reason is Madame Merle. As another woman who had sought her freedom in Europe, she gains Isabel's confidence as well as her admiration. The older woman is thereby empowered to lead the younger woman into the same dilemma she herself has been living out for the past fifteen years. The blame for Isabel's fate as an unloved wife, therefore, cannot be placed on Osmond but on American idealism, which in the new, postwar, female equation had led Merle to believe an illicit relationship with a man would bring her happiness or satisfaction, or at least something different—not marriage, but the courtly lover whom

Isabel herself is unconsciously trying to combine with the convention of a husband.

In *The Portrait of a Lady* James produced the new American romance, the one in which the American male quester returns from the sea, the West, the war, as a woman in society. He combined the American romance about the isolato with the British preoccupation with the morals and manners of contemporary society.[11] Isabel is this new American quester, but the quest is no longer confined to the rebirth of the self but broadened to include the indictment if not the refashioning of society. Like her male precursors in the Emersonian paradigm, she also thinks that "society scatters your force."[12] Yet as a woman in this paradigm, she may suspect that the traditional opposition to society, the male sense of individuality, also scatters *her* force. James is not, however, writing a feminist novel. Surely *The Bostonians* (1886) demonstrates his lack of sympathy for that social paradigm. What he has done instead is to relocate the American hero (now "heroine"), to move her from the gothic landscape of the Manichean Mind to the social setting of the sexes, or society. He has shifted the focus of his "international novel" from the male to the female; in a sense, he has not only moved the American back to European society but the protagonist into the double bind of womanhood to demonstrate that the desire for rebirth has as much to do with society as anything else. For the New American Woman (as perhaps for the Old One in Hester), society is the newest frontier.

The Portrait of a Lady is a romance in the sense of the individual quest; yet it also signals an important change in American fiction, anticipating the American writer's concern in the last twenty years of the century with the social forces that help to shape our perception of the human dilemma. Isabel's search for identity involves some very concrete details. For one, it is not God but the institution of patriarchal marriage that seems to be the problem. Isabel may ultimately desire, as it were, to navigate the globe, sail to the South Pole, or find God on the shores of Walden Pond, but first she has to navigate the circumstances of her social condition. It is here, I think, that the feminist concern has to be considered—even in a work of the nineteenth century, before the emergence of the working woman, or professional, made feminism in America more clearly relevant to the "human condition." Which is to say that the social condition of the woman *is* part of the human condition that can, at its most profound depth, cast the spirit into the same "damp, drizzly November" dramatized in *Moby-Dick*.[13] Of course, society affects the traditional male American hero's condition as well, but mainly in the sense that he must someday return to it. Before the Civil War, the woman—or lady—on the other hand, can never quite avoid or run away from society any more than she could ignore the limits of her domestic sphere. It *is* the closest thing she has to a frontier: to the sea, to the West, to a war; she begins and ends there. Hence, Isabel's American quest is social from the very outset. There is no international ship's company of women that she can join, no same-sex territory to "light out" to, no female army in which to enlist. In other words, the American woman—this outsetting virgin—is from the start what we used to call "in the family way." Her quest is always social and quickly defined as involving marriage; hence, when Ralph asks his father to make Isabel a rich woman, the only acknowledged danger is that a fortune hunter will precede a worthier candidate for her hand in *marriage* (p. 162). Isabel herself sees her destiny in these terms. She might tell Goodwood that she may never marry, but no one (including Goodwood) is misled by the ploy. Subconsciously perhaps, she agrees with his advice that "an unmarried woman . . . isn't independent."

This seems to be the case for Isabel, who is pursued by suitors not one after another but all together. It is not the case, however, for Henrietta Stackpole, who is described by Isabel as "decidedly pretty" (p. 79). She has only one suitor, Bob Bantling, who laughs "immoderately" at everything Henrietta says and is generally patient in his pursuit of her (p. 126). The main difference is that Henrietta does something that few characters do in James's world of fiction: she *works*. In his New York preface James suggested that he had gone too far with Henrietta—had *overtreated* her character rather than undertreated it (p. 15). As a result of James's retrospective attitude toward a character created more than a quarter of a century earlier, readers have tended to see Henrietta as something of a caricature. Even the name "Henrietta" suggests something other than the traditional object of male infatuation. Not only is there something of "Henry" James in her (in the sense, for example, that both are writers), but there is something masculine in her name—really a blending of a masculine name with that of a diminutive ending that traditionally denotes the female, not a Henry but a Henrietta. She is the first significant working woman in the novels of Henry James. As such she has stepped out of the traditional female role and thus runs the risk—then as well as now—of being taken less seriously than Isabel or even Serena Merle.

Henrietta is not a quester but a questioner. Warburton remarks of her that "I never saw a person judge things on such theoretic grounds" (p. 119). Yet her "theory" is simply the Emersonian distrust of the past or tradition. As Isabel tells Ralph, "there's something of the 'people' in her. . . . she's a kind of emanation of the great democracy—of the continent, the country, the nation" (p. 87). Ironically, it is not Isabel but Henrietta, the woman who resists the European tradition of class, who finds happiness in Europe, in England with Mr. Bantling. Henrietta has no illusions about the Old World, but she makes constant allusions to the New One. Consequently, James never has to ask the question that he does of Isabel—"what was she going to 'do' with herself?" He adds significantly that this "question was irregular, for with most women one had no occasion to ask it. Most women did with themselves nothing at all; they waited, in attitudes more or less gracefully passive, for a man to come that way and furnish them with a destiny." Obviously, Henrietta has plenty to do. Less obvious is that Isabel has nothing to do in spite of giving the impression "of having intentions of her own" (p. 64). She is, as Martha Banta suggests of the postwar American *femme*, echoing James's sentiments in the essay "Saratoga," all dressed up with no place to go.[14] Unlike Henrietta, Isabel is never defined by what she can do—only vaguely by what she desires (i.e., a consumer instead of an artisan in the same technological society that subverts her male counterparts). Although she is introduced to the reader in terms of her sex (and potential sexuality), Isabel is ultimately regarded in terms of her bank account. The problem in asking what she will do, not only with her life but with her sexuality and money, is that the question is historically out of order. The question is "irregular" for Isabel because as long as she lives in a society where women do not "work," she must be defined solely in terms of marriage and motherhood. Isabel, in truth, seeks to become the kind of woman Walt Whitman idealized—the one that had existed "before time was." James, of course, has invented one in time for the twentieth century, when work will define the woman as well as the man. Yet Isabel is no working woman, merely her precursor in American fiction.

It is clear in this "portrait" of a lady that women have yet a long way to go. And just as Pearl is not much improvement over Hester in terms of the female condition, Pansy even represents a certain backsliding on the "woman question." She symbolizes not only Isabel's dilemma but Madame Merle's as well. Merle, of course, wants Osmond to marry Isabel for Pansy's sake. She practically begs her exlover to meet and to marry the young woman. "Come and make a beginning; that's all I ask," she says to Osmond, who replies, "A beginning of what?" "I want you of course to marry her" is the reply. Osmond claims not to undertand her "ambitions," but Merle replies that she thinks he will understand once he has met Miss Archer. Yet he should have understood immediately once Merle added that "Pansy has really grown pretty" (p. 209). Pansy has also grown up in a convent, not exactly a finishing school for the New American Girl. Osmond in fact likes very much what the nuns have "made of her"—thinking his daughter "as pure as a pearl" (p. 210). This exchange occurs in a bitterly poignant scene in which the now middleaged ex-lover and secret mother of Pansy struggles with the father in a surrealistic anticipation of a child-custody dispute. At stake is the pearl that Serena purchased at such a great price. Ironically, she will sacrifice another woman to the same fate in the attempt to rescue Pansy, who is probably already beyond assistance.

In other words, Pansy is beyond freedom, or that condition that Isabel had sought first in her travels around Europe and second in her marriage to Osmond. Pansy from the start has been reduced to a type—the virgin and the *jeune fille* to be sacrificed to the needs of society. Thanks to her father and the nuns who raised her, Pansy is even beyond the help of a Ralph Touchett (or a Lord Warburton) because she has no imagination to exercise. She is the total product of the society that Isabel (and perhaps Merle before her) had tried to elude. Isabel sought out Osmond instead of Warburton because the former appeared to represent an escape from the traditions of womanhood, or wifehood as it was then defined. As Richard Poirier has pointed out, Isabel refuses Warburton precisely because she should not have—because he was what organized society would choose for her. "It is just that which she rejects in declining his offer of marriage—conventionalized society and all that it implies about 'system' in human effort and conduct."[15] Isabel is also a reflection of James's reluctance to fall into the cycle of love and marriage himself; she is the projection of his sexual frigidity, which often protects an individual from marriage in the first place. Yet James ultimately abandons his heroine much in the manner of Hawthorne with his Hester, whose spontaneity is initially celebrated only to be condemned or seriously qualified in the final chapters of *The Scarlet Letter*.[16] When Isabel is last seen, James has sent her back to Rome and to Osmond, where she will continue to be afraid to "publish" her mistake by divorcing him. Rather, she is being "punished" for her mistake, in which she mistook freedom for the egotism that prompted her to choose Osmond. Excessively self-reliant, she has defined her freedom in terms of controlling him, in thinking that she would launch her husband's boat. Isabel enjoys the same authorial protection afforded Hester during the first half of her story as long as she remains single, if not solitary; once married, James allows us to peer into her mind to discover all sorts of inconsistencies. It is even suggested, however obliquely, that Isabel is jealous of Pansy for receiving Warburton's affections. She denies it vigorously, of course, but it is because of that vigor that we have to doubt finally her sincerity. And of course she is fearful of revealing to the world her mistake with Osmond. She is also somewhat vain with Ralph on his deathbed, more concerned, it seems, with the mess she has made of her life than with the approaching end of Ralph's life.

The question "What will she 'do'?" is asked and answered twice in the novel, in the beginning and at its close. In both cases, the answer is the same, and painfully clear. Isabel must marry, and she must remain married. Ralph knows this (speaking for the author) when he tells his father, in answer to what he will receive out of Isabel's receiving an inheritance—"that of having met the requirements of my imagination" (p. 163). The money is not for the exercise of Isabel's imagination, but for his own. He knows that she cannot "do" anything but marry as long as she is intent on becoming "happy" or fulfilling herself. He also knows that Isabel will not be able to overcome the Victorian disapproval of divorce and hence will remain married. With seventy thousand pounds, he has paid for his entertainment in which he views the dissolution of one who dwells under the illusion that she enjoys freedom of choice. Terminally ill, Ralph himself is free of the illusions that make life a drama, the illusions that brought Isabel to Europe and eventually to Florence. These are the illusions that brought her to the home of Dante, to the bridge over the Arno, as it were, where the poet first encounters his Beatrice and the "vita nuova." Ralph knows as a veteran expatriate of American idealism that the new life is the next life, the one he is coming to before his time, and that all that remains to him is Isabel's life. She is in this sense his Beatrice, his "vita nuova," which he must "ruin" with the seventy-thousand-pound legacy in order to share it vicariously.

The Portrait of a Lady is Henry James's magnum opus (in 1881 as well as 1908) because it connects the autobiographical impulse with the biographical one to tell a story. All his great works do this, but this novel, its first edition, comes at a crucial time in the author's life, when he had given up all illusions of finding a Minnie Temple (on whom Isabel is partially based). James is also no longer Isabel Archer, full of American self-reliance and the illusions of life, but Ralph Touchett, the involuntary observer of life. As Ralph, he faces in his love for Isabel the competition of two male worthies in Warburton and Goodwood. In his secret quest for Minnie Temple, fifteen years earlier, the rivals had been Oliver Wendell Holmes, Jr., and John Chipman Gray, two Civil War veterans who were destined to become two of America's great jurists.[17] As Edel remarks, the drama largely resided in James's mind—where of course the drama for the writer belongs. Minnie Temple is larger than life in this respect. James adored his cousin, according to Edel; yet it may be more prudent to say that he adored the idea of Minnie. Which is to say that Isabel "is perhaps [to Quentin Anderson] a study of the Minny Temple [*sic*] one might have known, rather than the Minny Temple of the [autobiographical] *Notes of a Son and Brother.*"[18] Like Poe, whose work he ironically disliked and whose reputation he may have parodied in *The Aspern Papers* (1888),[19] James was fascinated with the "death" of this beautiful woman. Yet James is more vicarious than even Poe, indeed as homoerotic as Whitman (who is probably more erotic than sexual as a poet).[20] The "portrait" of Isabel Archer is the last book published by "Henry James, Jr." It is a product not merely of the "middle years" but of the mid-life of a man longing for more than a Daisy Miller; it is the achievement of one who seeks out in his fiction a female who was not yet allowed to exist. The character of Isabel brings together the body and the soul, heart and intellect, in a mix that was stronger than plausibility in the nineteenth century. Not only does her body have a mind (of its own), but the mind has a body, or a new presence after the Civil War. Frankly, she belongs in the twentieth century of working women and women working out a new design for themselves; for left back in the nineteenth century (where her creation began in the early 1880s), Isabel is, like the women of her era, all dressed up—mentally and physically—but with nowhere to go.

Isabel's strengths are largely maternal—in the sense that her responses and reactions are often correctives to seemingly foolish or "immature" questions, the kind asked by Warburton, Goodwood, and even Ralph Touchett in their anxious ploys to win her. In other words, James may have invented merely the precursor of the female character of the twentieth century, not her prototype, but the literary sister of George Eliot's Dorothea in *Middlemarch* (1871–72); his model of maidenhood may more resemble Whitman's model of womanhood because motherhood is the role Isabel faces at the end of the novel. Which is to say that she is all dressed up but with nowhere to go but back to Rome and Pansy, and probably to Osmond. Pansy is the pearl whose price is yet to be calculated, though the future seems clear enough for Isabel now. The "trap" is motherhood, the same thing that essentially helps to keep Hawthorne's Hester with her Pearl and away from Dimmesdale. We can see in both Hester and Isabel a willingness to do what Edna Pontellier of *The Awakening* will not do, and that is give herself (rather than her life) for her family. Like Edna, Hester and Isabel have the potential of becoming artists, of having an identity outside their traditional gender roles, but it is only Edna who actually tries to become one. The difference may be that Edna is the creation of a female writer, whereas Hester and Isabel are not. The difference may be that Hawthorne and James, like Whitman in his idea of "the woman," stop short of letting her go.

For the author, as it was for Hester's "Arthur," the character of Isabel is a meditation on the human condition as it wakes up female. Like Rip Van Winkle, it wakes up to find the world changed. Rip as the prototypical male after the Revolution is now freed of the termagant wife and can devote himself to the creative (and apparently indolent) act of storytelling. As the prototypical American woman after the Civil War, Isabel can also vary from the straight and narrow of ladyhood. She can go to Europe and even think of affronting her destiny, which before had been forlornly "manifest." As I will concede in my next chapter, on *The Awakening*, Chopin's novel is as much a feminist argument as it is one devoted to the enigma of the "human condition." James's concern, however, has much less to do with the "woman question." He is much more interested in the question of the woman facing the human condition. Ultimately, Isabel's problem is not with her gender but with her (American) idealism, which invites her to become everybody *but* herself. As Anderson aptly puts it, "In her declaration of principle ('Her life should always be in harmony with the most pleasing impression she should produce; she would be what she appeared, and she would appear what she was.') James indicates Isabel's worst error. She puts herself at the mercy of 'the most pleasing impression' she has made on others; she proposes to live up to the portrait instead of the demands of the inner life."[21] This judgment, while sound enough, overlooks the fact that such impressions are internally generated: in conducting herself as an independent woman, Isabel initiates or creates the impressions she receives from others. She convinces herself that this megaportrait is also a composite of what others desire of her.

Perhaps this is why Isabel never understood Unitarianism (p. 363). Although the bedrock of Transcendentalism, which launched the first American Renaissance, Unitarianism held that human beings were essentially social animals. They may have been relieved of the Puritan burdens of innate depravity, original sin, and the son of God who died for their sins (Christ now vaguely reduced to the status of archangel), but Unitarianism retained two important Puritan concepts: the validity of Scripture and the right of the religious community to influence secular affairs. Transcendentalism, of course, did away with these two principles, replacing Scripture with nature and social responsibility with the idealistic notion that a society of potentially good men and women will govern itself without the social engineering of very much external regulation (hence, Emerson's and Thoreau's refusal to join the Brook Farm utopian experiment and their reluctance toward political involvement). Isabel does not *want* to understand Unitarianism any more than Emerson or Thoreau did because all three are Transcendentalists—who believe in the "slumbering giant" of self-reliance. They believe they are "part or parcel of God" and hence fated for a destiny in which society (as indirectly regulated by Scripture) has very little effect on their lives. In other words, Isabel thought she could marry Osmond and have ideas of her own.

Isabel simply does not share the Unitarian commitment to society. She has no compunction whatever about coming into the Touchett family and departing as a rich heiress. She shows little sensitivity to either Warburton's or Goodwood's feelings—or, for that matter, for Ralph's hopeless infatuation. She acts more like the Transcendentalist, one to whom "there is properly no History; only Biography."[22] *The Portrait of a Lady* was of course spiritual autobiography for James. He projected in it his sense of the woman's condition as it came under the limits of the human condition. Isabel was the woman in him—his feminine side that led to such a fine psychological portrait of the opposite sex. Yet it is nevertheless the achievement of a male writer because Isabel is more logical than emotional in the face of defeat. I am not falling back on the traditional stereotype that ascribes the head to the male and the heart to the female. Isabel accepts her destiny logically, if not altogether calmly, because as a representative American woman in post–Civil War fiction, she has yet to wake up *as* a woman, or as one who faces not only the absurdity of cosmic restrictions but those of an unfair social situation as well. After Ahab, there was probably no reason to rail against the universe; but social oppression was another matter, whose resistance called for both the head and the heart. In neither the first nor the second edition of *The Portrait* is Isabel clearly confronted with the limitations of the female condition. The mistakes she makes in pursuit of matrimonial happiness are essentially the result of the same brand of American idealism that defeats Christopher Newman in *The American*. No marriage laws really imprison her (except possibly that Osmond would get Isabel's fortune in the event of a divorce, but money is never a major concern with Isabel); no male code calls her into that particular marriage in the first place (indeed, she goes against social expectations in marrying Osmond); and no condition of motherhood (Pansy aside) restricts her social or professional movement. In a phrase, Isabel is not a working woman—working against a misogynistic tradition. At best, she is the androgynous product of a male author whose protagonist "affronts" her destiny and suffers the same fate as the male questers before her. James's "portrait," we should not forget, is that of a "lady," not a woman. That achievement would have to wait for a "lady" author.

In a more revisionist strain, it might be argued that James sets up Isabel for failure—as Alfred Habegger has recently insisted[23]—by having her marry an older man, a father-lover who attempts to shape her life as effectively as he has his daughter's. Yet Warburton is also an "older" man, if not exactly the "father"-lover. Goodwood is almost a caricature of carnal dominance. Yes, she chooses the wrong man, but where is the male in the novel who will allow his boat to be launched by a woman? Indeed, where is the male either during the period of the novel or today whose sexual drive conforms so neatly with the feminist ideal that informs Habegger's thesis? James may have been influenced by his father's antifeminist views (even though he spoke somewhat disparagingly in 1885 about Henry Sr.'s writings to his brother William[24]), but James was also the first important American storyteller to introduce the woman's complex situation into the enigma of the human condition. He tried to pass through the customhouse of gender like Melville's "unincumbered travellers in Europe," but he could go no farther than Twain in his attempt to cross the Color Line, another taboo whose political and psychological perils we tend to discount in the post-Vietnam era. What also stopped James on this social frontier, however, was his deeper concern about experience regardless of gender. His shortcoming, then, was to explore the woman's world as a man, nothing more.

11 : Chopin's
Twenty-Ninth Bather

t almost goes without saying that Henry James could never have written *The Awakening* (1899). The nearest he probably came to creating a character as corporeal as Kate Chopin's Edna Pontellier is Kate Croy in *The Wings of the Dove* (1902), and this sexy lady (an oxymoron in nineteenth-century America, if not at the turn of the century) is motivated as much by money as by sex or infatuation. His women, if not relatively docile, are more or less sexless, some almost helpless as in the case of the other *jeune fille* in that novel, Milly Theale. Isabel Archer of *The Portrait of a Lady*, James's predecessor in the working out of his fanciful dreams about his lost cousin Minnie Temple, is powerfully beautiful but also passionately intellectual and—if her nervous reactions to Caspar Goodwood are any indication— downright fearful of sex. This lack of a body in James's women may stem from his personal reluctance about matters of sex.[1] Yet the question has to be asked as to whether *any* American male writer could have created the character of Edna. Even a casual survey of Chopin's short fiction and work previous to *The Awakening* shows that (1) her main idea comes out of the sentimental plots of the 1850s that Hawthorne complained about, and (2) her central theme is the romantic and often thwarted quest for love. Of Chopin's male precursors in the depiction of such a questing female (or male, for that matter), Whitman was the most successful, not James. In section 11 of "Song of Myself," he identifies and empathizes with a sexually frustrated "lady":

Twenty-eight young men bathe by the shore,
Twenty-eight young men and all so friendly;
Twenty-eight years of womanly life and all so lonesome.

She owns the fine house by the rise of the bank,
She hides handsome and richly drest aft the blinds of the window.

Which of the young men does she like the best?
Ah the homeliest of them is beautiful to her.

Where are you off to, lady? for I see you,
You splash in the water there, yet stay stock still in your room.

Dancing and laughing along the beach came the twenty-ninth
     bather,
The rest did not see her, but she saw them and loved them.[2]

In this rare departure from the "I" in "Song of Myself," Whitman identifies with the American woman in hiding as a "lady"—he empathizes with her as an actively sexual (and thus frustrated) human being. Yet Whitman, as I have argued in chapter 7, was otherwise as fantastic in his depiction of women as his "twenty-ninth bather" is vicarious in her participation in group sex. The woman "aft the blinds" never literally takes the plunge but stays "stock still" in her room. She nevertheless entertains the possibility of expressing her sexual feelings and thus advances the cause of woman's emancipation beyond James's "portrait" of Isabel.[3] Indeed, Isabel is *portrayed* by her author instead of being "photographed" the way Whitman's lady is—that is, caught in action or on its threshold. In a word, Whitman's lady thinks to *act* (however vicariously), whereas James's lady in *The Portrait*, being much more Emersonian and hence scholarly, mainly *reflects* (however fitfully). Though constrained from overt action, the "twenty-ninth bather" thinks about what *could* happen—not (like Isabel) about what has happened and its devastating significance.

Because she is a transcendentalist, or one for whom action is subservient to thought, Isabel must remain a lady. Whitman's "lady," on the other hand, is less ladylike—at least in her daydreams. Edna differs from both because she wakes up neither to the "slumbering giant" of Transcendentalism nor from the slumber of a sexual fantasy exactly, but to the problem of not being able to either accept or transcend the social constraints of her gender. Chopin's generic theme of an awakening was established in her earliest recorded fiction, "Emancipation: A Life Fable" (1869–70). It tells the story of a caged animal: "Awaking one day from his slothful rest."[4] Like Whitman's animals who "do not sweat and whine about their condition,"[5] Chopin's caged beast rushes into the "Unknown." The fable sets the pattern in her fiction, in which the female "beast" risks what she has for the romance and affection she craves. It culminates, of course, with the story of Edna Pontellier, who is in deed as well as desire the first authentic twenty-ninth bather in American literature.

If American fiction of the late nineteenth century and early twentieth was in any way factual, it reflected the reality that it was risky business for a woman to have such a mind (and body) of her own. At about age twenty-eight James's Isabel finds her options as limited or exhausted as those of other twenty-eight-year-olds, Whitman's "twenty-ninth bather" and the woman in *The Awakening* who learns to swim so that she can ultimately drown. Trina Sieppi in Frank Norris's *McTeague* (1899) pays the ultimate penalty for hoarding of the means of male autonomy, and Maggie in Stephen Crane's *Maggie: A Girl of the Streets* (1893) blossoms "in a mud puddle" only to die in the streets. In the twentieth century, these women who dare to improve their lot at the expense of the male's dominance fare hardly better. Edith Wharton's Lily Bart in *The House of Mirth* (1905) learns (too late) that the truth is irrelevant: "Where a woman is concerned, it's the story that's easiest to believe."[6] Elizabeth Willard in Sherwood Anderson's *Winesburg, Ohio* (1919) learns the same lesson about the perils of "a somewhat shaky reputation" in her youth.[7] More important, she learns that the sought-after marriage can kill off the very thing it initially nourished. The mother of George Willard is forty-five, not twenty-eight. Yet the dream of freedom and romance persists because love, or its relentless pursuit, was still the woman's primary field of adventure.

The question, therefore, of "What will she 'do'?" in *The Portrait of a Lady* pertains to *whom* she will marry. Likewise, the impetus for Edna's abandonment of her marriage is the need for love instead of the freedom to be an artist. When she ignores her Tuesdays at home because, as she tells her husband, she feels "like painting," Leonce counters that Madame Ratignolle, the ideal wife and mother, keeps up her household duties and is "more of a musician than you are a painter." Edna then has to confess that "it isn't on account of painting that I let things go."[8] She may demand, as Willa Cather observed in her review of *The Awakening*, "more romance out of life than God put into it." Women of the Bovary type, she wrote, "really expect the passion of love to fill and gratify every need of life, whereas nature only intended that it should meet one of many demands." One of Cather's recent biographers notes that her harsh observation "reveals Cather's own belief in romantic love as a destructive force and helps to explain her own avoidance of entangling emotional relationships."[9] For whatever reasons of her own, Cather passes over the larger significance of Edna's desire for freedom and sex. First, whereas romance may meet only "one of many demands," it is the central demand of the woman in the nineteenth century who was compelled to live primarily for marriage and motherhood.[10] Second, it was virtually the only way she could find relative freedom and autonomy in a male-dominated society. Edna Pontellier cannot become a fulfilled or completely successful artist in last-century America any more than her real-life counterpart in France, for example, can be a sculptor in the age of Rodin. Just as Camille Claudel's life was destroyed by her love (and then hate) for the creator of *Le Penseur*, few American women found social acceptance in careers outside the home and, accordingly, few in the fiction of Kate Chopin are able to detach their (love) lives from their work. One exception is Paula Von Stoltz in "Wiser Than a God" (1889), and even here "love" threatens to win out ultimately.[11]

Rather than try to compete in the male marketplace, even of art, or strike out for "the eternal rights of women" (p. 65),[12] Edna sets out to improve not the lot of women exactly but mainly her own place in the female sphere of romance. Like her creator, Edna is, "in many ways, a lone wolf." This is Felix Chopin's description of his mother, who as a widow wore clothing that was often more "eccentric" than it was fashionable and who never voiced her positive opinion of women's suffrage, the burning question of the 1890s.[13] In other words, Chopin is interested primarily in "the eternal rights" of one woman to control her destiny with at least as much freedom and authority as the male wields in the structuring of one's social life. This means, of course, that Edna wants—like Isabel in *The Portrait*—the upper hand in her relationships. Andrew Delbanco remarks in a recent essay that *The Awakening* "is about a woman passing for a man."[14] He points out her developing taste for ownership, her smoking cigars, the description of her as "rather handsome than beautiful," and the fact that her relationship to her children's governess and to her children is not very different from her husband's relationship to herself. We could add to these details the fact that Edna seems to thrive on the courtly nature of Robert's attentions, that she rather enjoys her control over Alcée Arobin, and of course she finds it easy not only to disobey her husband but generally to disregard him.

Edna's rebellion begins in a dream of courtly love. As a "courtly lover" Robert is ideally suited for this necessarily illicit romance. He is (a little) younger, socially or professionally beneath her husband and thus in a position to worship Edna as he does at Grand Isle. He is the Prince Charming who tells her after her autoerotic nap on "the big, four-posted bed, snow-white," at Madame Antoine's on *Chênière Caminada*, "You have slept precisely one hundred years" (pp. 37–38). As in Perrault's fairy tale of "Sleeping Beauty" (and *any* fairy tale), her awakening is not subject to the tyrannies of time and place. Even before her sleep, while sailing across the bay, "Edna felt as if she were being borne away from some anchorage which had held her fast" (p. 35). Robert's suggestions that they go tomorrow to Grande Terre and the next day to Bayou Brulow are filled with the phallic imagery of romance: "She gazed away toward Grande Terre and thought she would like to be alone there with Robert, in the sun, listening to the ocean's roar and watching the slimy lizards writhe in and out among the ruins of the old fort" (p. 35). Edna does not want to wake up from this dream; the awakening is merely what happens to her.

Her creator had been living a dream as well—in terms of her success as a writer. Since 1889 Chopin had been selling short stories and sketches that were mistaken for local color when they were in fact mostly romances that happened to be set mainly in one section of the country. Her "rude awakening" (also the title of a mediocre story published in 1891) came with the moralistic reaction to her second novel about love and betrayal. Indeed, much of her life, despite its tragedies, resembled a happy fiction. Brought up in a prosperous Catholic family in St. Louis, she became the belle of that city or her set and married a Creole gentleman who turned out, from most appearences, to be an ideal husband.[15] Leonce, too, fits this description—at least to the extent of being a good provider and a benevolent if not intensely warm and loving husband. He does, however, love his wife—as his patience for her strange behavior involves more than mere appearances for the sake of business. Though Chopin lost her husband early and was left with six children, she managed first to run the plantation in Natchitoches (in northwestern Louisiana, where the family had moved after Oscar's business had failed in New Orleans) for a year, and afterwards to make a successful transition for herself and her children to St. Louis. Though she once noted that she would have given up the successful writing career in exchange for the return of her dead husband and mother (who died a year after Oscar Chopin), she must also have felt like the woman in "The Story of an Hour" (1894) who secretly savors her newfound freedom upon being told erroneously that her husband has died in an accident. Louise Mallard of that story wakes up to the fact that her husband lives and promptly dies of a heart attack.[16] It was also a "heart attack" that woke up Chopin as a writer. In a reverse of Hawthorne, it is the heart that rules the head of most of her characters, and certainly that of Edna Pontellier. Like the caged beast of "Emancipation," her characters commit the pardonable sin of losing themselves in the romantic impulse for freedom. Chopin herself was carried away by the same impulse in her writing—not merely to show her characters in love but to show them in search of the same ineluctable satisfaction that drove the more celibate male characters to sea or to Walden Pond. Those white males of the American Renaissance (the one we designate between the publication of Emerson's *Nature* and Whitman's *Leaves of Grass*) taught that one had to balance the nagging impatience of the intellect against the unruly passion of the spirit. They dramatized the dangers of satisfying one at the expense of the other in works as varied as the essay "Experience" and the "Calamus" poems. Chopin knew these lessons too, having read Emerson and Whitman as well, no doubt, as the other major writers of the Renaissance who had not waked up or responded to the special dilemma of the woman facing the human condition. Her work therefore articulates the need—felt more keenly in the late nineteenth century, when the gender gap in social opportunity became more apparent—for love in spite of its impossible odds. In other words, *The Awakening* and the shorter works that precede it do not expand the realm of women's writing (into the male domain) but embrace the concept of the "sentimental" and the domestic in experience: if the woman is to be left in the domestic sphere, should she not be better satisfied? This, it seems, is the nature of "the eternal rights of women" in *The Awakening*. Today the book appears to have a clear feminist theme, and because of the social needs of our day (the fact that the majority of married women work outside the home), it does. Edna, however, does not want equality exactly, not primarily the kind of intellectual and professional equality that the Renaissance "upstart" Margaret Fuller had argued for in *Woman in the Nineteenth Century* (1845). She seeks instead "equality" in love, which means the superiority of the female in the courtly love tradition that probably never existed as anything other than a *literary* tradition. She seeks to become the active, even aggressive, partner in all affairs of the heart.

This is the aspect of Edna that most displeased the critics and the moralists of Chopin's day, not merely her adultery with Arobin, which contemporary reviewers of *The Awakening* failed to mention directly. Even the Creole culture encouraged her to flirt with the Roberts of Grand Isle and New Orleans. And who is to say that the convention was as harmless as Madame Ratignolle suggests when she warns Robert against overstimulating Edna's feelings? The very necessity of the warning suggests the dangers of such a convention. Rather, Edna is asserting her civil rights in the realm of romance. This means for the woman not only flirtation and adultery, but autonomy. It would certainly be the case for an attractive twenty-eight-year-old woman who has every other creature comfort she can imagine. It is obviously the case with the woman who dwells in "the fine house by the rise of the bank." In *The Awakening* Chopin brought to the fore the truth that in society money meant sex for the male, and sex meant money for the female. This Dreiserian equation (which dictates the fates of Carrie and Hurstwood in *Sister Carrie*) was the index of social success for both sexes, especially in turn-of-the-century America, where the Robber Barons were romanticized. The difference arose only in the approach: since the male was the financial provider because he also existed in a world outside the home, he came to sex as the superior "partner." Edna wants to change all that, at least for herself, not by going outside the home but by returning it, or sex, to an illicit affair of the heart in which the woman is master—or mistress—again. She searches for a realm where sex is unconnected to money—and, of course, reality. Her gambling, albeit successful, suggests her abandonment of a world in which money is invested for the future for one in which it (or one's emotional resources) is risked for the present. She is given to unrealistic declarations—such as giving her life but not herself for her children. In fact, the life she desires leaves little room for her children—little or no room for anybody but herself. Even Robert, as she concludes shortly before her suicide, would ultimately fail to satisfy her hunger for life without labor. In other words, Edna desires a lover outside of the social restraints whom she can dominate, thus shaping the terms of "romance." In *At Fault* (1890), Chopin's first completed novel, this is the achievement of the moralistic Thérèse Lafirme, who orchestrates her "romance" by persuading David Hosmer to remarry his alcoholic wife. In the disjointed melodrama that follows, the heroine's superior qualities become even clearer to Hosmer, and (aided by Fanny's accidental death) the two are finally united. The exchange of the two lovers at their reunion on a train after a year's separation is worthy of a Harlequin Romance, if not the pen of Chrétien de Troyes:

> "You knew I was on the train?" he asked.
> "Oh, no, how should I?"
> Then naturally followed question and answer.
> Yes, he was going to Place-du-Bois.
> No, the mill did not require his presence. . .
> Yes, she had been to New Orleans. . .
> Yes—quite likely there would be rain next month. . .
> [And shortly thereafter:]
> It was a royal love; a generous love and a rich one in its revelation.[17]

For the wealthy Thérèse the dream of love has a happy ending, but for Edna (mainly because the power of money resides with the male) it is a dream with a rude awakening.

Edna's awakening, therefore, is not at Grand Isle or *Chênière Caminada* but in New Orleans when she discovers the truth about Robert and sets out for seashore again. "Despondency," Chopin writes in chapter 39, "had come upon her there in the wakeful night, and had never lifted. There was no one thing in the world that she desired" (p. 113). If we wanted the title of her novel to indicate her sexual awakening, we would call it "The Big Sleep" because the sexual and emotional ecstasy she wished to have on a continued basis can only be sustained in a dream. The true "awakening" occurs when the illusions run out and only the brooding, love-starved self remains. Edna realizes that only the self can fully satisfy the self, and to an individual whose "self-reliance" depends on personal love instead of transcendence that is an admission of loneliness and hopelessness. Whereas Whitman's protagonists in "Out of the Cradle Endlessly Rocking" and "As I Ebb'd with the Ocean of Life" approach the land's edge, that dividing line between life and death ("the solid marrying the liquid," as Whitman noted in *Specimen Days*), Edna crosses the line in search of life and love *in* death.

Actually, Whitman's persona crosses the line, too, or attempts to do so—which amounts to the same thing. In "As I Ebb'd," the poet stands on the seashore much like Edna at the close of *The Awakening* and asks more of poetry than it can give. The response he hears is "peals of distant ironical laughter at every word I have written." [18] Edna, as Cather remarked, had demanded "more romance out of life than God put into it." Both protagonists run the risk of mockery for their near-suicidal boldness, and indeed suicide is the only alternative to compromise. Whitman changed the course of *Leaves of Grass* in "As I Ebb'd"—from a focus on himself to all those other selves he represented in society. He stopped asking too much of poetry and started asking how his poetry could neutralize the harshness of the human condition. The result was a focus on Love *and* Death, as he announces in "Out of the Cradle Endlessly Rocking." Chopin, on the other hand, never gave up her search for romance as the key to life, never quite *celebrated* the inevitable exchange of passion for pathos. Sex, or its significance, was her subject (even more than it was Whitman's), and she did not compromise that emphasis even after going as dangerously far as she had in *The Awakening*. In "The Storm" (1898), written soon after the novel but before its denunciation by reviewers, she celebrates the "Children of Adam" theme of "native moments" and "libidinous joys only." It is doubtful whether this bold depiction of adultery could have been published at a time when Dreiser had to send Carrie offstage for sexual trysts with Drouet and Hurstwood. "When he touched her breasts," Chopin wrote of another Alcée in his passionate embrace of the married Calixta (indeed, both are married), "they gave themselves up in quivering ecstasy, inviting his lips."[19] Chopin's graphic description of sex here would have shocked perhaps even her French master in the realistic depiction of male-female relationships, Guy de Maupassant, who avoided such details. As Per Seyersted writes, "The story leaves aside all suspense of plot . . . [and] concentrates instead on the delights of *sexe pur*. There is nothing to hide in this naked pleasure, she seems to say."[20] Chopin, it is already agreed, owed a great deal to Whitman for the idea that sex in and of itself was a worthy subject for literature. In his famous open letter to a writer who was not so open about sex, Ralph Waldo Emerson, Whitman speaks of the "infidelism about sex. By silence or obedience the pens of savans, poets, historians, biographers, and the rest, have long connived at the filthy law, and books enslaved to it, that what makes the manhood of a man, that sex, womanhood, maternity, desires, lusty animations, organs, acts, are unmentionable and to be ashamed of, to be driven to skulk out of literature with whatever belongs to them."[21] It was this insistence on "amativeness of Nature" that got Whitman in trouble throughout his career, that made *Leaves of Grass* the first book to be "banned in Boston." *The Awakening* was "banned," too, in St. Louis. It was kept out of the St. Louis Public Library, and Chopin herself was refused membership in the city's Fine Arts Club.[22] In her only published defense of Edna's "indecency," Chopin wrote on 28 May 1899 that she had "never dreamed of Mrs. Pontellier making such a mess of things and working out her own damnation as she did. If I had had the slightest intimation of such a thing I would have excluded her from the company. But when I found out what she was up to, the play was half over and it was then too late."[23] It is important to note that this tongue-in-cheek but also serious response to the barrage of hostile reviews was written by the same person who had recently penned "The Storm" on 19 July 1898 and was now threatened with the abrupt conclusion to a highly successful writing career. We should also observe that the play was already "half over" in the very first line of the novel, which introduces the caged bird. The scene harks back to "Emancipation." This time the caged animal, a parrot, has the capacity for language, but its speech is also unanchored from any sense of even its own incarcerated condition. It represents, of course, the woman in the gilded cage of marriage. The parrot speaks not only "a little Spanish" but "also a language which nobody understood, unless it was the mocking-bird that hung on the other side of the door" (p. 3). It is, of course, a mockingbird that laments the loss of its mate in "Out of the Cradle Endlessly Rocking."

Edna cannot fully articulate the reasons for her unhappiness in marriage. Certainly, she cannot justify it either to her Creole friends or her white Protestant relatives. For all her education (and reading of Emerson), she is almost as verbally helpless as the relatively ignorant Athénaïse in the short story of the same name (one of Chopin's longest) published in the *Atlantic Monthly* for August and September 1896. "Athénaïse" is about a young Creole woman who marries early because of convention and then (after less than two months of marriage) regrets it. Like Edna, she does not have the excuse of a cruel or improvident husband. Nor does she have the support of her parents (only a brother who dislikes her husband, Cazeau). She also does not dislike her husband: "It's jus' being married that I detes' an' despise. I hate being Mrs. Cazeau, an' would want to be Athénaïse Miché again."[24] After a mild flirtation with a gentleman in New Orleans, where she has gone to live after leaving her husband, Athénaïse—for no other reason than the discovery that she is pregnant—suddenly undergoes a change of heart and returns to her husband. There is simply no way to explain the pull of motherhood any more than there is the desire to be free from such an obligation. "Her whole being," Chopin writes, "was steeped in a wave of ecstasy. When she finally arose from the chair . . . and looked herself in the mirror, a face met hers which seemed to see for the first time, so transfigured was it with wonder and rapture."[25] Ironically, this usually inevitable responsibility of the woman domesticated into a wife offers the same sense of freedom to Athénaïse as the thought of living without her husband offers to Edna. That is to say, she has become enraptured with the expectation of giving life instead of merely living it. Athénaïse feels that as a future mother she is becoming a woman in the sense of living life instead of only making wifely sacrifices for it. In other words, the "family" condition and its results will occupy her now—as it did Edna until she reached the magical number of twenty-eight years.

The number represents the lunar cycle or the menstrual cycle; it matters only that it signifies one of the cycles of life from ecstasy to resignation. At twenty-eight Edna, though not having satisfied the youthful dream of love, is about to enter another stage of life where youth or youthfulness is about to belong to someone else. The woman's "right" Edna seeks is endless passion and effortless creativity as an artist—a condition not of this world for either gender. It had been merely the illusion of the first twenty-eight years. Chopin deals with the female passion for life and love more successfully than any of her literary predecessors, including James. Her depictions are rarely sentimental because this female passion also represents the desire for the inscrutable in both sexes. It becomes, however, exclusively the woman's condition because the female is confined in the nineteenth century to the "sentimental" or domestic sphere. In "Athénaïse" Chopin is careful to point out all that Cazeau has to occupy himself in addition to seeking love. After eating a solitary dinner on the eve of his wife's initial departure, he "had many things to attend to before bed-time; so many things that there was not left to him a moment in which to think of Athénaïse."[26] In reproaching his wife for "her inattention, her habitual neglect of the children," Leonce Pontellier excuses himself with the fact of his brokerage business in New Orleans: "He could not be in two places at once; making a living for his family on the street, and staying at home to see that no harm befell them." He spoke, Chopin notes, "in a monotonous, insistent way" (p. 7). It is monotonous to Edna because it is the old male excuse. Indeed, neither husband seems that emotionally troubled over the desertion of his wife. Of course, each wants her back, but not at the expense of expending any true, sometimes crippling emotion. Cazeau refuses to do anything irrational (even when Athénaïse's hostile brother almost begs for a thrashing) but merely waits—really without much hope—for Athénaïse's return. Leonce takes a long business trip to New York rather than look for the obvious if merely ostensible cause for Edna's rebellion, namely Robert and later Alcée. Cazeau gets his wish; Leonce does not (or does he?). In both cases the male wins, however, because he never has to compromise. In the case of the female, the protagonist loses either her independence or her life. Athénaïse gives up her autonomy to become a mother-lover who will give herself as well as her life for husband and children; Edna "wins" by losing her life. The loss may be a "victory" for Edna, as some have argued.[27] Yet her "choice" merely mocks the unsatisfied love for life. What else has she won but freedom from the human condition?

The human condition is that state in which there are, finally, no true choices. In "The Road Not Taken," Robert Frost wisely observes that the two paths through life were worn "about the same." In *Freedom of Will*, Jonathan Edwards notes that we do not choose our will or selves and hence can merely act out what has been doled out. If she chooses life, Edna can only act out the circumstance of her social condition. Yet if this circumstance were to be suddenly changed—that is to say, if we view *The Awakening* as a feminist argument—what would finally change in Edna's condition? She might, if possessing enough talent, become a productive and successful artist, but she would also have to endure the disappointments and insatiable desires of a Whitman. She might actively choose her lover and perhaps husband, but she could not expect to enjoy the endless passion she seems to think her marriage to Leonce prevents. She would merely rise from the female condition to the human condition. *Voilà!* The feminist concern—so far as it argues for equal gender rights in both the domestic and public or professional spheres—*is* part of the human condition and thus a worthy subject of "Literature." It is also a part that has been traditionally underrated and relegated to the "sentimental." Indeed, this vast body of domestic or "sentimental" (using the word pejoratively now) work between Lydia Maria Child's *Hobomok* (1824) to Sara Parton's *Ruth Hall* (1855) or Elizabeth Stoddard's *The Morgesons* (1862) prepared the way for Kate Chopin—as such "women's literature" allowed Emily Dickinson to make one's confrontation with a snake or a housefly as memorable in literature as Ahab's pursuit of the White Whale. Edna Pontellier's main or initial problem is that she is a woman in the late nineteenth century; her ultimate problem is that she is a human being subject to an imperfect world.

Yet how can she be expected to confront the "higher" problems when her gender is such a distraction to her imagined happiness? This leads to the question of whether Edna is being truly reasonable in her demands. In "Athénaïse" the heroine is described (by her husband) as being "nothing but a chile in character." "Besides that," Cazeau adds, "she's my wife."[28] By all standards of adult behavior, Athénaïse does act foolishly. But she acts like a child because she is treated like one. She is also treated like property—Cazeau's wife. On the couple's return from Athénaïse's first desertion of her husband, they pass a "solitary oak-tree" at which Cazeau remembers his father allowed a runaway slave to rest on his return to the plantation. We are told that "Cazeau's father was a kind and considerate master, and every one agreed at the time that Black Gabe [the runaway] was a fool, a great idiot indeed, for wanting to run away from him."[29] The analogy between slavery and marriage is hard to miss. Gabe is a fool for running away from a benevolent master, and so is Athénaïse. They are fools because they have no other options than to endure—indeed, to "enjoy"—their bondage. In this light Athénaïse's seemingly petulant behavior takes on a new sense and justification. And thus does Edna's.

The Awakening, therefore, is first and foremost about emancipation of the individual, then about the cycle of anticipation and resignation that characterizes the human condition. Where it concerns women's rights, the focus is probably on their "eternal rights" as human beings rather than on their political rights as women. Yet the clear implication is present in the novel that the absence of "political" rights—whether in the home or outside it—renders women special victims of the human condition. Without a woman's complete social emancipation, the normal anticipations of life become inflated and its satisfactions grow even more elusive, and perhaps even illusory, than they are for the male. It is little wonder that Edna apparently lacks the independence for the life of the struggling artist; she is too busy with the life of the struggling female in a male-oriented society. To ask her to worry about the metaphysical aspect of the human condition is to ask this woman, now twenty-*nine*, to pretend that life, or this world, is even more insignificant than the neo-Kantians of the American Renaissance (the one that ends with Whitman, if not slightly *before* him) would admit. The fact remains that Edna as a married woman in nineteenth-century New Orleans (or America, for that matter) is not as free as her husband. As an upper-class white woman, she may be freer than most women of her day, but she is not free enough. This is because she is not free of the world of romance or the illusions about love (and sex) that keep her from a full appreciation of the human condition. In other words, she is not free of the woman's sphere in the nineteenth century, where the closest approach to the metaphysical was Love and Marriage. The Emersons and the Whitmans could transcend the quotidian with art based on an almost exclusively male tradition, and the Cazeaus and the Leonces could escape it, or marriage, with the outside world of male occupations. These points bring us back to the truth that Henry James could have never created Edna Pontellier. For it required a female writer, and one as gifted as Chopin, to teach us that the "woman's condition" imprisoned her in two important ways. It restricted her social and political movements, of course. But more important, it kept her in a relatively perpetual state of adolescence with regard to an understanding of the human condition.

Isabel Archer, as noted in chapter 10, does not view her lack of freedom as necessarily connected to her gender; hence, she never acts as recklessly as Edna. Isabel is also (unlike Edna) never at a loss for words in defending her position. Indeed, she is possibly the freest character in. *The Portrait of a Lady*, certainly freer than all the male characters. This is due not to gender but to the fortuitous results of wealth and health (even Lord Warburton suffers from a retarded state of adolescence because of his nobility and good looks). James created a "portrait" of a "lady"—not only with regard to how the other characters see her as advancing their own fortunes but how Isabel sees herself. And she sees herself as a *woman* with the same psychological and social options as a man in the Jamesian world where few work for a living anyway. Gender is not a problem until it is *perceived* as one. Emerson wisely remarked, after being invited to the Woman's Rights Convention held at Worcester, Massachusetts, in 1850: "The fact of the political & civil wrongs of woman I deny not. If women feel wronged, then they are wronged."[30] If James's mildly antifeminist theme in *The Bostonians* (1886) is not an indication of his lack of empathy with the "woman's condition," the fact of his refusal to dwell at the close of *The Portrait* on Isabel's lack of financial options with Osmond at least suggests his determination to keep his heroine in the (male) sphere of the "life of the mind." Here the "universal" truths dominate, everything else being relegated to the secondary world of action (always, as has been remarked, subservient to the life of the "scholar" or intellectual). Emerson, at least, was ready to allow for the possible legitimacy of feminist complaints, but he was not prepared to attend the Woman's Rights Convention in Worcester. James was ready to introduce the New Woman or the *jeune fille* into American fiction, but he was not prepared to let in also her special problems with the human condition. It was left to Kate Chopin, heir not only to the male writers of the (first) American Renaissance but to the Fanny Ferns and others who had to clear the political way for the more talented female writer by focusing on the quotidian. Whenever they would do both, that is, focus on the world of the body *and* soul, as Stoddard tries so admirably but does so ineptly in *The Morgesons*, for example, their fictions fracture into melodrama, fragmented plots, or incomplete characterizations. This was the fate of *At Fault*. "One reason for her writing it," writes Per Seyersted, "was that [Chopin] had to get her irritation with moral reformers out of her system. This explains in part the artificiality of plot, the occasionally stilted language, and the woodenness of the central characters." Chopin, as a relative newcomer to the writing of fiction (her first publication coming only the year before), was stymied by the quotidian. On the other hand, Seyersted notes that several of the supporting characters "are true to life and fully convincing, and a number of scenes are effectively realized."[31] These figures, namely Grégoire and Aunt Belindy, do not derive from a political or social argument but from life itself—the situation of being human first and social or political second.

Chopin shared with Emily Dickinson the literary capacity to embrace both worlds in original ways. Dickinson may have written, as I have said elsewhere, "on the second story" of life, where the experience of life is more important than the sum of its transient adventures,[32] but she was never strictly a "metaphysical" poet any more than she was as mundane as the other well-known Amherst-born poet, Helen Hunt Jackson. Dickinson's poetry emerges, like Whitman's (as *he* said), out "of my own emotional and other personal nature—an attempt, from first to last, to put *a Person*, a human being (myself, in the latter half of the Nineteenth Century, in America), freely, fully and truly on record."[33] Dickinson, as *she* wrote biographically, "never lost as much but twice"; and that experience, or its cycle of anticipation and resignation, was the basis of her great body of poetry. Early readers and later critics of Dickinson assumed this loss to be that of a lover, expecting only domestic drama from a woman's verse. Yet this is where all great poetry comes from—the cycle of Love and Death, or gain and loss. This is her link with Kate Chopin as well as the one with Emerson, Whitman, Hawthorne, Thoreau, Poe, and others. And it is Chopin's link to the great American literature of the nineteenth century.

It seems historically appropriate that Chopin, like Dickinson in terms of her critical reception, was forgotten during the first three or four decades of the twentieth century. It should also be remembered that Melville's reputation sank into oblivion until the 1920s, and that it was mainly because of Whitman's band of Camden disciples that his reputation was kept alive, if not altogether healthy (until the 1940s). These figures and others came to replace the Schoolroom Poets and the editors of the *Atlantic Monthly* and other prestigious magazines because they introduced the irrational into literature. Beginning with Irving, American literature presented not a world of conventional thought in which Longfellow's "nature" is motherly or Whittier's condition of being "snowbound" is womblike, but one in which the mother is also a lover and the womb a projection of the tomb. They brought in not works of social reform but the psychological evidence that "reform"—even for women's rights and black emancipation— was incomplete without the reformation of the individual to find his or her way in a world of constant change. The mind is a customhouse, as Hawthorne suggested in the preface to *The Scarlet Letter*, through which the individual was always passing. It is this pattern of waking up to new worlds in the old one of human necessity that characterizes American (or "New World") literature from Washington Irving to Kate Chopin. For Chopin's Edna, however, the awakening results not (as in Irving's case) with the birth of a storyteller but with the end of the story. As the "twenty-ninth bather," Edna drowns in her own auto-erotic desire. In other words, she wakes up to discover that the story of life had been a fiction all along.

It was, indeed, the fiction of autoeroticism, best illustrated by Whitman's twenty-ninth bather, whose example opened this chapter and which, I believe (without any evidence other than the parallel between this passage from "Song of Myself" and the novel), directly suggested Edna's dilemma to Chopin. The realm of romance, as Edna discovers, is the state of infatuation, of being in love with the idea of being in love. Only the self can perpetuate this self-reflexive state. In this context, I would qualify my earlier note (#10) that Chopin privileges heterosexuality in the novel. There is an element of homosexuality in the story in the sense that homosexual acts are—to borrow the words of Michael Moon—"symmetrically reversible in ways that corresponding heterosexual acts are not."[34] It would be gross exaggeration to say that Edna seeks this kind of "romance" in either Madame Ratignolle or Reisz. Yet she is at least androgynous enough to look for a truly reciprocal, reversible kind of love. In "Fedora" (1895) the female protagonist is attracted to a male, "though his nearness troubled her." Fedora is more drawn to his sister, who bears a "vivid, poignant" resemblance to her brother and upon whom she bestows "a long, penetrating kiss upon her mouth."[35] Here, I think, Chopin is exploring the options of the woman confined to the world of romance. The kiss is neither returned nor appreciated by the astonished sister. With Edna the options also disappear. She cannot find someone as loving as herself—someone feminine enough to reciprocate her version and vision of romance. All that remains is the self-begotten self that Whitman also dramatized in section 11 of "Song of Myself."

12 : Dreiser's Novel About a Nun

In this final chapter on authorship in the American Renaissance as extended to 1900 and to *Sister Carrie*, I want to begin with two assertions that run counter to the critical consensus about Theodore Dreiser's work. The first is that Dreiser's first novel is his finest, not *An American Tragedy* (1925), essentially his last. The second is that Dreiser is not—at his best—an awkward stylist per se. Such assertions would no doubt take up my entire chapter, but they will have to wait for another chapter in possibly another book. For my present purpose, they are merely preliminary to my task of examining Dreiser's success in *Sister Carrie* as the culminating fiction about the American woman (waking up) at the end of the nineteenth century. Suffice to say that whereas Clyde Griffiths is largely a composite of actual victims of the American Dream of material success, Carrie—as Ellen Moers and others have observed—comes almost exclusively from the author's life and that of his family, especially his wayward, working sisters. Carrie's story, for example, does not depend on court documents and newspaper accounts (relating to the Chester Gillette case and others in *An American Tragedy*) but on the inevitable myth about courtly (and of course illicit) love as it is transformed into a concupiscence for worldly goods after the Industrial Revolution and the evolution of capitalism. On the second point it may be observed that Dreiser's colloquial redundancies often serve his story by underpinning its realism. Carrie is described (in an example often cited as indicative of the author's prose style) as having "four dollars in money" as she journeys toward Chicago.¹ Yet this is a precisely apt expression of one who had little "money" to speak of in the small town of Columbia City that she is leaving for the first (and last) time. Indeed, the expression, reflecting the vagaries of currency speculation, was heard often in America during the era in which *Sister Carrie* takes place. Generally, Dreiser's language comes directly from his origins in the American heartland of hard knocks. His first novel most urgently reflects the memory of his adolescence and family troubles, beginning with the title of the book, which legend has it he scrawled across the top of a half sheet of copy paper without knowing exactly what story it would introduce.² *Sister Carrie* is about "sisters"—the girl next door or, better, one's own sister, who would often be called by family members "Sister" or "Sis." In the ideal she was imagined as virginal as a nun; in the real (where fantasy is also never absent) she was potentially voluptuous in her innocence.

As Richard Lingeman points out in the latest biography, Dreiser saw his future wife, Sarah Osborne White, in precisely these contradictory terms. In the ideal of Jug (her nickname) "the sensual and the saintly had coalesced."³ Jug offered Dreiser the stable background he lacked from his itinerant family originating in Terre Haute, Indiana. Yet as his partially censored (by Jug, who saved them) courtship letters reveal, Dreiser longed to despoil the virgin in a multitude of ways that often led to frantic autoeroticism. Jug was the woman imagined onto the pedestal of courtly, illicit love (he once pictured her in Union Square, posing in various "classical attitudes"), but the reality of her and of their marriage soon doomed them to a lifelong separation. Carrie, of course, is the embodiment of these counteracting forces, which Dreiser characterizes generally as duty and desire. Although her first lover, Charlie Drouet, sees her initially as an easy addition to his string of sexual conquests, the virgin in her comes out to conquer, not only Drouet but his rival, George Hurstwood, when she plays the part of Laura in Augustin Daly's *Under the Gaslight*. As Moers notes, "When Carrie launches into her grandiloquent curtain speech, about the pricelessness of a woman's love, Hurstwood feels the appeal is directed straight at him and can hardly repress his tears, while Drouet bubbles over with resolutions: 'He would marry her, by George! She was worth it'" (p. 192).⁴

Hurstwood is the dubious winner in this dance of desire and ultimately stands under another gaslight as the price he pays for the elusive Carrie. This is because *Sister Carrie* is neither the story of a nun nor the portrait of a lady. As a sister of charity, her attention span is all too brief, forgetting almost completely about the bedraggled Hurstwood after giving him nine dollars during their chance meeting on Broadway (p. 477). And unlike Isabel Archer, Carrie will not endure a marriage very long after it becomes apparent that she has been deceived. Drouet and Hurstwood become infatuated finally with the stage version of Carrie, the character of Laura in Daly's play, a child of the slums who, adopted by aristocracy, takes up the role of a lady. Though actually highborn herself, she is always in danger of falling. The character is played by Carrie "Madenda," yet another fiction for Caroline Meeber, whose surname is phonetically close to "amoeba." Carrie's career literally comes to life through the fiction of romantic love. Beginning with only the slightest chance of success, Carrie moves through her world by projecting herself (offstage as well as on) as something she is not—a warm-blooded creature in a cold-blooded world. Generally, Carrie has been seen as Dreiser saw most of his characters: as wisps in the wind—in Carrie's case, the virgin cast into urban nature. Yet Dreiser's admiration for the strong was as operative as his pity for the weak, and thus he presents Carrie as one of the survivors. Later Dreiser would celebrate this type more fully in "The Trilogy of Desire," but in *Sister Carrie* he was the first to introduce the woman in such a role. As such, Carrie is the first working woman in American fiction to be realistically drawn from a world measured exclusively by money. Dreiser knew of such lives firsthand from the earthy experiences of his five older sisters, especially Mame and Emma, who, like Carrie, used their bodies as the only commodity they had to barter themselves out of poverty. Such a class of women, when not directly prostituting themselves as mistresses to rich men, worked long hours in arduous, assembly-line jobs where they were often seduced by money. Carrie, however, is not a "worker" per se; her experience in the shoe factory in Chicago proves that. Rather, she is Lily Bart without the social pedigree. Bart's social standing as a "lady" in Edith Wharton's *The House of Mirth* (1905) is, of course, what finally damns her. Carrie, on the other hand, is beyond this kind of compromise. While she shares with Lily the need for money (from men), this is the only thing Carrie shares. Born poor instead of rich, she is free from the constraints of the nineteenth-century male idea about women—which is to say, the doctrine of ladyhood instead of womanhood.

Money is the major problem to these otherwise liberated women of the turn-of-the-century middle class, but of course it had been a problem for Dame Van Winkle, the "termagant wife" who labors to keep up the patrimonial farm that Rip has allowed to fall into disrepair. Long ago seduced into marriage, she now finds herself in the state of wifehood (and then widowhood) that ought to make anyone "termagant." Mrs. Chillingworth finds herself in the same abandoned situation and after the birth of her illicit child is forced to work as a seamstress. In both cases, the woman is also cut off from love *and* money. For all their imagined ability to "swim, row, ride, wrestle, shoot, run, strike, retreat, advance, resist, defend themselves," Whitman's women were idealized versions of his mother and one sister who married alcoholics, as well as another who married an uncaring, egotistical landscape painter. In all three cases, these husbands to the Whitman women were also unlucky in the world of money. Dickinson felt that women were cut off after marriage not only from the sisterhood of youth and female friendship but from the kind of control that money ultimately determines. Isabel Archer, for all her questing after the ideal mate, is married for her money, and Edna Pontellier is martyred by her desire to separate men from money. Carrie, it might be said, is the first survivor in this matrimonial jungle. We follow her as if in a silent movie in which the heroine's movements are described in legends as melodramatic as Dreiser's chapter titles: "A Magnet Attracting: A Waif Amid Forces," "What Poverty Threatened: Of Granite and Brass," "We Question of Fortune: Four-Fifty a Week," and so on for forty-seven chapters. Yet the melodrama *is* the drama in such lives which set dreams against the drama of defeat. Dreiser has Carrie view the world with such a lens because that is the way he had seen life in the great cities from Chicago to New York.

As Larzer Ziff observes, "When he came to write, Dreiser had to pour his entire energy into the material he wished to present and depend upon matter rather than manner for his meanings."[5] This is not merely because he lacked formal training (having only one year of college, at Indiana University), but because his life up to the 1890s had been full of "true stories" about his brothers and sisters. There was the oldest, Paul Dresser the Broadway songwriter (whose pre-ragtime hits included "On the Banks of the Wabash" and "My Gal Sal"); he represented for the young Theodore the possibilities of American material success. There was Emma, the second-oldest sister, who ran off to New York with embezzler L. A. Hopkins; her experience was the basis for *Sister Carrie*. There was Sylvia, who became pregnant by the son of a wealthy merchant in Terre Haute who refused to marry her; hers is the "story" that led to *Jennie Gerhardt* (1911). There was Rome Dreiser, the second-eldest son, the wandering petty criminal, and Dreiser himself, who once embezzled funds from an employer; together they probably suggested how an economically deprived American could, faced with the relentless promise of material success, very possibly go the way of Clyde Griffiths in *An American Tragedy*. *The "Genius"* (1915) is closely autobiographical in its recall of Dreiser's authorial and personal life after the initial publication of *Sister Carrie*. *The Financier* (1912) and *The Titan* (1914), though paradigmatic adaptations of Herbert Spencer's idea of "the survival of the fittest" (his phrase before Darwin's), are brought down to real life by the impoverished background of Frank Cowperwood. A storyteller above all else, Dreiser was indeed moved by the matter of life much more than its manner.

In the case of women, this was doubly true. He had watched his beloved mother struggle against economic adversity and a husband whose religious fanaticism kept her children for too long out of the proper schools. He had seen his sisters become—largely because of that difficult life—kept women. It might be said that Dreiser did in fiction for the American working woman what Henry James did for the nonworking American female, especially in *The Portrait of a Lady*. He appears to have employed a sixth sense in depicting their heartfelt aspirations, their dreams of material success and the leisure to enjoy it. The cover of *Ev'ry Month: The Woman's Magazine of Literature and Music* (as it was eventually subtitled), which Dreiser edited in the mid-1890s, pictured a young woman reading and dreaming, dressed in the smartest fashion of the day. Established to sell sheet music (including Paul Dresser's works), the magazine also sold the American Dream to the New American Woman who could not afford to look to Europe for her liberation. In other words, Dreiser's women never have the chances of James's women but are locked into the cycle of the American middle-class economy. They live vicariously much of the time, waiting for their chance. Note, for example, Dreiser's description of Carrie's fanciful reaction to landing the job at $4.50 a week in the Chicago shoe factory:

> For the next two days Carrie indulged in the most high-flown speculations. An excellent essay on the art of high living might well be compiled out of the thoughts of those who, like her, are anxiously anticipating the arrival of a small income. . . . Carrie plunged recklessly into privileges and amusements which would have been more becoming had she been cradled a child of fortune. With ready will and quick mental selection she scattered her meagre four-fifty per week with a swift and graceful hand. It was spent many times over in car fare alone, sight-seeing. . . . The round of theatres with delightful seats was a simple matter. Her certain income covered it all. Her purse, now unchangingly filled with it, was carried into every avenue and every store. Portions of its fullness were passed over every counter and broken into small change a thousand times, and yet it did not fail. Silks, woolens, lingerie and fine feathers— the necessities and frivolities of fashion as she understood it—all strained its marketing power, but it did not break. (pp. 29–30)

Thus Carrie's dream as she sits in her rocking chair. Dreiser immediately contrasts it with the crushing reality of a woman in Carrie's economic class. "Her sister Minnie," he writes, "knew nothing of these rather wild cerebrations. . . . She was too busy scrubbing the kitchen woodwork and calculating the purchasing power of eighty cents for Sunday's dinner" (p. 30).

Her grim sense of reality becomes Carrie's the next week when Carrie begins her labor in the shoe factory, subsequently becomes ill, and finally succumbs to Drouet's seductions. Dreiser suggests that her working conditions might have been better under "the new socialism" (p. 39), but that is of course not what saves her. Later, in discussing Hurstwood's weak "chemism" (the balance of duty and desire in one's moral constitution), Dreiser hints at the utopianism of Spencer that suggests that "men are still led by instincts before they are regulated by knowledge" (p. 269). He had also subscribed briefly to the pseudopsychology of Elmer Gates, but these notions gave priority to his belief in the other Spencerian idea of "the survival of the fittest." Carrie does not succeed through any social programs or even through

Emersonian self-reliance (which, it has been recently forgotten, recognized the larger needs of society), but by luck and pluck. As Richard Lehan remarks, "The world of *Sister Carrie* . . . is not totally a realm of gratuity. Chance is 'only another name for our ignorance of causes,' Dreiser says in his 'Notes on Life.' Behind what appears to be a series of disconnected and random events in the novel is a realm of causality."[6] Carrie, of course, has only a naive sense of causality, but she looks out for herself in ways Isabel Archer and even Edna Pontellier never would have considered. She neither gives her allegiance to one man nor allows herself to become completely lost in the illusions of romantic love. The concessions she makes with her body are amorally regarded because her youth and beauty are the only currency she possesses in a world where women still lack political suffrage and the means of making a fast fortune.

Carrie is the newest American Woman, one who breaks out of the domestic cycle and survives in the world of men and money. Although she comes close to suffering the fates of her predecessors in American fiction (not only the Isabels but the Maggies), she escapes because she is committed to nothing but the male notion of material success. Accordingly, she lacks Hester Prynne's capacity for atonement, Isabel Archer's ethical considerations, Edna Pontellier's semiromantic reasoning—in a word, the ideology of the domesticated female. This woman wakes up to the reality of her prefeminist condition, which marks off the ethereal presence of the woman in the nineteenth century from her absolute physicality in the twentieth. Dreiser, of course, was no feminist and in fact a philanderer who once bragged that he had wooed away the girlfriend of Floyd Dell.[7] Women to him were directly symbolic of material success. In *Dawn* (1931), the first volume of his autobiography (though published after *Newspaper Days* [1922]), he confesses to his weak "chemism" with regard to the sexual appeal of women: "Let us say that my blood has been either ill or well compounded, as you will. But because of this pre-arranged system . . . I have thrilled again and again from head to toe, the sight of this particular formula (female) resulting in the invasion of homes, the destruction of happy arrangements among others, lies, persuasions, this, that. In short, thus moved, I have adored until satiated."[8] Although he personally (and so vigorously) viewed the woman as an object of lust, he could—because of his sisters' example—also appreciate the

Dreiser's Novel About a Nun

dilemma of her workaday world. In one of the scenes omitted from the Doubleday version of *Sister Carrie*, where Carrie tries to get on the stage in Chicago after quarreling with Drouet, Dreiser captures the cynicism of the stage manager who tries unsuccessfully to seduce her, dismissing her to a fellow employee as "just another pair of tights" for the chorus line (p. 255). Dreiser knew well, especially from his observations of brother Paul's lowbrow society, what the single working woman was mainly valued for. And certainly Drouet and Hurstwood know it. The original version of the novel reveals them both as more excessive philanderers, Drouet even having secret trysts while living with Carrie. The Old Butterfly, we are told, "was a man whom it was impossible to bind to any one object long. He had but one idol—the perfect woman. He found her enshrined in many a pretty petticoat" (p. 105). Hurstwood, too, "loved to go out and have a good time"—which occasionally included "the gilded chambers of shame with which Chicago was then so liberally cursed" (p. 44). Dreiser speaks here with a divided mind that sees social morality as possibly good but beyond the reach of most human beings; in its place there was only sham and hypocrisy. In an earlier chapter, I have remarked that the difference between Hester Prynne and Carrie Meeber is that the first fell in love with a druid while the latter became involved with a "drummer." That is to say, money replaces the power of religion (and thus the source of the male's social prominence) in postcolonial America. Yet Carrie is seduced by the same kind of authority figure. Drouet possesses the material burnish Carrie craves, and Hurstwood merely outdoes Drouet in this department. They both claim to want to make "an honest woman" of Carrie, yet each desires her for her sexuality and vulnerability (the latter made clearer when she plays the character of Laura in Daly's play). Both are rather avuncular in their appeal to Carrie's materialism.

This is true of Dreiser as well, as he paints the portrait of Carrie. Much in the way Hawthorne fell in love with his Galatea in *The Scarlet Letter*, the author of *Sister Carrie* sketched out the autobiographical picture of the woman whose aspirations were kindred to his own. Both writers ultimately changed that relationship in midstream, so to speak. Hawthorne, as I have argued in chapter 2, backed away from the rebellious Hester and her identity with his inmost sexual longings by concocting the editorial pose in "The Custom House" sketch and

[202]

by bringing her back into the ideological fold of the Puritans in the last three chapters of his book. Dreiser, as Donald Pizer and others have pointed out, cleaned up Carrie's image considerably between the original manuscript and the Doubleday version.[9] In both cases, the authors were concerned about the reception of their books with regard to the current standard of morality. Dreiser, of course, was compelled to make the changes because of Doubleday's objections. Writing fifty years after Hawthorne (both novels were written in the space of half a year), Dreiser was prepared to take more chances and speak of life as he had seen it. Yet there is a much more important reason for his candor, and it has to do with his view of women.

Carrie rises as Hurstwood falls. It is her good fortune to be blessed with good looks and a wit ready enough to tell her when it is time to move on to the next lover. Mainly, it is her luck to be born female. That is, if one is to be born poor, it is possibly better to possess something the (male-controlled) world dearly wants—sex. As Walter Benn Michaels remarks, "Feminine sexuality thus turns out to be a kind of biological equivalent to capitalism."[10] In fact, *Sister Carrie* as a story is most compelling in its appeal to our fear of poverty. Dreiser had grown up probably poorer than most literate white people would experience today. There were times in Indiana when he and his siblings would even have to search for loose coals along the railroad tracks to heat their home. He started out in the world with relatively few opportunities, and this is the way Carrie begins her life in the novel. Mainly because of her sex (appeal) she ends that fictional life at the top. Hurstwood, on the other hand, has by the time we meet him in the book already spent his sex appeal in his climb to the manager's position at Chapin and Gore's (Fitzgerald and Moy's in the Doubleday version). In other words, he has already invested his youth in the American economy and must now be satisfied with what he has accumulated. This dilemma as well as its dangers is underscored and projected long before his financial fall. Not only has he spent his youth, but because of the social restrictions of his position in Chicago, he cannot enjoy to the full the Dreiserian fruits of his success—a meaningful (perhaps the wrong word in the world of *Sister Carrie*) relationship with a woman other than his wife, in this case Carrie. He cannot have Carrie without losing his job. Now, of course, many a married male in both Hurstwood's time and today has managed this balancing act either through promiscuous sexual activity or in extra-marital contact with one particular woman who becomes his "mistress." If in the latter case his affair becomes emotionally binding, however, the financial reality of his situation often threatens to reveal his involvement as a romantic illusion. That is, he is soon brought back to reality by a mistress who seeks to become the mistress of his house and home. This is not exactly Hurstwood's situation, but it becomes so when the money begins to run out in New York City and Hurstwood loses his amorous interest in Carrie. Like the word "affair" (discussed in chapter 3), the word "mistress" cuts both ways. Carrie becomes Hurstwood's "mistress" in the modern sense, but she ultimately becomes the "mistress" of the situation, no longer a paramour but a woman in a position of authority (over Hurstwood). The end result is that Hurstwood, already restricted in Chicago by his social status (as a married man and responsible citizen-worker), loses Carrie completely in New York City.

The point I am developing here is that there is in Dreiser's regard for Carrie—for young women in general—a divided feeling, imbedded deeply no doubt in his attitude dating back to puberty and his sexual debut with the baker's daughter in Warsaw, Indiana.[11] On the one hand, he supports his little soldier of (sexual) fortune, but on the other there is a tinge of jealousy. And this feeling is conveyed generally by the juxtaposition of Carrie's rise and Hurstwood's fall. For the woman to get ahead, the male must lose not only his sexual advantage (connubial rights in Hurstwood's case because once he loses his job in New York, Carrie stops sleeping with him) but his ability to compete with the traditional male advantage. In other words, in a capitalistic society of true equals (gender included now), if one is to earn excessively more than *she* needs, somebody else may have to lose more than *he* can afford. This Marxist observation is the basis of Michaels's economically based study of the novel. He sees Dreiser generally applauding Carrie's desire for more and more material goods. Yet as Lehan notes in a helpful corrective to Michaels's rather one-dimensional approach, "by concentrating so heavily on one trope, Michaels represses as much narrative meaning as he explains. . . . Such a reading negates Dreiser's criticism of the sweatshops that he so graphically described at the beginning of the novel, and such a reading belies a kind of higher beauty that the novel is constantly glimpsing and toward which Ames points."[12]

At fault here in this disagreement may be Dreiser himself, who, as I have said, both pitied the victims of capitalism and admired its captains. The same bipolar view obtained when he turned to women. For Dreiser, like Hawthorne with Hester, fell in love with only half of Carrie. This was because the spirit of Carrie as an object of affection was not based altogether on Jug, Dreiser's first wife, who, though she was sexually attractive to Dreiser, impressed him mainly by her level of education and social training. Rather, Carrie is based as much on a woman like Emma, Dreiser's most attractive sister as well as the lover of the main model for Hurstwood. The latter is a woman to be *possessed* mainly for her physical appeal. She symbolizes the good life, and if Hurstwood cannot continue to have her, it must mean that his fortune is turning downward. Of course, in the plot of the novel this is exactly what it means. Dreiser, however, presents in *Sister Carrie* something far more complicated than an economics lesson. For as Ellen Moers has taught us, not only was Carrie a projection of the author's anxieties, but Hurstwood was as well. Indeed, the psychological composite of the author is most acute when both the male and the female are down and out, and it is the female who has the advantage. Three years after the move to New York City, Hurstwood is no longer anyone's object of physical (and thus materialistic) desire, no symbol of success, because by his age (mid-forties) he ought to have already had the money which would have made him desirable, which would have made up for his lost youth (or the energy to make money from nothing). Without youth, of course, Carrie would also be out of luck; but then she would also be out of this novel, which is about feminine sexuality as the symbol of material success. *Sister Carrie* is a novel about a "nun"—about a woman who *looks* innocent but is surely not. Carrie represents the sum of Dreiser's mixed feelings about women.

Her every step upward (the salary increases) is carefully juxtaposed with Hurstwood's decline (the measured count of his dwindling funds). Carrie is the first New Woman in major American fiction (and probably only second to the protagonist in Fanny Fern's *Ruth Hall*) to come away successfully from her encounter with men. Both Isabel and

Edna are doomed by the "Daisy Miller" paradigm which says that middle-class women are of no value after they have abandoned their husbands or violated social decorum. Dreiser's Carrie gets away, but not—it is important to say—without the censure of Hurstwood's decline. Which is to repeat my earlier point that if the woman gains financial and social control of her body, some male must lose his social and sexual advantage. Carrie's sexuality ultimately proves to be stronger than the purses of either Drouet or Hurstwood. In the end, of course, it frees her from having sex with all men, including Ames (who indicates at one point that he is coming to one of her plays not to see the production but to see her). And who is Ames but Dreiser himself? Ames is the fellow who tries to get Carrie to consider bettering herself by taking on more challenging theatrical roles. He also advises her that money will not bring her the inner peace she is evidently (if not too consistently) seeking. First of all, what does this electrical engineer know (or what can we credibly expect him to know) about theater? Second, why should this friend of the materialistic Mrs. Vance (initially Carrie's neighbor in New York) be so genuinely objective? Rather, is not Ames, in his pretentious and moralistic urgings on Carrie, really trying to get the psychological upper hand in the absence of superior capital? Ames may be several cuts above the likes of Drouet and Hurstwood, but he is also a male with sexual longings. If he had met Carrie when she was in economic difficulty, he could—and would—have used his position and (at least ample) money to impress her and thus possess her sexually. As it is, he is superior to Carrie only in education (and not necessarily "inner peace"), and it is this advantage that he subtly uses in his attempt to seduce Carrie (in the original version of the manuscript). This is also Dreiser's last-ditch attempt to hold onto Carrie and thus his total creature comfort. The original version ended with Hurstwood's suicide, and this was its proper ending. For Carrie is lost to both the author and the reader after her success frees her from having to have sex with men for money. Indeed, to bring her back into the novel as listlessly rocking to and fro and wondering what went wrong is to suggest that a woman without a man cannot be happy or fulfilled. This notion is clearly secondary to Dreiser's message that materialism can lead to unhappiness, but the subtext is that the *woman* cannot be satisfied without the product to which such materialism leads—the protection (and thus sexual dominance) of a man.

This point rather abruptly brings us back to Lehan's suggestion about the "kind of higher beauty that the novel is constantly glimpsing and toward which Ames points." There are, as Roger Asselineau has shown us, definite elements of Emersonian romanticism in Dreiser's realism.[13] It was this tradition that no doubt led him to both the pseudophilosophy of Spencer, which sees the ultimate advancement of the species in spite of its earthly condition, and the pseudopsychology of Gates, which holds out for a kind of spiritual (and physical) release. There may also be the tendency in such critics as Asselineau and Lehan (as well as myself) to discover in Dreiser, if not also in the other naturalistic writers beginning with Zola, something other than stark nihilism and pathos. This is, in other words, the Emersonian desire to find beauty in even the worst aspect of nature, something which, when seen in the broader context of the creation, transcends all sordidness and pettiness and their implications for the human race. Yet the "higher beauty," as perhaps Whitman and later Freud have taught us, may ultimately reside in the libido. Dreiser, speaking through Ames, somehow wants Carrie to be *carried away* from the social rabble and enshrined back on that pedestal of lust and love. She is a woman who waits for all of us (men and women alike in the sense of American romanticism), the one who the poet says in a similar poem, "To a Common Prostitute," will make "an appointment" and who will "make preparation to be worthy to meet me." As I have noted in chapter 7, it was redundant of Whitman to call a prostitute "common"; yet it was necessary, one would suppose, to emphasize her rather miraculous capacity for change—miraculous, of course, only in the imagination charged by both sexual desire and spiritual hope. Somehow, Dreiser implies the same hope with his Doubleday ending to the novel, that Carrie will save us all by saving herself—but also that she will *serve us* by serving herself.

This desire for a new beginning at the end of the story is what I have referred to throughout this study as the literary awakening that characterizes great American literature. In *Sister Carrie* Dreiser contrasts his worst fears about society with his highest hopes, and in doing so he discovered the "higher beauty" of life's contradiction and its irony.

Carrie, like Poe's Helen, is finally a "whore," but she is also every American male's sister or mother. The contradiction collapses our idealism, while the irony enshrines our desires. It is this desiderative aspect of life, of course, that makes it interesting, not the utopian solution we might seek out after realizing only its contradiction. American literature, or any literature for that matter, becomes mere social rhetoric without the innate desire to transcend the quotidian. It has often been said that *Sister Carrie* is really Hurstwood's story, but without Carrie the novel would not differ that markedly from Upton Sinclair's *The Jungle* (1906), in which a struggling protagonist is oppressed by the ruthless forces of capitalism. We would pity Hurstwood, of course, as we pity Jurgis in *The Jungle*, but life would nevertheless be reduced to a social or economic problem. Carrie keeps the novel open-ended and thus leaves the reader with his or her possibilities about the meaning of life, or its lack of meaning, and thus the meaning of desire.

  Sister Carrie, it should be said, is Dreiser's first and only "story," the identity-theme that is played out again and again in his subsequent novels. Every writer has such a story, and it is usually his or her "first." It was Hawthorne's first novel (not counting *Fanshawe*), and it was Chopin's first (not counting *At Fault*, which was her apprentice novel)—both of which came at the end of years of writing short stories and sketches. *The Sketch Book* was Irving's "first" in the sense that it was his first single-authored, book-length collection of short stories tied together by the psychological thread of displacement. Though *Moby-Dick* was certainly not Melville's first, it was his first book to be "damned by dollars" *after* its publication instead of before its composition—his first full-length commercial failure (*Mardi* having followed in part the popular paradigm of the travel novel) and his first purely literary success. *The Narrative of Arthur Gordon Pym* is, of course, Poe's only book-length novel. *Walden*, as I have suggested in chapter 6, was the book Thoreau had subconsciously in mind since his earlier memory, which was of Walden Pond. Emerson's "Experience," as Carl F. Strauch has pointed out, was where the essayist's Neoplatonic writings were headed all along.[14] *Leaves of Grass* was Whitman's only "book," indeed what he viewed in "A Backward Glance O'er Travel'd Roads" as an extension of his personality, and "Song of Myself" is his most seminal poem. For Twain it was *The Adventures of Huckleberry Finn*, which brought him back to his childhood memories of innocence and corruption, and *The Portrait of a Lady* was the first novel authored by Henry James instead of Henry James, Jr., and his last as an American writer instead of America's "foreign correspondent." Dickinson's complete oeuvre can probably be reduced in terms of her central theme to be embodied in "Because I Could Not Stop for Death." In other words, there is something primitive and primary about these works that sets them aside from the others they wrote. In Dreiser's case, it is the sister who never returned home (the subject of Paul Dresser's song, "Just Tell Them That You Saw Me"), the prostitute that she may have become, the girl next door who got away, or the mother of twelve who kept the family together. It took Dreiser two major novels before he could write centrally about a male protagonist. He worked somewhat away from this autobiographical subject in the Cowperwood books, only to return in *The "Genius"* and in *An American Tragedy* with Clyde Griffiths. If Carrie is the author's sister, Clyde is his brother. He is the person the youthful Theodore Dreiser might have become, the one who has the same desire but gets a different fate. Which is to say that he believed that the wrong opportunity would not only keep one from developing one's natural talent (in this Dreiser is not only Emersonian but puritanical) but possibly lead that person down the wrong path—much in the way of the subjects of Paul Dresser's sentimental songs.

In American literature of the nineteenth century, the wrong opportunity always leads, however, to the right novel, poem, or "story." It is the central story of "the Bad Boy" or Girl, and never that of the man or woman because the quest is for a lost innocence. Dreiser returned to his boyhood of hardworking mothers and wayward sisters in *Sister Carrie* as earnestly as Irving returned to the mythical past in *The Sketch Book*. These protagonists as well as those studied throughout this book seek out good in evil, or prelapsarian innocence in the trauma of the human condition. Carrie culminates this paradoxical quest for the American ideal. Afterwards—in the twentieth century— such characters tend often to become lost to the pessimism of psychological and economic naturalism as well as to the self-invention of modernism and the relative nihilism of postmodernism. Yet even today—as the narrator of "Night-Sea Journey" attests—the American desire for rebirth (birth in Barth's case) persists. This is because, as in the case of Carrie and the other American protagonists, there always remains the faintest chance of reform and rebirth—a kind of literary and philosophical "Symmes Hole" that will save the protagonist as it (initially) does Pym and, in yet another literary miracle, Ishmael in *Moby-Dick*. Even Edna of *The Awakening*, some (American) critics argue, has achieved a "victory" in her suicide! Isabel might even, in this singularly American point of view, divorce Osmond and start over. Carrie, then, is every American's sister. She is as resilient as Lady Liberty herself, for she represents the freedom to err fatally and yet survive for a new day. Carrie may, as Dreiser observes in the Doubleday ending, "dream such happiness as you may never feel,"[15] but the dream is the reality in America.

Epilogue

uring the fall of 1989, soon after drafting the Dickinson chapter in this book, I had the opportunity of teaching as a Fulbright lecturer at La Sorbonne Nouvelle (Université de Paris-III) and—because Walt Whitman was one of the topics to be covered on that academic year's national examination—giving lectures on the Good Gray Poet at about a dozen universities around France. American professors on their first visits abroad are often surprised at the lack of student participation in class and learn to attribute it to the greater formality of the student-professor relationship in Europe and to the fact that the student is supposed to communicate his or her questions to the visiting professor in what is (to the student) a second language. What surprised me on my third academic sojourn abroad (once to Leningrad and twice to Paris) was how eagerly and intelligently my French students did ask questions. Of course, they had a strong need-to-know because of the *agrégation*, a massive preliminary to qualifying for the doctorate in literature. They asked me, for example, how Whitman originally implemented the ideas of Emerson, what philosophers he had read, what edition of *Leaves of Grass* to study, why the poet kept rewriting and expanding the same book, what is the poet's reputation in the United States today, what is the structure of "Song of Myself" (anybody's guess), and so on.

One question posed repeatedly (after class) by my French students struggling to take in as much information as possible for the *agrégation* was the following. It was first asked in Paris, and then in Bordeaux,

and then in Nice, where I was showered with questions. "If you had
to choose one book to learn as much about Whitman and his work as
possible in a relatively short period of time, what book would that be?"
In the United States, the question is equivalent, of course, to asking
what material will appear on the exam. Students will be students the
world over, but the French version of the old student question in-
trigued me because it reminded me that Whitman was an enormous
topic and as such only one of several large areas of literature and
history that the students had to master for one of their most important
examinations. Other topics on the syllabus that year as well as in years
past had been, for example, only one novel or play per author, but in
Whitman's case one title (and not even all its poems) meant many
books because *Leaves of Grass* had gone through six official, significantly expanded editions and nearly a dozen reprintings equipped
with supplements and revisions during the poet's lifetime.

Even a direct answer to the question (if such were possible) was
problematic. Should I have suggested the second volume of Roger
Asselineau's biography of the poet, which in the best French tradition
treats the work separate from the life? Even here Asselineau's study
depends on his first volume indirectly. I could have recommended
Gay Wilson Allen's definitive life of the poet (meaning that an analysis of the works is woven into the biography), but a more systematic
treatment of the poems is to be found in Allen's *New Walt Whitman
Handbook* (1975), and naming both would have broken the rules of
this challenging French question. A work that seemed to fit better its
confining limits was James E. Miller, Jr.'s *Critical Guide to "Leaves
of Grass"* (1957) or, since "Song of Myself" was receiving most of the
attention, a work by the other Miller of Whitman studies, Edwin Haviland Miller's recently published *Walt Whitman's "Song of Myself": A
Mosaic of Interpretations* (1989). The reader conversant with Whitman
scholarship will note that with the exception of the last title named
here, all these are old books by established scholars (as is Edwin Haviland Miller with his multi-volume edition of *The Correspondence*
[1961–67] and the study entitled *Walt Whitman's Poetry: A Psychological Journey* [1968]). These individuals along with others retrieved
Whitman's reputation from the New Critics and their scorn in the
1920s and 1930s for biography and the poem with ragged edges; they
established the first reliable texts and launched the first modern theo-

ries about *Leaves of Grass*. Their humanistic approach to a poet who found his roots in Transcendentalism is now out of fashion in the United States, or at least at the Modern Language Association, where Whitman is now valued for his resistance to Cartesian fictions, his celebration of homosexuality, his subversive calls for social reform in the poetry—in short, the New Historicist approach with which Betsy Erkkila cleverly "re-visions" the barbaric bard in *Whitman the Political Poet* (1989) or M. Wynn Thomas's *The Lunar Light of Whitman's Poetry* (1987) or Ezra Greenspan's *Walt Whitman and the American Reader* (1990). I mention here the strongest of the titles in this new methodology, not the weakest—of which there is a growing number.

I had come to Paris the first time as an "Old Historicist," which is to say a scholar who combines the most empirically based history and biography with the imaginative techniques of the New Critics. Such practitioners were already going out of style in the United States (though that news had not yet reached Texas and the other academic enclaves outside of Yale and Johns Hopkins—at least not to the extent that Deconstructionism and its neo-Marxist offshoots were becoming mandatory approaches for a successful career). Between the time of my first visit to Paris in the winter and spring of 1984 and my second in 1989, these methodologies had swept through American English departments, turning the MLA convention programs into highbrow versions of a popular culture association agenda. Not unaffected by these changes, I was prepared this time to offer my French students the trendiest methodologies and New Historicist approaches to Whitman—Whitman and gender, Whitman and politics, Whitman and sexuality, Whitman and language, Whitman and skepticism, and so on. The response I generally received even to the suggestion of such avenues of investigation reminded me that I had missed the intellectual/political heyday of Sartre and Lacan in France, if not Derrida's in America. "Teach the poetry!" my students (and French colleagues) declared—for the topic to be studied for the *agrégation* was *Leaves of Grass*, not primarily (or exclusively) the linguistic and social forces that had supposedly brought the poems into existence. Many American academics sold on these postmodern approaches to literature think that merely because the critical "revolution" started in Paris French intellectuals one and all have converted as they have. The French as well as their fellow Europeans are interested in literature not only as a function of language but as a miracle of the imagination. With Whitman, the French were interested in such topics as *Leaves of Grass* as an epic of the self, Whitman's poetics of space, the poet's obsession with the body beautiful, his celebration of both unity and multiplicity, and so on.

This observation brings me back to the question about the single wonderbook for the study of Walt Whitman. That book is, of course, *Leaves of Grass*. Teaching in France allowed me the freedom to teach the poetry without any apologies, to teach literature generally without having to wink every time the word "metaphysical" was implied. This is not to say that the French are not acutely aware of the challenges to traditional literary approaches but merely to suggest that they are not, as I have already suggested, as enamored of the "new" as their American counterparts. The difference is that healthy European skepticism which resists the (American) notion that Original Sin is a venial sin. This American idealism, what Terence Martin calls the "negative structures" of our ideology, is probably what distinguishes the United States from other countries and cultures. American idealism began with the antinomianism of the Puritans and fructified with the Arminian reforms that introduced Unitarianism, Emerson, and (later) secular humanism. It has been most clearly and recently seen in the antiwar movement of the Vietnam era as well as its postwar cynicism with regard to the old liberal consensus that American society, despite its ills, is the best, last hope for democracy. Since their beginnings, Americans have wanted to start anew, to wake up without sin. One of the most useful discussions of this phenomenon is Martin's essay in *American Literature*, which helped me to open this study about literary awakenings. In it he cites the speech of a "mentor-type" character in Sylvester Judd's *Margaret*—in which it is suggested that much of "the Old World on its passage to the New was lost overboard":

> We have no monarchical supremacy, no hereditary prerogatives, no
> patent nobility, no Kings, . . . There are no fairies in our meadows,
> and no elves to spirit away our children. Our wells are drugged by
> no saint, and of St. Winifred we have never heard. . . . We have no
> resorts for pilgrims, no shrines for the devout, no summits looking
> into Paradise. . . . All these things our fathers left behind in
> England. . . . Our atmosphere is transparent, unoccupied, empty

from the bottom of our wells to the zenith, and throughout the entire horizontal plane.[1]

It is not surprising, therefore, that American critics in the post-Vietnam era would want to cast off the old part of the New that they think got their country into Vietnam in the first place. Hence, the rampant revisionism in the apprehension of literature, which is suspected of reinforcing "imperialistic" attitudes while passing as subversive commentary on American society.

None of these changes would have surprised Whitman, who—as I have noted—was the first to challenge the genteel notion of literature. As a former printer and newspaper editor aware of the rapid changes in print technology, he sensed a broader audience for "literature" and with it a need for the American vernacular's emphasis on the real as well as the ideal.[2] The book that most students read opens with a cluster called "Inscriptions" and a little poem that attempts to sum up the main ideas in *Leaves of Grass*. But Whitman's "book," what he came to view as his other self, truly begins with "Song of Myself," a poem so personal and yet at the same time so universal that it was probably beyond naming when it was first published (it had no title in the first 1855 edition and became "Song of Myself" only in the 1881–82 edition). If *Leaves of Grass* is the one book to read, this is probably its best poem. It is about starting over with oneself. Emerson called it, or the book of twelve poems that appeared in 1855, "the beginning of a great career"—unaware that the writer was already thirty-seven years old and had written more than a few conventional poems and stories. Not only is the poem a new beginning, it is full of beginnings. "The press of my foot to the earth," the poem announces in section 14, "springs a hundred affections."[3] In section 28 he asks, "Is this then a touch? quivering me to a new identity" (p. 57). Whitman may be waking up to a new world in the best American tradition, but he is not so lost in that discovery as to fall victim to the idealism of Judd's "mentor-type" character. First of all, the poet is a "brother" figure, not a father type. He does not "repel the past" (p. 711) but absorbs the old into the new. Like Emerson (in a different vernacular), Whitman merely tells the sibling-reader what he sees and urges him or *her* (Whitman's usage long before it became prescribed by the MLA's manual on non-sexist language) to see it alone: "You shall not look through my eyes either, nor take things from me,/You shall listen to all sides and filter them from your self" (p. 30). Second, Whitman (unlike the early Emerson) does not leave out "evil" or the body and its preoccupation with decay and death. He might be "satisfied," "see, dance, laugh, sing" (p. 31) at one point in the poem, but at another he is "the hounded slave":

> I wince at the bite of the dogs,
> Hell and despair are upon me, crack and again crack the
> marksmen,
> I clutch the rails of the fence, my gore dribs, thinn'd with the ooze
> of my skin,
> I fall on the weeds and stones,
> The riders spur their unwilling horses, haul close,
> Taunt my dizzy ears and beat me violently over the head with
> whip-stocks. (pp. 66–67)

"Agonies," the poet says, "are one of my changes of garments" (p. 67). In fact, Whitman is the quintessential quick-change artist of American literature. One never quite knows where he will turn up. "Failing to fetch me at first keep encouraged," he states at the end of the poem, "Missing me one place search another" (p. 89).

Admitting that he constantly contradicted himself, Whitman said he contained "multitudes." This is because he saw life as a miraculous contradiction—the contradiction of life and death, of the body and the soul:

> Has any one supposed it lucky to be born?
> I hasten to inform him or her it is just as lucky to die, and I know
> it.
> I pass death with the dying and birth with the new-wash'd babe,
> and am not contain'd between my hat and boots. (p. 35)

This last line, we should remember, comes from the "poet of the Body" as well as the "poet of the Soul" (p. 48). Rather than insist upon resolving the contradictions of life (as even Emerson tried in his writings up to and perhaps beyond "Experience"), Whitman revels in their paradoxical nature. His original appreciation and articulation of life's dualities are probably what keeps the poet "modern" in the postmodern age, that is to say ever up-to-date with the American love of change. In 1855 he was ahead of his time. In 1892 time (his time) caught up with him. Yet slightly more than one hundred years later, Whitman remains ahead of our time—always one step beyond our fashionable paradigms about language and politics. *Leaves of Grass*—the one book for Whitman study—is, like death itself, simply unde-constructible because it resists the worst aspects of postmodernism, the tendency to see life as *posthumous*. Every time we read that book we startle over his way with words, the psychic power he somehow derives from language, and thus we start over with the poet. As in "The Sleepers," we wander all night in his vision to wake up as one of the "journeymen divine" (p. 426). This poem, about the most fa-mous dream in American literature, exemplifies Whitman's *literary* capacity to "merge" with the night in order to reinvent the day when we first surmised ourselves as sleepers in the amniotic waters of mor-tality. "O night," the poet addresses the darkness, which stands not only for death but for the mother of life,

Why should I be afraid to trust myself to you?
I am not afraid, I have been well brought forward by you,
I love the rich running day, but I do not desert her in whom I lay
    so long,
I know not how I came of you and I know not where I go with you,
    but I know I came well and shall go well.
I will stop only a time with the night, and rise betimes,
I will duly pass the day O my mother, and duly return to you.
    (p. 433)

Thus, the recent centennial of this *person's* death was merely another *birth*day for the poet's life in a literature that refuses to be fully ex-plained by one critical study—or any of them, for that matter. "If you want me again," the poet tells the twentieth century at the close of "Song of Myself," "look for me under your boot-soles" (p. 89). Ad-dressed to contemporary readers, it is as if the poet died right after writing the poem. And so he does—only to wake up again to the be-ginning every time we begin the poem. For this is the life of literature, whose language is more than the sum of words or barren signifiers in a book: "Camerado, this is no book,/Who touches this touches a man, /.../I spring from the pages into your arms—decease calls me forth" (p. 505).

Epilogue

And so it is with the other great works discussed in this volume. As acknowledged classics of American literature, they remain beyond deconstruction or the exclusive definition of any one approach or "book" of criticism, including this one. The "office" of *The Scarlet Letter* or *Moby-Dick* or *The Portrait of a Lady* is literature, the unique combination of internal and external human landscapes. The "one book" for Whitman or any of the other writers studied here is his or her greatest book—that is, not a "book" at all but the recorded genius of the person who wrote it. It is the work in which the absolute best of that genius "springs" from the pages into the arms of the reader, the "book" that always brings the author back to life for us. It is the American work that brings *us* back to life as Americans. We "start over" in the best American fashion with Dreiser in *Sister Carrie* as we do with Irving in *The Sketch Book*. This is so because such works reflect the nature of the American experience, which is—always—to begin again, regardless (or perhaps *because*) of previous national origin or ethnic heritage. Just as the epilogue in *Moby-Dick* serves that story as a prologue, the American experience as it is dramatized in the other classics discussed here always ends at the beginning of the story.

Notes

1. IRVING'S PARADIGM

1. *The Sketch Book*'s only competitor, as James M. Cox observes in *Recovering Literature's Lost Ground: Essays in American Autobiography* (Baton Rouge: Louisiana State University Press, 1989), p. 19, is Franklin's *Autobiography*. Yet that book, while the first to define the American Post-Puritan Self, comes from the world of work and politics, not from the underworld of dreams that informs the work of Hawthorne, Melville, and other writers discussed in this volume. Another candidate in this competition for "Number One" (always an American fascination) is Crèvecoeur, yet his primary interest is with the absence of everything European—kings, feudalism, and so on—political rather than philosophical or literary in its desire for a new world. For the most recent and best "cross-cultural" study of this French-American, see Gay Wilson Allen and Roger Asselineau, *St. John de Crèvecoeur: The Life of an American Farmer* (New York: Viking, 1987), especially pp. 32–45.

2. *The Sketch Book of Geoffrey Crayon, Gent,* ed. Haskell Springer (Boston: Twayne Publishers, 1978), p. 10. Subsequent references to *The Sketch Book* are to this edition.

3. See Albert J. von Frank, "The Man That Corrupted Sleepy Hollow," *Studies in American Fiction* 15 (Fall 1987), pp. 129–43.

4. *Collected Works of Ralph Waldo Emerson,* ed. Joseph Slater et al. (Cambridge: Harvard University Press, 1983), III, p. 27.

5. See Jeffrey Rubin-Dorsky, "Washington Irving: Sketches of Anxiety," *American Literature* 58 (December 1986), pp. 499–522. See also his *Adrift in the Old World: The Psychological Pilgrimage of Washington Irving* (Chicago: University of Chicago Press, 1988), pp. 65–122.

6. Kenneth S. Lynn, "Washington Irving Saw the American Past—Sunnyside Up," *The Smithsonian* 14 (August 1983), p. 92.

7. "The American Scholar," p. 70.

8. William L. Hedges, *Washington Irving: An American Study, 1802–1832* (Baltimore: Johns Hopkins University Press, 1965), p. 145.

9. Terence Martin, "The Negative Structures of American Literature," *American Literature* 57 (March 1985), pp. 1–22.

2. HAWTHORNE'S AWAKENING IN THE CUSTOMHOUSE

1. *The Scarlet Letter*, ed. William Charvat et al. (Columbus: Ohio State University Press, 1962), p. 43. Further references to the novel are to this text.

2. Arlin Turner, *Nathaniel Hawthorne: A Biography* (New York: Oxford University Press, 1980), p. 188. See also Nina Baym, "Nathaniel Hawthorne and His Mother: A Biographical Speculation," *American Literature* 54 (March 1982), pp. 12, 20. Baym's is a feminist interpretation of the mother's influence on Hawthorne's fiction, but one that also stresses Hawthorne's vague sense of guilt about his mother, which is implied in the character of Dimmesdale.

3. Turner, p. 189.

4. Turner, p. 193.

5. *Letters of Herman Melville*, ed. Merrell R. Davis and William H. Gilman (New Haven: Yale University Press, 1960), p. 142.

6. Edwin Cady, Introduction to *The Scarlet Letter* (Columbus, Ohio: Merrill Publishing Company, 1969), p. xiv.

7. *Letters of Herman Melville*, p. 133.

8. *Nathaniel Hawthorne: The Letters, 1843–1853*, ed. Thomas Woodson, et al. (Columbus: Ohio State University Press, 1985), XVI, p. 312.

9. *Hawthorne: The Letters, 1843–1853*, p. 305.

10. Nathaniel Hawthorne, *Twice-Told Tales*, ed. William Charvat et al. (Columbus: Ohio State University Press, 1974), p. 435.

11. David S. Reynolds, *Beneath the American Renaissance: The Subversive Imagination in the Age of Emerson and Melville* (New York: Alfred A. Knopf, 1988).

12. Edwin Haviland Miller, *Salem Is My Dwelling Place: A Life of Nathaniel Hawthorne* (Iowa City: University of Iowa Press, 1991), p. 291.

13. Turner, p. 189.

14. *The Blithedale Romance and Fanshawe*, ed. William Charvat et al. (Columbus: Ohio State University Press, 1964), p. 1.

15. For a "public" reading of *The Scarlet Letter*, see Sacvan Bercovitch, *The Office of the Scarlet Letter* (Baltimore: Johns Hopkins University Press, 1991), which subordinates the personal and psychological aspects of the novel to the influence of American "ideology": that the New

World (from Puritan theocracy to mid-nineteenth-century democracy) distinguished itself from the Old World (of failed revolutions beginning with Cromwell) through the historically pre-ordained process of "peaceful amelioration" and "spreading enlightenment." In other words, Hester's "return" to America and the dictations of the Letter A ("America"?) reflected Hawthorne's belief that the American historical process is providential in terms of social order over individual freedom. This ideological reading may account for Dimmesdale's return from the Dark Wood of passion as well as that of his creator from the customhouse of the imagination, as I argue. It does not, however, explain Hester's acquiescence to Dimmesdale's final insistence that they can never be together because of the "law" they broke: she accepts this "office" of the letter only when no other choice is available. "Shall we not meet again? . . . [she pleads as her lover dies] Surely, surely, we have ransomed one another, with all this woe!" (p. 256). The question maintains the same level of social defiance of her earlier invitation to him in the Dark Wood (p. 197, cited earlier). Later Hester returns to New England "of her own free will," as Hawthorne concludes (p. 263), but, as Bercovitch concedes, perhaps inadvertently (*The Office*, p. 91), "Hawthorne must bring her back, and, more than that, must force her [and himself] to resume to the A 'freely and voluntarily,' of her own free will." Hawthorne ultimately backs out of his romance (of the self). Yet it is only after he has returned from the flight that only fiction can allow that he creates the "ideological" fiction of her social automatism.

16. See Jerome Loving, "Pretty in Pink: Young Goodman Brown and New World Dreams" in *Critical Essays on Hawthorne's Short Stories*, ed. Albert J. von Frank (Boston: G. K. Hall, 1990).

17. John Winthrop, *The History of New England*, ed. James Savage (Boston: Phelps and Farnham, 1825), I, p. 166.

18. *Hawthorne: The Letters, 1843–1853*, p. 421.

19. *Hawthorne: The Letters, 1843–1853*, p. 402.

20. Turner, p. 193.

21. *Nathaniel Hawthorne: The English Notebooks*, ed. Randall Stewart (New York: Russell and Russell, 1941, 1962), p. 225.

22. Turner, p. 194.

23. *Hawthorne: The Letters, 1843–1853*, p. 313n.

24. Rose Hawthorne Lathrop, *Memories of Hawthorne* (New York: AMS Press, 1969 [1897]), p. 173. For a more critically avant-garde reading of Sophia Hawthorne's headache, what David Leverenz calls "a rare moment in the history of American reader responses," see his *Manhood*

and the American Renaissance (Ithaca: Cornell University Press, 1989), pp. 259–78.

25. Turner, pp. 140–41.

26. *Moby-Dick*, ed. Harrison Hayford and Hershel Parker (New York: W. W. Norton, 1967), p. 378.

3. MELVILLE'S HIGH ON THE SEAS

1. *Moby-Dick*, ed. Harrison Hayford and Hershel Parker (New York: W. W. Norton, 1967), p. 127. Further references are to this text.

2. *The Sketch Book of Geoffrey Crayon, Gent*, ed. Haskell Springer (Boston: Twayne Publishers, 1978), p. 11.

3. The raft scene appeared in chapter 3 of *Life on the Mississippi* (1883); "The Town-Ho's Story" appeared in the October 1851 issue of *Harper's New Monthly Magazine*.

4. Edwin Haviland Miller, *Melville* (New York: George Braziller, 1975), passim.

5. Oliver Sacks, *Awakenings* (New York: E. P. Dutton, 1983), pp. 75, 79.

6. Jerome Loving, *Emily Dickinson: The Poet on the Second Story* (Cambridge: Cambridge University Press, 1986), p. 8.

7. *Moby-Dick As Doubloon*, ed. Hershel Parker (New York: W. W. Norton, 1970), p. 12.

8. *Letters of Herman Melville*, ed. Merrell R. Davis and William H. Gilman (New Haven: Yale University Press, 1960), p. 128.

9. *Nathaniel Hawthorne: Tales and Sketches*, ed. Roy Harvey Pearce (New York: Library of America, 1982), p. 288.

10. Ishmael, as William B. Dillingham writes, "is like another kind of Hawthorne who is writing a 'romance' but insisting all the time that it be accepted as a 'novel.'" See his *Melville's Later Novels* (Athens: University of Georgia Press, 1986), p. 28.

11. *Letters*, p. 130.

12. *Letters*, p. 124.

13. *Letters*, p. 125.

14. *The Divine Comedy*, ed. Ernest H. Wilkins (New York: The Modern Library, 1957), p. 144.

15. *The Education of Henry Adams* in *Henry Adams*, ed. Ernest Samuels and Jayne N. Samuels (New York: Library of America, 1983), p. 1071.

16. *Doubloon*, pp. 7–8.

17. *The Scarlet Letter*, ed. William Charvat et al. (Columbus: Ohio State University Press, 1962), p. 48.

18. *Doubloon*, pp. 247–49.

19. Cf. Dillingham, who states that Ishmael "suggests that, ironically, the closer a work of art follows actual life, the more deeply symbolic it is" (*Melville's Later Novels*, p. 34).

20. *Collected Works of Ralph Waldo Emerson*, ed. Alfred R. Ferguson et al. (Cambridge: Harvard University Press, 1971), I, p. 56.

21. Harold Bloom, *Poetry and Repression: Revisionism from Blake to Stevens* (New Haven: Yale University Press, 1976), p. 7.

22. *Collected Works of Ralph Waldo Emerson*, ed. Joseph Slater et al. (Cambridge: Harvard University Press, 1983), III, p. 30.

23. *Nature* in Emerson's *Complete Works* (Boston: Houghton, Mifflin, 1883), I, p. 16.

24. "A Figure a Poem Makes" in *Complete Poems of Robert Frost* (New York: Holt, Rinehart, and Winston, 1961), p. vi.

25. *Lectures and Essays in Criticism*, ed. R. H. Super (Ann Arbor: University of Michigan Press, 1962), p. 270.

26. *Edgar Allan Poe: Poetry and Tales*, ed. Patrick F. Quinn (New York: Library of America, 1984), p. 829.

4. POE'S VOYAGE FROM EDGARTOWN

1. *Edgar Allan Poe: Poetry and Tales*, ed. Patrick F. Quinn (New York: Library of America, 1984), p. 1180. Further references are to this text.

2. Leslie Fiedler, *Love and Death in the American Novel* (New York: Stein and Day, rev. ed., 1966), p. 392. See also Benjamin Franklin Fisher IV, *The Very Spirit of Cordiality: The Literary Uses of Alcohol and Alcoholism in the Tales of Edgar Allan Poe* (Baltimore: Enoch Pratt Free Library, 1978), passim.

3. *Moby-Dick*, ed. Harrison Hayford and Hershel Parker (New York: W. W. Norton, 1967), p. 470.

4. Daniel Hoffman, *Poe Poe Poe Poe Poe Poe Poe* (New York: Doubleday & Company, 1972), p. 277.

5. See William B. Dillingham, *Melville's Later Novels* (Athens: University of Georgia Press, 1986), p. 33.

6. James M. Cox, "Edgar Poe: Style As Pose," *Virginia Quarterly Review* 44 (Winter 1968), p. 73.

7. Fiedler, p. 391.

8. *The Poems of Emily Dickinson*, ed. Thomas H. Johnson (Cambridge: Harvard University Press, 1955), I, p. 116.

9. Hoffman, p. 273.

10. Hoffman, p. 267.

11. Judith L. Sutherland, *The Problematic Fictions of Poe, James, and Hawthorne* (Columbia: University of Missouri Press, 1984), p. 29.

12. Cf. Taylor Stoehr, "Young Goodman Brown and Hawthorne's Theory of Mimesis," *Nineteenth Century Fiction* 23 (March 1969), pp. 393–412.

13. Larzer Ziff, *Literary Democracy: The Declaration of Cultural Independence in America* (New York: Viking Press, 1981), p. 83.

14. Ziff, p. 84.

15. Terence Martin, "The Negative Structures of American Literature," *American Literature* 57 (March 1985), pp. 1–21.

16. See, for example, "The Rites of Assent: Rhetoric, Ritual, and the Ideology of Consensus" in *The American Self: Myth, Ideology, and Popular Culture*, ed. Sam B. Girgus (Albuquerque: University of New Mexico Press, 1981), pp. 5–42.

17. "Water" in *The Early Lectures of Ralph Waldo Emerson*, ed. Stephen E. Whicher and Robert E. Spiller (Cambridge: Harvard University Press, 1959), I, p. 63.

18. *Selected Poetry and Prose of Edgar Allan Poe*, ed. T. O. Mabbott (New York: The Modern Library, 1951), p. 365.

19. Stanley Fish, *Surprised by Sin: The Reader in Paradise Lost* (Berkeley: University of California Press, 1971).

20. Cox, p. 87.

21. Poe claimed that he did not "assume the position of husband" for the first two years of their marriage. See Kenneth Silverman, *Edgar A. Poe: Mournful and Never-Ending Remembrance* (New York: Harper-Collins, 1991), p. 124.

5. EMERSON'S BEAUTIFUL ESTATE

1. Ralph L. Rusk, *The Life of Ralph Waldo Emerson* (New York: Columbia University Press, 1949), p. 508.

2. *Collected Works of Ralph Waldo Emerson*, ed. Joseph Slater et al. (Cambridge: Harvard University Press, 1983), III, p. 29.

3. *The Journals and Miscellaneous Notes of Ralph Waldo Emerson*, ed. William H. Gilman and Alfred R. Ferguson (Cambridge: Harvard Uni-

versity Press, 1963), III, p. 227. For more on Emerson's supposed lack of grief, see Evelyn Barish, *Emerson: The Roots of Prophecy* (Princeton: Princeton University Press, 1989), pp. 29–31 n, who observes that Emerson attested (to his children) that he had not grieved at his father's death in 1811. In that case, the reason was not transcendental—according to Barish—but traumatic in the sense that William Emerson had not been very affectionate to his son. This lack of male parental love was probably part of the reason Emerson responded so warmly to his firstborn son and, accordingly, could not have treated his death in the stoic manner he suggests in "Experience."

4. Gay Wilson Allen, *Waldo Emerson; A Biography* (New York: Viking Press, 1981), p. 438.

5. James M. Cox, "R. W. Emerson: The Circles of the Eye" in *Emerson: Prophecy, Metamorphosis, and Influence*, ed. David Levin (New York: Columbia University Press, 1975), pp. 62–63; this essay is reprinted in James M. Cox, *Recovering Lost Ground: Essays in American Autobiography* (Baton Rouge: Louisiana State University Press, 1989), pp. 78–96. See also B. L. Packer, *Emerson's Fall: A New Interpretation of the Major Essays* (New York: Continuum, 1982), p. 157, and Barish, pp. 99–115 passim (where Hume's influence on the adolescent Emerson may be overstated).

6. *Collected Works of Ralph Waldo Emerson*, ed. Alfred R. Ferguson et al. (Cambridge: Harvard University Press, 1971), I, p. 7.

7. Jerome Loving, *Emerson, Whitman, and the American Muse* (Chapel Hill: University of North Carolina Press, 1982), pp. 178–83.

8. Cox, p. 61. Even this attenuated vision of God in nature can be seen, of course, as the discovery of a "fresh high Romanticism"; see Mark Edmundson, "Emerson and the Work of Melancholia," *Raritan* 6 (Spring 1987), pp. 120–36. Edmundson argues that Emerson reinvented the Self at the expense of his son, whose memory denies the father's Transcendental present.

9. Kenneth Marc Harris, "Reason and Understanding Reconsidered: Coleridge, Carlyle and Emerson," *Essays in Literature* 13 (Fall 1986), pp. 263–81.

10. *Leaves of Grass; Comprehensive Reader's Edition*, ed. Harold W. Blodgett and Sculley Bradley (New York: New York University Press, 1965), p. 81.

11. *The Journals and Miscellaneous Notes of Ralph Waldo Emerson*, ed. A. W. Plumstead and Harrison Hayford (Cambridge: Harvard University Press, 1969), VII, pp. 143–44.

12. *Emerson's Complete Works* (Boston: Houghton, Mifflin, 1883), IX, p. 137.

13. *Collected Works of Ralph Waldo Emerson*, ed. Joseph Slater et al. (Cambridge: Harvard University Press, 1979), II, p. 66.

14. *Emerson's Complete Works*, IX, p. 134.

15. *Collected Works of Ralph Waldo Emerson*, I, p. 10.

16. *The Early Lectures of Ralph Waldo Emerson*, ed. Robert E. Spiller and Wallace E. Williams (Cambridge: Harvard University Press, 1972), III, p. 279.

17. *Journals and Miscellaneous Notes*, ed. William H. Gilman and J. E. Parsons (Cambridge: Harvard University Press, 1970), VIII, p. 108.

18. *Journals and Miscellaneous Notes*, VIII, p. 139.

19. *Journals and Miscellaneous Notes*, VIII, p. 95.

20. John Winthrop, "Speech to the General Court" in *The Puritans*, ed. Perry Miller and Thomas H. Johnson (New York: American Book Co., 1938), pp. 205–7.

21. For partial support for what is admittedly my own speculation, see Allen, pp. 351–52.

22. James Elliot Cabot, *A Memoir of Ralph Waldo Emerson* (Boston: Houghton, Mifflin, 1887), II, pp. 697–702.

23. Michael Herr, *Dispatches* (New York: Alfred A. Knopf, 1968), p. 49.

24. See Wesley T. Mott, *"The Strains of Eloquence": Emerson and His Sermons* (University Park: Pennsylvania State University Press, 1989), p. 162, where it is observed—quoting J. A. Ward—that in "Experience" Emerson tried "to affirm a faith independent of experience."

25. Barton Levi St. Armand, *Emily Dickinson and Her Culture: The Soul's Society* (Cambridge: Cambridge University Press, 1984), p. 66.

26. *Collected Works of Ralph Waldo Emerson*, III, p. 150.

27. See Lawrence Buell, *Literary Transcendentalism: Style and Vision in the American Renaissance* (Ithaca: Cornell University Press, 1973), pp. 284–96, for a helpful discussion of Emerson's increasing use of the personal anecdote in the essays following "Experience."

28. Loving, pp. 139–42.

29. *Collected Works of Ralph Waldo Emerson*, I, p. 8.

30. *Collected Works of Ralph Waldo Emerson*, II, p. 40.

31. *Collected Works of Ralph Waldo Emerson*, I, p. 15.

32. *Emerson's Complete Works*, VI, p. 51.

6. THOREAU'S QUARREL WITH EMERSON

1. Walter Harding, *The Days of Henry Thoreau* (New York: Alfred A. Knopf, 1970), p. 464.

2. *Journal* (Boston: Houghton, Mifflin, 1906), III, p. 134.

3. *Journal*, II, p. 406; see also Walter Harding and Michael Meyer, *The New Thoreau Handbook* (New York: New York University Press, 1980), p. 125.

4. Sharon Cameron, *Writing Nature: Henry Thoreau's Journals* (New York: New York University Press, 1985), p. 6 passim.

5. Robert D. Richardson, *Henry Thoreau: A Life of the Mind* (Berkeley: University of California Press, 1986), p. 154.

6. *The Illustrated Walden*, ed. J. Lyndon Shanley (Princeton: Princeton University Press, 1973), p. 28. Further references to *Walden* are to this text.

7. Richard Bridgman, *Dark Thoreau* (Lincoln: University of Nebraska Press, 1982), passim.

8. Richard Lebeaux, *Young Man Thoreau* (Amherst: University of Massachusetts Press, 1977), pp. 172–204.

9. Harding, p. 136.

10. For an extended treatment of *Walden* in this regard, see Stanley Cavell, *The Senses of Walden* (San Francisco: North Point Press, 1981).

11. *Journal*, IV, p. 445.

12. Richardson, pp. 265, 257.

13. *The Correspondence of Henry David Thoreau*, ed. Walter Harding and Carl Bode (New York: New York University Press, 1958), p. 283.

14. H. Daniel Peck, *Thoreau's Morning Work: Memory and Perception in A Week on the Concord and Merrimack Rivers, the Journal, and Walden* (New Haven: Yale University Press, 1990), p. 158.

15. *Emerson in His Journals*, ed. Joel Porte (Cambridge: Harvard University Press, 1982), p. 142.

16. *Collected Works of Ralph Waldo Emerson*, ed. Joseph Slater et al. (Cambridge: Harvard University Press, 1979), II, p. 31.

17. Richardson, pp. 224ff.; "Walking" in *Excursions* (Boston: Houghton, Mifflin, 1893), p. 251.

18. "Walking," pp. 276–77.

19. "Walking," pp. 284–85.

20. *Collected Works of Ralph Waldo Emerson*, III, p. 43.

21. *The Correspondence of Henry David Thoreau*, pp. 441–42.

22. Frederick Garber, *Thoreau's Redemptive Imagination* (New York: New York University Press, 1977), p. 123.

23. *The Maine Woods*, ed. Joseph J. Moldenhauer (Princeton: Princeton University Press, 1972), p. 70.

24. *Journal*, II, p. 406.

25. "Walking," pp. 251–52.

26. For a discussion of the linguistic barriers to "at-homeness" in nature, see Frederick Garber, *Thoreau's Fable of Inscribing* (Princeton: Princeton University Press, 1991).

7. WHITMAN'S IDEA OF WOMEN

1. John S. Haller, Jr., and Robin M. Haller, *The Physician and Sexuality in Victorian America* (Urbana: University of Illinois Press, 1974), pp. 55–56; *With Walt Whitman in Camden*, ed. Horace Traubel (New York: Mitchell Kennerley, 1915), II, p. 331.

2. Haller and Haller, p. 38.

3. *Leaves of Grass; Comprehensive Reader's Edition*, ed. Harold W. Blodgett and Sculley Bradley (New York: New York University Press, 1965), p. 74. Further references to Whitman's poetry are to this text.

4. *Walt Whitman: Prose Works 1892*, ed. Floyd Stovall (New York: New York University Press, 1964), II, p. 389.

5. Harold Aspiz, *Walt Whitman and the Body Beautiful* (Urbana: University of Illinois Press, 1980), p. 211.

6. *Prose Works 1892*, II, pp. 389, 364.

7. Aspiz, p. 215.

8. *With Walt Whitman in Camden*, III, pp. 452–53.

9. Haller and Haller, pp. 62–63.

10. Gay Wilson Allen, *The Solitary Singer: A Critical Biography of Walt Whitman* (New York: New York University Press, 1955), p. 177.

11. *Walt Whitman; The Correspondence*, ed. Edwin Haviland Miller (New York: New York University Press, 1961), II, p. 137.

12. *Correspondence*, II, p. 136.

13. *Correspondence*, II, p. 140. For the latest information on Gilchrist's relationship with Whitman and her life in general, see Marion Walker Alcaro, *Walt Whitman's Mrs. G; A Biography of Anne Gilchrist* (Rutherford, New Jersey: Farleigh Dickinson University Press, 1991).

14. Arthur Golden, "Nine Early Whitman Letters, 1840–1841," *American Literature* 58 (October 1986), pp. 342–60.

15. Aspiz, p. 223.

16. James M. Cox, "Walt Whitman, Mark Twain, and the Civil War," *Sewanee Review* 69 (Spring 1961), pp. 185–204.

17. R. W. B. Lewis, *Trials of the Word: Essays in American Literature and the Humanistic Tradition* (New Haven: Yale University Press, 1965), p. 12.

18. Michael Orth, "Walt Whitman, Metaphysical Teapot: The Structure of 'Song of Myself,' " *Walt Whitman Review* 14 (March 1968), pp. 16–24.

19. Cox, pp. 187–88.

20. *The Education of Henry Adams* in *Henry Adams*, ed. Ernest Samuels and Jayne N. Samuels (New York: Library of America, 1983), pp. 1070–71.

21. R. W. B. Lewis, *The American Adam: Innocence, Tragedy and Tradition in the Nineteenth Century* (Chicago: University of Chicago Press, 1955), p. 52.

22. *Correspondence*, V, p. 73.

23. See, however, Betsy Erkkila, *Walt Whitman the Political Poet* (New York: Oxford University Press, 1988), passim.

24. Myrth Jimmie Killingsworth, "Whitman and Motherhood: A Historical View," *American Literature* 54 (March 1982), pp. 28–43. See also his expanded argument about the poet's evolving view of women in *Whitman's Poetry of the Body: Sexuality, Politics, and the Text* (Chapel Hill: University of North Carolina Press, 1989), pp. 62–73, 89–96.

25. William White, "Fanny Fern to Walt Whitman," *American Book Collector* 11 (May 1961), p. 9.

26. Milton E. Flower, *James Parton: Father of Modern Biography* (Durham: Duke University Press, 1951), p. 48.

27. *With Walt Whitman in Camden*, III, pp. 235–36; *Ruth Hall and Other Writings*, ed. Joyce W. Warren (New Brunswick: Rutgers University Press, 1986), p. 384.

28. "Peeps from under a Parasol" in *Ruth Hall and Other Writings*, p. 272.

29. See Justin Kaplan, *Walt Whitman; A Life* (New York: Simon and Schuster, 1980), pp. 216–17.

30. This consensus has been recently challenged. See Larry D. Griffin, "Walt Whitman's Voice," *Walt Whitman Quarterly Review* 9 (Winter 1992), pp. 125–33.

31. Flower, p. 242.

32. Jerome Loving, *Walt Whitman's Champion: William Douglas O'Connor* (College Station: Texas A&M University Press, 1978), pp. 100–102.

33. Flower, p. 38; see also Harriet Prescott Spofford, "James Parton," *Writer* 5 (November 1891), pp. 231–34. Spofford, a neighbor of Par-

ton in his later years, states that the marriage was a difficult one: Parton "had married Fanny Fern in a moment of chivalrous impulse. . . . Before a month had passed he discovered his mistake. Generous, noble, and true, Fanny Fern had suffered trials which made her morbid and difficult; and he had the hot, impetuous temper of youth. Separating at once but coming together out of regard to propriety and expediency, they lived under the same roof, sometimes in friendly habit, sometimes in a state of armed neutrality." Flower doubts that the couple actually separated but accepts Spofford's description of their turbulent marriage.

34. *Hobomok and Other Writings on Indians*, ed. Carolyn L. Karcher (New Brunswick: Rutgers University Press, 1986).

35. Edwin H. Miller, *Walt Whitman's Poetry: A Psychological Journey* (Boston: Houghton, Mifflin, 1968), p. 73.

8. TWAIN'S CIGAR-STORE INDIANS

1. Manuscript in the Beinecke Library, Yale University; reprinted in *Camden's Compliment to Walt Whitman*, ed. Horace Traubel (Philadelphia: David McKay, 1889), pp. 64–65. Twain's listing of nineteenth-century achievements resembles the catalog he would later use in "Queen Victoria's Jubilee" (1897); see Alan Gribben, *Mark Twain's Library: A Reconstruction* (Boston: G. K. Hall, 1980), II, p. 763.

2. James M. Cox, *Mark Twain: The Fate of Humor* (Princeton: Princeton University Press, 1966), p. 175; see also his *"Pudd'nhead Wilson* Revisited" in *Mark Twain's Pudd'nhead Wilson: Race, Conflict, and Culture*, ed. Susan Gillman and Forrest G. Robinson (Durham: Duke University Press, 1990).

3. George M. Frederickson, *The Black Image in the White Mind: The Debate on Afro-American Character and Destiny* (New York: Harper & Row, 1971), p. 201.

4. *The Adventures of Huckleberry Finn*, ed. Walter Blair and Victor Fischer (Berkeley: University of California Press, 1988), p. 341; further page references to this novel are indicated in the text, preceded by "*HF.*"

5. Frederickson, p. 172.

6. John Howard Griffin, *Black Like Me* (Boston: Houghton, Mifflin, 1961), p. 129.

7. Forrest Robinson, *In Bad Faith: The Dynamics of Deception in Mark Twain's America* (Cambridge: Harvard University Press, 1986), p. 20.

8. Louis J. Budd, *Mark Twain: Social Philosopher* (Bloomington: Indiana University Press, 1962), p. 105.

9. W. E. B. Du Bois, *The Souls of Black Folk* (New York: New American Library, 1969), pp. 45–46.

10. Justin Kaplan, *Mr. Clemens and Mark Twain; A Biography* (New York: Simon and Schuster, 1966), p. 314.

11. *Mark Twain in Eruption: Hitherto Unpublished Pages about Men and Events*, ed. Bernard DeVoto (New York: Harper & Brothers, 1940), p. 34.

12. *Mark Twain in Eruption*, p. 8.

13. William C. Gibson, *Theodore Roosevelt among the Humorists* (Knoxville: University of Tennessee Press, 1980), p. 41.

14. *Mark Twain in Eruption*, pp. 31–32.

15. Frederickson, p. 300.

16. *No. 44, Mark Twain's Mysterious Stranger Manuscripts*, ed. William M. Gibson (Berkeley: University of California Press, 1982), p. 187.

17. See William Bedford Clark, "The Serpent of Lust in the Southern Garden," *Southern Review* 10 (Fall 1974), pp. 805–22.

18. *Pudd'nhead Wilson* and *Those Extraordinary Twins*, ed. Sidney E. Berger (New York: W. W. Norton, 1980), p. 8.

19. Alan Gribben, "Reconstructing Mark Twain's Library," *Bookman's Weekly* for 11 August 1980, p. 756; see also Gribben's "The Dispersal of Samuel L. Clemens' Library Books," *Resources for American Literary Study* 5 (Autumn 1975), pp. 147–65.

20. John Seelye, *The True Adventures of Huckleberry Finn* (Urbana: University of Illinois Press, 1971), p. 121.

21. Seelye, p. 337. Originally, Seelye had written one further chapter (33) in which Huck decides to become an abolitionist, but he wisely canceled it, sensing that such a resolution would undermine the argument for white ambivalence toward blacks.

22. T. S. Eliot, "An Introduction to *Huckleberry Finn*" in *Adventures of Huckleberry Finn* (New York: W. W. Norton, 1977), pp. 334–35.

23. Eliot, p. 329.

24. Eliot, p. 330.

25. Leslie Fiedler, *Love and Death in the American Novel* (New York: Stein and Day, rev. ed., 1966), pp. 25–26.

26. W. H. Auden, "In Memory of W. B. Yeats" in *Collected Poems, 1927–1957* (London: Faber and Faber, 1966), p. 142.

27. See Eric J. Sundquist, "Mark Twain and Homer Plessy" in *Mark Twain's Pudd'nhead Wilson* (pp. 46–72), where he suggests how

Twain's novel reflected the nation's recurring racial biases as they led to the doctrine of "separate but equal" in *Plessy v. Ferguson* (1896).

28. Eldridge Cleaver, *Soul on Ice* (New York: Dell Publishing Co., 1970), p. 18.

9. DICKINSON'S UNPUBLISHED CANON

1. Jerome Loving, "Dickinson's Deconstruction in the Eighties," *ESQ: A Journal of the American Renaissance* 32 (1986), p. 201.

2. Cynthia Griffin Wolff, *Emily Dickinson* (New York: Alfred A. Knopf, 1986), p. 99.

3. *Letters of Emily Dickinson*, ed. Thomas H. Johnson (Cambridge: Harvard University Press, 1958), I, pp. 54–55.

4. Richard B. Sewall, *The Life of Emily Dickinson* (New York: Farrar, Straus and Giroux, 1974), pp. 360–61.

5. *Letters*, I, p. 60.

6. *Letters*, I, p. 67.

7. *Letters*, II, p. 460.

8. *Letters*, I, p. 58.

9. *Letters*, II, p. 475.

10. Wolff, p. 42.

11. *Letters*, I, p. 66.

12. See Harold Bloom, *The Anxiety of Influence* (New York: Oxford University Press, 1973), and Sandra M. Gilbert and Susan Gubar, *The Madwoman in the Attic: The Woman Writer and the Nineteenth-Century Literary Imagination* (New Haven: Yale University Press, 1979).

13. Fred Lewis Pattee, *The Feminine Fifties* (New York: D. Appleton-Century Co., 1940).

14. In Dreiser's case, the problem was the *lack* of reviews because Doubleday, though compelled by a legal contract to publish *Sister Carrie* in 1900, refused to advertise or promote the book.

15. Karen Dandurand, "New Dickinson Civil War Publications," *American Literature* 56 (March 1984), pp. 17–27.

16. David S. Reynolds, *Beneath the American Renaissance: The Subversive Imagination in the Age of Emerson and Melville* (New York: Alfred A. Knopf, 1988).

17. *Walt Whitman: Prose Works 1892*, ed. Floyd Stovall (New York: New York University Press, 1964), II, p. 716.

18. *Letters*, II, p. 404.

19. *Letters*, II, p. 421.

20. *Poems by Emily Dickinson*, ed. Mabel Loomis Todd and T. W. Higginson (Boston: Roberts Brothers, 1890), p. vi.

21. *Critical Essays on Emily Dickinson*, ed. Paul J. Ferlazzo (Boston: G. K. Hall, 1984), p. 31.

22. *Critical Essays*, p. 32.

23. Barton Levi St. Armand, *Emily Dickinson and Her Culture: The Soul's Society* (New York: Cambridge University Press, 1984).

24. *Critical Essays*, p. 32.

25. *The Poems of Emily Dickinson*, ed. Thomas H. Johnson (Boston: Harvard University Press, 1955), II, pp. 417–18. Unless otherwise indicated, the texts of Dickinson's poems are taken from these volumes.

26. See Emerson's "New Poetry" in *Uncollected Writings: Essays, Addresses, Poems, Reviews and Letters*, ed. Charles C. Bigelow (New York: Lamb, 1912), p. 139.

27. St. Armand, p. 5.

28. Louis J. Block, "A New England Nun," *Dial* 18 (1 March 1895), pp. 146–47; reprinted in *Critical Essays*, pp. 42–44.

29. *A Poet's Parents: The Courtship Letters of Emily Norcross and Edward Dickinson*, ed. Vivian R. Pollak (Chapel Hill: University of North Carolina Press, 1988), pp. 109–11.

30. *Austin and Mabel: The Amherst Affair & Love Letters of Austin Dickinson and Mabel Loomis Todd*, ed. Polly Longsworth (New York: Farrar, Straus and Giroux, 1984), p. 153.

31. *Moby-Dick*, ed. Harrison Hayford and Hershel Parker (New York: W. W. Norton, 1967), p. 128.

32. Van Wyck Brooks, *The Ordeal of Mark Twain* (New York: E. P. Dutton,1920); Bernard DeVoto, *Mark Twain's America* (Boston: Little, Brown, and Co., 1932).

33. According to John Evangelist Walsh, *This Brief Tragedy: Unravelling the Todd-Dickinson Affair* (New York: Grove Weidenfeld, 1991), pp. 112–14, Susan Dickinson was discouraged from publishing her sister-in-law's poems in 1886 by Thomas Wentworth Higginson.

34. *Letters*, I, p. 241.

10. HENRY JAMES'S PEARL AT A GREAT PRICE

1. *The Portrait of a Lady*, ed. Robert D. Bamberg (New York: W. W. Norton, 1975), p. 238. Further references are to this text, which reflects the

revisions made for the 1908 version in the New York Edition. My reading of *The Portrait* acknowledges the possibility that the Isabel of 1908 is more "intellectual" and less "emotional" than the Isabel of 1881 (for detailed discussions of the textual alterations, see Anthony J. Mazzella, "The New Isabel" in the Norton edition of *The Portrait*, pp. 597–619, Nina Baym, "Revision and Thematic Change in *The Portrait of a Lady*" in *Modern Critical Interpretations of Henry James's "The Portrait of a Lady*," ed. Harold Bloom [New York: Chelsea House, 1987], pp. 71–86, and Philip Horne, *Henry James and Revision: The New York Edition* [Oxford: Clarendon Press, 1990]); yet I also view the 1908 *version* as a subtle revision of the 1881 novel without the conscious intent of creating a separate work with a separate theme. (I have examined this issue further in "The Death of Romance: Lily Bart and the 1908 *Portrait of a Lady*" in *The "Other" Romance*, ed. Donald Pease and Jeffrey Rubin-Dorsky [in progress].) Whether James intended or succeeded at creating a significantly different story is, of course, debatable. The argument for a "new" Isabel (Mazella) or a more "conservative" James with regard to the "woman question" (Baym) is largely based on a semantic interpretation of James's revised words and phrases. Sometimes these arguments are based on misreadings; see, for example, Baym (p. 79), who claims that "Henrietta (in the 1908 edition) is no longer 'decidedly pretty' but only 'delicately . . . fair.'" In fact, both phrases appear in the 1908 edition (Norton, p. 79).

2. Quoted in *The Recognition of Nathaniel Hawthorne*, ed. B. Bernard Cohen (Ann Arbor: University of Michigan Press, 1969), p. 129. Indeed, Pansy is the only "sequel" to Isabel's quest. The word derives from the French *pensée*, or fanciful "thought"; hence, its derogatory connotation both today and in James's time. In other words, Pansy is not active as a shaper of her destiny, and she thus reflects Isabel's situation at the end of the novel.

3. "The Education of Henry Adams" in *Henry Adams*, ed. Ernest Samuels and Jayne N. Samuels (New York: Library of America, 1983), p. 1071; see also Martha Banta, "They Shall Have Faces, Minds, and (One Day) Flesh: Women in Late Nineteenth-century and Early Twentieth-century American Literature" in *What Manner of Woman: Essays on English and American Life and Literature*, ed. Marlene Springer (New York: New York University Press, 1977), pp. 235–46.

4. Jeffrey Rubin-Dorsky, *Adrift in the Old World: The Psychological Pilgrimage of Washington Irving* (Chicago: University of Chicago Press, 1988), p. 68.

5. Banta, p. 236.

6. Gay Wilson Allen, *Waldo Emerson: A Biography* (New York: Viking Press, 1981), p. 495.

7. Baym, p. 81.

8. Leon Edel, *Henry James; A Life* (New York: Harper & Row, 1985), pp. 85, 549.

9. *Letters of Emily Dickinson*, ed. Thomas H. Johnson (Cambridge: Harvard University Press, 1958), III, p. 755.

10. Edel, p. 216.

11. For the most recent summary of the ongoing debate over the definition of the "American Romance," see George Dekker, "Once More: Hawthorne and the Genealogy of American Romance," *ESQ: A Journal of the American Renaissance* 35 (1st Quarter 1989), pp. 69–83. See also Dekker's *The American Historical Romance* (Cambridge: Cambridge University Press, 1987).

12. *The Collected Works of Ralph Waldo Emerson*, ed. Joseph Slater et al. (Cambridge: Harvard University Press, 1979), II, p. 31.

13. Joan Templeton, "The *Doll House* Backlash: Criticism, Feminism, and Ibsen," *Publications of the Modern Language Association* 104 (January 1989), p. 31.

14. Banta, p. 239.

15. Richard Poirier, "Setting the Scene: The Drama and Comedy of Judgment" in *Henry James's "The Portrait of a Lady,"* p. 36.

16. See Quentin Anderson, "News of Life" in *The Merrill Studies in "The Portrait of a Lady,"* ed. Lyall H. Powers (Columbus, Ohio: Charles E. Merrill Publishing Company, 1970), p. 77: "Isabel suggests spontaneity and intellectual grace in the first volume, and a dogged, manly husbanding of creative energy toward the end of the novel."

17. Edel, p. 76.

18. Anderson, p. 78.

19. J. Gerald Kennedy, "Jeffrey Aspern and Edgar Allan Poe," *Poe Studies* 6 (1973), pp. 17–18.

20. Introduction to *Henry James's "The Portrait of a Lady,"* p. 12.

21. Anderson, p. 77.

22. *Collected Works of Ralph Waldo Emerson*, II, p. 6.

23. Alfred Habegger, *Henry James and the "Woman Business"* (Cambridge and New York: Cambridge University Press, 1989), pp. 4–12, 27–62, 150–81, passim.

24. Leon Edel, *Henry James: The Middle Years, 1882–1895* (Philadelphia: J. B. Lippincott Company, 1962), p. 63.

11. CHOPIN'S TWENTY-NINTH BATHER

1. Leon Edel, *Henry James; A Life* (New York: Harper & Row, 1985), pp. 85, 549.

2. *Leaves of Grass: Comprehensive Reader's Edition*, ed. Harold W. Blodgett and Sculley Bradley (New York: New York University Press, 1965), p. 38. For other Chopin-Whitman connections, see Elizabeth Balkman, "*The Awakening*: Kate Chopin's 'Endlessly Rocking' Cycle," *Ball State University Forum* 20 (1979), pp. 53–58, Lewis Leary, *Southern Excursions: Essays on Mark Twain and Others* (Baton Rouge: Louisiana State University Press, 1971), pp. 169–74, and Kenneth M. Price, *Whitman and Tradition: The Poet in His Century* (New Haven: Yale University Press, 1990), pp. 114–21.

3. Even in this remarkable section of "Song of Myself," of course, Whitman probably falls short—because of his maleness—of complete female identity. Whereas his homosexual tendencies may give him the best male advantage, the twenty-ninth bather may be only a means to a homosexual end in which the speaker in the poem appropriates the woman's position for his own. For the most recent homosexual reading of this passage, see Michael Moon, *Disseminating Whitman: Revision and Corporeality in Leaves of Grass* (Cambridge: Harvard University Press, 1991), pp. 38–47.

4. *The Complete Works of Kate Chopin*, ed. Per Seyersted (Baton Rouge: Louisiana State University Press, 1969), p. 37.

5. *Leaves of Grass*, p. 60.

6. *The House of Mirth*, ed. Elizabeth Ammons (New York: W. W. Norton, 1990), p. 176.

7. *Winesburg, Ohio*, ed. John H. Ferres (New York: Viking Press, 1966), p. 45.

8. *The Awakening*, ed. Margaret Culley (New York: W. W. Norton, 1976), p. 57. Further references to this novel are to this text.

9. James Woodress, *Willa Cather; A Literary Life* (Lincoln: University of Nebraska Press, 1987), pp. 142–43. See also Sharon O'Brien, *Willa Cather: Emerging Voice* (New York: Oxford University Press, 1987), pp. 117–46.

10. By "romance" I am privileging—for the nonce—heterosexual desire because Chopin privileged it in virtually all her stories and novels. There is also little or nothing in any of the biographies to suggest that she entertained homosexual feelings. In what they admittedly call a "hyperbolic" reading of the novel, Sandra M. Gilbert and Susan Gubar see

Edna's quest in terms of sexual desire—where the protagonist faces "inevitable crucifixion by a culture in which a regenerated Aphrodite has no viable role." See *No Man's Land: The Place of the Woman Writer in the Twentieth Century* (New Haven: Yale University Press, 1989), II, pp. 83–119.

11. *Complete Works of Kate Chopin*, pp. 39–47.

12. In *Kate Chopin; A Critical Biography* (Baton Rouge: Louisiana State University Press, 1969), pp. 93, 102, passim, Per Seyersted argues that Chopin was not interested in social issues as much as she was preoccupied with the issues of the individual in society—most clearly the issue for Edna.

13. Emily Toth, *Kate Chopin* (New York: William Morrow, 1990), p. 184.

14. Andrew Delbanco, "The Half-Life of Edna Pontellier" in *New Essays on "The Awakening,"* ed. Wendy Martin (New York: Cambridge University Press, 1988), pp. 98, 104.

15. For the fullest treatment of Oscar Chopin's character (and financial problems), see Toth pp. 133–62.

16. The actual title of this story is "The Dream of an Hour" (as it appeared in *Vogue* in 1894). See Toth, p. 431n.

17. *Complete Works of Kate Chopin*, pp. 871, 873.

18. *Leaves of Grass*, p. 254.

19. *Complete Works of Kate Chopin*, p. 595.

20. Seyersted, *Kate Chopin; A Critical Biography*, p. 166.

21. *Leaves of Grass*, p. 739.

22. Seyersted, *Kate Chopin; A Critical Biography*, p. 175. According to Toth, however, the banning was never official. She also questions not only the assertion that Chopin was refused membership in "a fine-arts club" (first proposed by Daniel Rankin in *Kate Chopin and Her Creole Stories* [1932]) but the notion that such a club even existed at the time *The Awakening* was published. See Toth, pp. 369, 422–25.

23. "Aims and Autographs of Authors," *Book News* 17 (July 1899), p. 612; reprinted in the Norton edition of *The Awakening*, p. 159.

24. *Complete Works of Kate Chopin*, p. 431.

25. *Complete Works of Kate Chopin*, p. 451.

26. *Complete Works of Kate Chopin*, p. 427.

27. See, for example, Anne Goodwyn Jones, *Tomorrow Is Another Day: The Woman Writer in the South, 1859–1936* (Baton Rouge: Louisiana State University Press, 1981), p. 182.

28. *Complete Works of Kate Chopin*, p. 439.

29. *Complete Works of Kate Chopin*, p. 433.

30. *Letters of Ralph Waldo Emerson*, ed. Ralph L. Rusk (New York: Columbia University Press, 1939), IV, p. 230.

31. *Complete Works of Kate Chopin*, p. 31.

32. Jerome Loving, *Emily Dickinson: The Poet on the Second Story* (Cambridge: Cambridge University Press, 1986).

33. *Leaves of Grass*, pp. 573–74.

34. Moon, p. 42.

35. *Complete Works of Kate Chopin*, pp. 467–69.

1 2. DREISER'S NOVEL ABOUT A NUN

1. *Sister Carrie*, ed. James L. W. West et al. (Philadelphia: University of Pennsylvania Press, 1981), p. 3; further references, unless otherwise indicated, are to this edition of the novel. While it remains debatable whether this text, which is the version of the novel before Dreiser made the concessions to the censors at Doubleday, is superior to the one published in 1900, I have found it useful as a better basis on which to analyze Dreiser's original intentions in presenting certain crucial scenes.

2. Richard Lingeman, *Theodore Dreiser; At the Gates of the City, 1871–1907* (New York: Putnams, 1986), p. 241.

3. Lingeman, p. 205.

4. Ellen Moers, *Two Dreisers* (New York: Viking Press, 1969), pp. 110–11.

5. Larzer Ziff, *The American 1890s: Life and Times of a Lost Generation* (New York: Viking Press, 1966), p. 335.

6. Richard D. Lehan, *Theodore Dreiser: His World and His Novels* (Carbondale and Edwardsville: Southern Illinois University Press, 1969), p. 74.

7. W. A. Swanberg, *Dreiser* (New York: Charles Scribner's Sons, 1965), p. 169.

8. *Dawn* (New York: Fawcett Premier Books Reprint, 1965), p. 153.

9. Donald Pizer, *The Novels of Theodore Dreiser: A Critical Study* (Minneapolis: University of Minnesota Press, 1976), p. 34.

10. Walter Benn Michaels, *The Gold Standard and the Logic of Naturalism* (Berkeley: University of California Press, 1987), p. 57.

11. Swanberg, p. 21.

12. Richard D. Lehan, "The Theoretical Limits of the New Historicism," *New Literary History* 21 (Spring 1990), p. 541.

13. Roger Asselineau, "Theodore Dreiser's Transcendentalism" in

Critical Essays on Theodore Dreiser, ed. Donald Pizer (Boston: G. K. Hall, 1981); reprinted in Roger Asselineau, *The Transcendentalist Constant in American Literature* (New York: New York University Press, 1982), pp. 99–114.

14. Carl F. Strauch, "The Importance of Emerson's Skeptical Mood," *Harvard Library Bulletin* 11 (1957), pp. 123, 139.

15. *Sister Carrie*, ed. Donald Pizer (New York: W. W. Norton, 1970), p. 369.

EPILOGUE

1. Terence Martin, "The Negative Structures of American Literature," *American Literature* 57 (March 1985), pp. 1–22.

2. For a similar observation, see Ezra Greenspan, *Walt Whitman and the American Reader* (Cambridge: Cambridge University Press, 1990), p. 31.

3. *Leaves of Grass: Comprehensive Reader's Edition*, ed. Harold W. Blodgett and Sculley Bradley (New York: New York University Press, 1965), p. 41. Further citations are from this text.

Index